AMERICAN COLORS are officially raised for the first time on Guam in front of III Amphibious Corps Headquarters on 27 July 1944.

THE RECAPTURE OF

GUAM

HISTORICAL BRANCH

G-3 DIVISION

HEADQUARTERS

U.S. MARINE CORPS

Major O. R. Lodge, USMC

1954

Marine Corps Monographs
in This Series

The Defense of Wake $1.25
The Battle for Tarawa $1.50
Marines at Midway $0.50
Bougainville and the Northern Solomons $2.00
The Guadalcanal Campaign $4.25
The Assault on Peleliu $2.50
Saipan: The Beginning of the End $3.25
The Seizure of Tinian $2.50
Marine Aviation in the Philippines $2.50
The Campaign on New Britain $3.75
Marines in the Central Solomons $2.75

For sale by the Superintendent of Documents, U. S. Government Printing Office
Washington 25, D. C.

COVER PICTURE: First assault waves of Marines take cover prior to moving inland on Guam. In the background smoke rises from a burning LVT hit by enemy fire.

Foreword

I have always had a feeling of deep satisfaction in having been the commander of one of the assault elements that returned the American flag to Guam. The island once more stands ready to fulfill its destiny as an American fortress in the Pacific.

The conquest of Guam was a decisive triumph of combined arms over a formidable Japanese defensive force which took full advantage of the island's rugged terrain.

The heroic action of the veteran Marines who seized Orote Peninsula and Apra Harbor gave the Navy a much-needed advance base for further operations in the Pacific. Once marine and Army units captured northern Guam, engineers moved in and cut from the jungle the airfields from which the Twentieth Air Force launched B–29 raids, bringing the full realization of war to the Japanese homeland.

LEMUEL C. SHEPHERD, Jr.
GENERAL, U. S. MARINE CORPS
COMMANDANT OF THE MARINE CORPS

Preface

THE RECAPTURE OF GUAM is the twelfth in a series of operational monographs prepared by the Historical Branch, G-3 Division, Headquarters U. S. Marine Corps, designed to give the military student and the casual reader an accurate and detailed account of the operations in which Marines participated during World War II. When sufficient of these monographs have been completed they will be integrated into a final Operational History of the Marine Corps in World War II.

With Army units fighting directly beside the Marines throughout most of the campaign, Army activities are treated herein with sufficient detail to give the proper perspective to the overall account.

Many officers and men who participated in this campaign have contributed to the preparation of this monograph by generously answering specific inquiries, commenting on preliminary drafts, or submitting to interview. Grateful acknowledgment is made herewith. Special recognition is extended to Office of Naval History, Naval Records and Library, and Office of the Chief of Military History, Department of the Army—in particular Dr. Philip A. Crowl and Mr. Thomas G. Wilds of the Pacific Section. Appreciation for the extensive research required in presenting an accurate and complete account of the campaign, especially as to the Japanese viewpoint, is extended to Mr. Henry I. Shaw, Jr. Finally, the help of Lieutenant Colonel Frank O. Hough in editing the manuscript is acknowledged with gratitude. Maps included herein were prepared by the Reproduction Section, Marine Corps Schools, Quantico, Virginia. Official Marine Corps photographs have been used to illustrate this monograph unless otherwise noted.

T. A. WORNHAM
BRIGADIER GENERAL, U. S. MARINE CORPS
ASSISTANT CHIEF OF STAFF, G-3

Contents

CHAPTER I

Background

In the early summer of 1944, with blaring headlines making all the world aware of the Normandy invasion and its follow-up operations, public attention in the United States was focused on Europe. Campaigns in the Pacific were dwarfed by the tremendous scale of the Allied drive against Germany. The full significance of the capture of the Southern Marianas, with the American return to Guam, was overshadowed by the more voluminous accounts of the European conflict. Yet, in two short months on these islands, the Japanese lost their last chance for victory in the Pacific.

THE BIG PICTURE

By June of 1944 the outer island screen of Japanese defenses had been riddled by American attacks. New bases in the Marshalls had been seized in February at Kwajalein, Majuro, and Eniwetok by forces of the Pacific Ocean Areas. In March and April, landings in the South and Southwest Pacific theaters had added the Admiralties, Emirau, Hollandia, and Aitape to the rapidly growing chain of Allied installations. Shore-based Army, Navy, and Marine air squadrons harassed and pounded by-passed strong points into neutralization. With practiced ease planes of Fast Carrier Task Force 58 struck repeatedly at Truk, the Western Carolines, and Southern Marianas. The outlook for the Japanese was dark, indeed. A strangling noose was tightening around the inner perimeter guarding the path to their homeland.

Threatened at all points on an arc from the Southern Philippines to the Southern Marianas, the Japanese leaders were well aware that the decisive actions of the war were at hand. The fall of the outer zone of defense was not only a tactical loss; it meant the collapse of the entire strategic concept of Imperial Headquarters.[1] Recognizing this, Admiral Soemu Toyoda, Commander-in-Chief, Combined Fleet, in a message to all of his commanding officers on 4 May 1944 warned:

> The war is drawing close to the lines vital to our national defense. The issue of our national existence is unprecedentedly serious; an unprecedented opportunity exists for deciding who shall be victorious and who defeated.[2]

In preparation for the expected amphibious strike at the inner ring, the Japanese concentrated most of their remaining carrier strength at Tawi-Tawi, north of Borneo. The enemy's

[1] Dr. Herbert Rosinski, a noted military analyst, states the basic Japanese plan was one of fighting a "limited war" and called for activities to be restricted to the occupation and defense of Southeast Asia. The attack on Pearl Harbor was only to cripple the American fleet, allowing the Japanese time to prepare outpost defenses. They would then wear out the Americans and finally cause them to "throw [in] the sponge." For a complete discussion of the Japanese strategic concept see Dr. H. Rosinski, "The Strategy of Japan," *Brassey's Naval Annual, 1946*, (New York, 1946), 99–113.

[2] USSBS(Pac), NavAnalysisDiv, *The Campaigns of the Pacific War*, (Washington, 1946), 223, hereinafter cited as *Campaigns*.

1

strategy was simple; at the first definite indication of an American assault, naval forces would assemble, attack, and annihilate the invasion fleet. The Japanese hoped that the first blow would be struck at Palau within easy range of shore-based air, and close to their naval bases. The Americans, however, did not intend to accommodate; they planned to hit a target closer to the homeland.

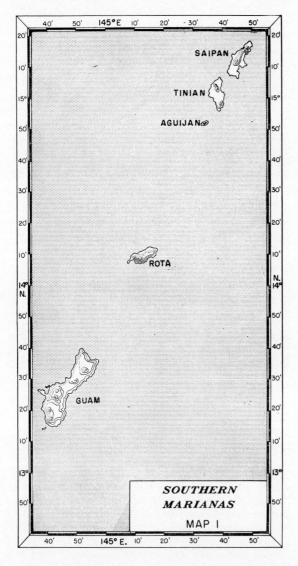

To most American planners the islands of the Southern Marianas were essential in the drive to shorten the war. They occupy a central position dominating the Western Pacific on an arc from Tokyo through the Ryukus to Formosa, the Philippines, and northern New Guinea.

Their capture would cut the strategic line of communication from Japan to its island holdings in the South Pacific and effectively isolate the garrisons there and would, for the first time during the war, permit Americans to operate on interior rather than exterior lines.[3] In addition, enemy planes could no longer stage through the airfields of Saipan, Tinian, and Guam to attack American forces hammering at the Japanese bases in the South and Central Pacific. But uppermost in the minds of the high-level strategists were three further considerations that made the target even more attractive. First, from the same airfields now being used by enemy planes and other sites selected for early development, B–29's of the Army Air Forces could initiate raids on Japan itself. Secondly, capture of Guam would permit the establishment of a submarine refueling point much closer to enemy areas. And finally, Apra Harbor offered a good anchorage for an advance naval base.

By first taking Saipan, headquarters of the defensive cordon in the Central Pacific, Americans could deal a fatal blow to Japanese hopes of retaining their dwindling island possessions. Furthermore, denial of the airstrips on this island to enemy planes would enable the Fifth Fleet to raise an effective air barrier over the Marianas and permit landings to be made on Guam and Tinian.

Guam's capture would return an important possession to American hands and provide a forward supply base for future operations in the Pacific. The flat terrain of Tinian would afford ideal heavy bomber strips from which round-the-clock strikes could be launched against Japan. If the Japanese accepted the challenge of an attack on these islands, a hoped-for showdown battle between the two fleets might take place.

The assault on Saipan,[4] 15 June 1944,[5] brought an immediate Japanese naval reaction.

[3] Ltr Adm R. A. Spruance to CMC, 3Dec52.

[4] See Maj C. W. Hoffman, *Saipan: The Beginning of the End*, MC Historical Monograph, (Washington, 1950), hereinafter cited as *Saipan*.

[5] A consistent effort has been made throughout the monograph to standardize dates and times. For the most part these are adjusted local times taken from the action reports of units involved in the operation.

2

The enemy's carrier task force came out of hiding and steamed toward the Marianas to meet the American amphibious effort. On 19–20 June 1944, planes from Task Force 58 engaged the enemy fleet, and the action that followed, the Battle of the Philippine Sea, proved disastrous for the Nipponese naval air arm. United States planes destroyed 402 planes, sank one carrier (*Hiyo*) and two attack oilers, and damaged four carriers, a battleship, and an oiler. In addition, on 19 June, torpedoes from American submarine pickets sank two carriers, the *Taiho* and *Shokaku*.[6] The badly mauled Japanese retired, but because of the shortage of fuel in destroyers and the disorganization caused by the necessity of taking planes on board during darkness, the U. S. Fifth Fleet could not press the attack further. Nevertheless, a crippling blow had been dealt to enemy naval air power and the danger of interference to the Marianas landings lessened. When Saipan fell on 9 July 1944, the Americans broke into the inner ring of the Japanese defenses and greatly reduced the enemy's potential for holding Guam.

GUAM AND THE GUAMANIANS

Dominated for years by the Japanese, the Marianas group forms an arc over 400 miles long across the Central Pacific extending from 13° to 20° north latitude and with the center of the group at 144° east longitude. Of its 15 islands, only Saipan, Tinian, Rota, and Guam are inhabited. The latter, with its 228 square miles, is the largest land mass in the group and approximates the total area of the remaining 14 islands. Long considered of great strategic importance, Guam was the only American territory in the Japanese Pacific stronghold.

The island's irregular shape defies glib description, but its narrow waist divides it roughly into two equal parts. (See Map 2, Map Section) The southern half, an oval about 8 by 16 miles, has its main axis north to south. Jutting to the northeast, the remainder is a rugged area approximately 7 by 14 miles. Fringing the entire island, except at the mouths of streams, is a coral reef shelf ranging from 20 to 700 yards wide.

Towering above the narrow coral sand beaches of the northern half are sheer cliffs 200 to 600 feet high that rim the shoreline from Fadian Point to Tumon Bay. Inland, a vast *cascajo* (coral limestone) plateau extends from the middle of the island to the northern tip and is broken by three mountain heights: in the south Mt. Barrigada (640 feet), in the east, Mt. Santa Rosa (840 feet), and in the extreme north, Mt. Machanao (576 feet). Growing through the thin layer of red topsoil that covers the *cascajo* is a tangled mass of tropical forest. Lianas, weeds, air plants, and dense undergrowth choke the space between the trees to form a virtually impassable barrier to cross-country movement. Marking the southern limit of the plateau is a 200-foot bluff that stretches across the island from the northwest slopes of Mt. Barrigada to the upper reaches of Agana [7] Bay.

The central lowland belt, dividing the island, extends from Agana Bay on the west coast to Pago Bay on the east coast. It is generally 100–200 feet above sea level and has many small, abrupt changes in elevation near the Pago River. The area contains several springs, the largest of which is located a few feet above sea level on the southern edge of Agana swamp. In this extensive swamp lies the source of a small river which empties into the bay.

Immediately to the south the land begins to rise abruptly and culminates in a wide, long mountain range that parallels the west coast. Once a plateau, this range has been eroded into numerous ravines, valleys, and gorges. Of volcanic origin, it extends from the vicinity of Adelup Point near the waist of the island to Port Ajayan on the southern tip. Just inland from Apra Harbor, rising to a height of 1,082 feet, is the Chachao-Alutom-Tenjo massif, largely composed of sedimentary rock from which the superimposed lava has rotted and fallen away.

South of this mass the range descends to a 400-foot saddle opposite Agat Bay. Then it rises to the Alifan-Lamlam-Bolanos-Sasalaguan ridge line which contains the highest point

---

[6] *Campaigns*, 213–215.

[7] In the spelling of Agana and other Spanish proper names the anglicized usage of American reports has been used throughout the monograph.

on the island, Mt. Lamlam (1,334 feet). The western slopes are steep and merge into low foothills and a narrow belt of rolling lowlands. On the other hand, the eastern slopes are more gradual, becoming, at an elevation of 400 feet a plateau that extends to the coast and ends in high bluffs above a narrow coastal flat. Covering this plateau is a carpet of sword, cogon, and bunch grass interspersed by short stretches of scrub forest.

The moist valleys of the numerous rivers and streams that rise in the central ridge are also heavily forested. Ravines and the lower mountain slopes are covered with the same type of jungle growth found in the northern part of the island. Rivers are all fordable by men afoot, but the steep banks in some cases prevent vehicles from making a crossing. As in the north, there is a large marsh area found in southern Guam; its treacherous depths border coral-jammed Apra Harbor and close most of the neck of Orote Peninsula. The peninsula itself is a *cascajo* formation with sheer cliffs ringing three-quarters of its perimeter. A matted tangle of low scrub growth stretches from Orote Point to the mangrove swamp on the shores of the harbor. Viewed as a whole, the terrain of Guam presents a formidable barrier to conquest, even without determined human defenders.

The island has another ally over which man has little control: the weather. From July to November, 20 to 25 days of every month are rainy, with more than two-thirds of the years' annual total of 90 inches of rain falling. Roads become quagmires and military operations are considerably hindered. Also from July to November a continuous succession of typhoons to the south and westward produce swells and rough landing conditions on the western beaches. The southern beaches are always bathed in surf from the prevailing trades. However, for the most part the climate is healthful and pleasant, with a constant, uniformly high temperature that varies little from the mean of 87 degrees. The Marianas area has often been called the "white man's tropics," and perhaps it was this beneficent climate that helped influence the original European colonization.[8]

The first white men to visit the Marianas were sailors of Magellan's globe-circling expedition who reached Guam in March of 1521. The natives actively resented the intrusion and made their displeasure so evident that the Spanish commander named their islands *Islas de los Ladrones* (Islands of the Thieves).

These original inhabitants, the Chamorros,[9] were an imposing people with "a lighter skin, a fine physique, a keen intelligence, and an aggressive spirit," [10] who orignally came from the mainland of Asia. They were sufficiently independent and warlike to resist the Spaniards who returned in 1565 with the intention of colonizing the islands and converting the heathens. Some estimates place the population of the Ladrones at this time very near 75,000. More than a century of continuous resistance to the missionaries and foreign soldiery, crippling inroads by white men's diseases, and steady migration to the Caroline Islands reduced the Chamorros to a mere handful by the time they were ready to submit to church and crown. In 1710, the first recorded census of the natives, who had all been forced to settle on Guam, showed that only 3,539 remained of the once flourishing population.[11]

Until 1898, the Marianas (the islands had been renamed for the Spanish queen in 1668) remained out of the main stream of world events. In that year, the USS *Charleston*, accompanying an expeditionary force bound for the Philippines, stopped off at Guam, informed the governor that the United States and Spain

[8] The geographical description above was taken from intelligence bulletins prepared for the Guam operation. It furnishes a picture of the island as it was in July 1944 before the bulldozers, graders, and dredges of the Seabees and engineers completely changed the topography. Especially helpful in compiling the description have been: ONI–99, Strategic Study of Guam, 1Feb44, hereinafter cited as *ONI–99*, and MIS, WD, Survey of Guam, 1943, hereinafter cited as *WD Survey*.

[9] The word "Chamorro" is considered obsolete at the present. "Guamanian" is considered the official designation of the peoples of Guam and is preferred by the natives of the island. Ltr 2dLt V. T. Blaz to author, 26Sept52.

[10] R. W. Robson, *The Pacific Islands Handbook–1944*, (New York, 1945), 136.

[11] L. Thompson, *Guam and its People*, (Princeton, 1947), 34.

MARINES of the first garrison on Guam shown on the steps of their barracks in an old photograph taken in October 1899. (Photograph courtesy of Walter Patterson.)

were at war, and promptly received the surrender of the defenseless island.[12] At the war's end the island became an American possession along with Puerto Rico and the Philippines for which a package price of 20 million dollars was paid. The rest of the Marianas, however, did not pass to control of the United States, and Spain sold them to Germany in 1899. Thus Guam became alien soil in a German sea. When World War I broke out, the Japanese seized the opportunity to expand and they occupied all the German territory north of the equator. The Versailles Treaty confirmed the seizure and the infant League of Nations gave Japan a mandate over these islands, effectively continuing the isolation of Guam.

Following World War I the U. S. Navy Department laid ambitious but abortive plans to make the island into a fortress guarding the routes to the Philippines and the Far East. The tremendous cost of such a project and an almost universal apathy towards military schemes combined to block these hopes. Not until Japan walked out of the League of Nations in 1935 did the average American become aware that something was wrong in the Pacific. The obvious reluctance of Japan to permit League inspection of the islands she held in trust stood as a warning for the future.[13] What little money the Navy had available in those depression years was spent to build up Pearl Harbor to insure that there would be at least one strong operating base in the Pacific. Guam remained virtually defenseless, a sitting duck waiting for the time the Japanese chose to strike.

While the military development of Guam had been held in abeyance, the lot of civilians on the island had improved considerably since the end of the Spanish rule. A presidential executive order of 23 December 1898 had placed the island under Navy administration and the

---

[12] The instructions to Capt Henry Glass, USN, commanding the *Charleston*, were to seize Guam, since information indicated that it was the only inhabited island of the group at that time. Consequently, the Spanish retained the rest of the Marianas at the conclusion of the war and were able to place them on the trading block. Lt F. J. Nelson, "Why Guam Alone Is American," *USNI Proceedings*, August 1936, 1132–1134.

[13] At the Washington Naval Conference of 1922 both Japan and the U. S. agreed not to fortify their holdings in the Central Pacific.

POWERFUL CARABAOS performed a wide variety of tasks for Guamanian farmers and townsmen and symbolize the prewar economy of Guam.

next year the first Marine garrison took up its duties there. A naval officer, usually a captain, was designated governor of Guam and exercised his powers directly under the Secretary of the Navy. For all practical purposes, although his staff of advisors included native leaders, the naval officer was the supreme executive with final legislative power, and the appointment and removal of all officials rested in his hands. Fortunately, this government, especially in its later stages, expressed itself as a form of benevolent paternalism that evidently suited the Guamanians, who by this time were a racial mixture of the original islanders, Spanish, and Filipino colonists. As one naval officer put it, ". . . the Chamorros never failed to show a kindly courtesy towards us. Their generous tolerance and compliance with our orders showed a most complaisant nature.[14]

By 1941 the native population had more than doubled from the original 9,000 that had been on the island when the Navy took over. About half of the people lived in the capital at Agana and another 3,000 in villages within ten miles' radius. The balance of the population was spread out in coastal villages and farming areas, with the greater percentage in the south. Fewer than 3,000 chose to live on the inhospitable northern plateau.

Although nominally townsmen, many of the Guamanians spent a great deal of their time working coconut plantations, rice fields, and garden plots in the interior. Those who lived on the farms tilled their own small areas and raised a few chickens, pigs, goats, and cattle. With the average ranch being small, cows and horses of the entire community often grazed on communal pastureland near the village. On the larger ranches, in addition to extensive cattle raising, the natives grew the main agricultural products. Vegetables, rice, tropical fruits, copra, and meat were transported to markets by the widely-used two-wheeled carabao carts. Only the most prosperous ranchers could afford motor vehicles to carry their products to town.

Population growth, improved economic and political status, and a vastly increased measure of tolerance on the part of the government were not the only benefits of American rule. The water supply had been augmented in 1940–41 to provide for the Apra Harbor area and garrison and island population in the vicinity of Piti and Sumay. The Navy supervised improvement and maintenance of 85 miles [15] of two-way roads. They circled the southern half of the island except for a stretch from Agat to Umatac, where the beach furnished the best route for traveling. In the north, from Ritidian Point to Yigo, the jungle had blocked construction of the proposed Agana-Yigo coast road. Throughout the interior a web of trails and carabao-cart tracks connected the farming hamlets with the main coastal roads. Extensive efforts to make the island economically self-sufficient had been fostered by the naval governors who encouraged the development of local island industries and the export of copra, Guam's biggest money crop. The island's real prosperity, however, derived from the naval facilities maintained there. Piti Navy Yard, the Marine Barracks at Sumay, and the various government departments (schools, hospital,

---

[14] Capt L. W. Johnson, (MC), "Guam—Before December 1941," *USNI Proceedings*, July 1942, 991, hereinafter cited as *Johnson.*

[15] According to RAdm G. J. McMillin, Governor of Guam at the time of the Japanese attack on 10Dec41, most of the 85 miles of road were built and maintained by Island Government funds, raised by local taxation. U. S. Government funds from the Navy Department were available for the so-called Federal roads, which were principally from Marine Barracks, Sumay to Agana. Ltr RAdm G. J. McMillin to CMC, 3Nov52, hereinafter cited as *McMillin.*

courts, police) employed a large number of Guamanians. These activities provided a market for most of the native products.

Although in 1941 Guam was only a fueling station for ships making the long runs to the Orient, it did have considerable strategic importance for other reasons. The station of the trans-Pacific cable and the naval radio station at Agana made it a focal point of the communication network in the Pacific. The clippers of Pan American World Airways landing in Apra Harbor on the San Francisco-Manila-Hongkong run provided an increasingly important link with the United States. Sites for airfields had been surveyed by late 1941, and plans were underway to initiate construction when the war broke out.[16]

The threatening situation in the Pacific had led the government to order the evacuation of all dependents from Guam, and the last of them left the island on 17 October 1941.[17] All classified matter was destroyed on 6 December and the island waited, as did all American Pacific outposts, for word of the outcome of the negotiations in Washington. At 0545, 8 December 1941,[18] the Governor, Captain George J. McMillin, USN, received word from the Commander-in-Chief, Asiatic Fleet, of the commencement of hostilities. Reinforcing the message were the first bombs from Saipan-based Japanese planes which fell at 0827.

The initial target was the mine sweeper USS *Penguin,* whose antiaircraft guns constituted the only weapons available to the garrison larger than .30 caliber machine guns. The attack continued throughout the daylight hours, with small flights of bombers hitting the various naval installations and strafing roads and villages. Agana was evacuated and the small number of enemy nationals rounded up and imprisoned. Among them were the Japanese who "owned the largest and most popular saloons, where the sailors and Marines liked best to hang out and argue the fine points of their professions." [19] Any such pleasant memories were soon dispelled when the first casualties of the bombings arrived at the hospital near Agana. Damage to installations was fairly extensive with houses,[20] barracks, fuel supplies, and roads being hit repeatedly. Enemy planes sank the *Penguin* after she put up a creditable fight, and her survivors joined the garrison ashore.

At daylight, 9 December, the bombers came again and repeated the pattern of attacks on naval installations. The Insular Force Guard, about 80 men who had been organized in early 1941 as an infantry unit to augment the native naval militia,[21] mustered in Agana and made preparations to protect the government buildings. The rest of the Guam garrison, including the 28 Marines of the Insular Patrol (Police), remained at their posts throughout the island. On Orote Peninsula the complement of the Marine Barracks, Sumay (6 officers, 1 warrant officer, 118 enlisted Marines) under Lieutenant Colonel William K. MacNulty, took up positions in the butts of the rifle range on the Marine Reservation. The inadequate garrison of

---

[16] The foregoing historical background is a synthesis of information contained in Thompson, *op. cit.;* Robson, *op. cit.;* T. Yanaihara, *The Pacific Islands Under Japanese Mandate,* (London, 1940) ; RAdm G. J. Rowcliff, "Guam," *USNI Proceedings,* July 1945; LCdr F. J. Nelson, "Guam—Our Western Outpost," *USNI Proceedings,* January 1940.

[17] One woman, Mrs. J. A. Hellmers, wife of a Navy CPO, who was too far along in pregnancy to be evacuated stayed on the island. She and her newborn daughter were taken prisoner when the Japanese occupied the island. They were both repatriated, together with the naval nurses taken on Guam, on the exchange ship *Asamu Maru* in June 1942.

[18] Capt G. J. McMillin, Surrender of Guam to the Japanese, official report to CNO, 11Sept45, hereinafter cited as *Surrender Report to CNO.*

[19] *Johnson,* 998.

[20] One of the houses demolished in Agana on 8Dec41 was that of RM 1/C George R. Tweed, USN. Tweed fled to the hills after the Japanese landing and with the help of loyal Guamanians managed to survive the entire period the Americans were gone from Guam. He was the only member of the garrison not killed or captured. Keeping him alive caused many natives to be beaten and robbed of their scarce food supplies, but his continued safety became a symbol of resistance against the Japanese.

[21] The members of the Insular Force Guard were in U. S. Government service and received 50 percent of the pay of corresponding ratings in the U. S. Navy. The native militia was a volunteer organization serving without pay or allowances and with no equipment except obsolete and condemned rifles. *McMillin.*

Guam made all possible preparations and waited for the Japanese assault.

About 0400, 10 December, flares appeared near Dungcas Beach above Agana and soon rifle fire could be heard in the plaza of the town. A Japanese naval landing party of about 400 men from the 5th Defense Force based on Saipan had run into the Guamanians of the Insular Guard who engaged them in a fire fight. About the same time the enemy's main force, a reinforced brigade of about 5,500 men, landed below Agat.[22]

Captain McMillin, aware of the overwhelming superiority of the enemy, decided not to endanger the lives of civilians by holding out against such heavy odds. He surrendered the island to the Japanese naval commander shortly after 0600. Scattered fights continued throughout the day as the invaders spread out over the island, but the defenders could offer only token resistance against the conquerors. The bombings and the action after the enemy landing killed 21 civilian and military personnel and wounded many others. But the small loss suffered by the Americans and Japanese on 10 December 1941 gave little indication of the high price to be paid by both sides when United

States forces retook the island two and a half years later.[23]

The enemy evacuated American members of the garrison to prison camps in Japan on 10 January 1942. Soon afterwards Japanese Army troops departed for Rabaul, and the Navy units that had been present at the surrender of the island remained to garrison and govern. At first, the yoke was light, with the Japanese making every effort to gain the good will of the natives. However, those regulations and changes put into effect seemed harsh to people accustomed to the easy-going American administration. Of great injury to the pride of the Guamanians was the changing of the name of their homeland to "Omiyajima" (Great Shrine Island) and that of their capital city to "Akashi" (Red or Bright Stone). In the same vein of keeping the populace always aware of the fact they no longer lived under American supervision, the military ordered schools to teach Japanese instead of English. Even with the institution of food rationing and a system of discipline whereby an entire family or community would receive punishment for the wrong-doings of an individual, the natives retained their attitude of watchful neutrality.

[22] This unit was the South Seas Detached Force under MajGen Tomitara Horii, organized in November 1941 for the purpose of assaulting Pacific bases. It was built around the 114th Inf Regt and reinforced by units of the Japanese 55th Div. MID, WD, Order of Battle for the Japanese Armed Forces, 1Mar45, hereinafter cited as *OB for Japanese*.

[23] The account of the defense and capture of Guam was taken from *Surrender Report to CNO*. The garrison of the island at the time of its capture was composed of 30 naval officers, six warrant officers, five naval nurses, 230 regular naval enlisted men; seven Marine officers, one warrant officer, 145 Marine enlisted men, and 246 members of the native Insular Force.

JAPANESE NAVAL TASK FORCE landing site at Dungcas Beach on 10 December 1941 and the route through Agana to Orote Peninsula is shown in this picture from an illustrated review of Japanese naval operations. (Army Photograph.)

They were not happy, but life was endurable.

When the Japanese began to build up Guam's defenses, forced labor supplemented the work of their own construction units. Men, women, and children worked with their hands, and little else, on the airfields being rushed to completion. The Japanese recognized the value of the preliminary work and surveys done by the Americans and proceeded to build airfields on the sites selected on Orote, at Tiyan, and in the vicinity of Dededo.[24] But this activity was just the start of the work planned for the unhappy Guamanians, and the worst was yet to come.

When Japanese army units began returning to the island as reinforcements in the spring of 1944, the enemy dropped all pretense of getting along with the natives. The military closed schools, forbade church attendance, and took over all government functions. As the garrison grew larger, an acute shortage of food developed and the Japanese seized all available stockpiles. In addition, they drastically increased forced labor demands and further reduced the already small pittance of food supplies of the natives. A bare subsistence ration was issued to the worker, and those too sick or weak to produce had even this withheld.

Finally, the Japanese ordered all people living in the military areas to evacuate their homes, and herded them into concentration camps in the interior. Medical supplies were limited, sanitation non-existent, and food inadequate. Hundreds died, and small children who did survive became stunted and deformed from disease and malnutrition. Human bodies were beaten and broken, but within them the spirit remained alive. Every bow to a Japanese officer, every blow received for some real or fancied offense, every violation of native customs and traditions only served to heighten the resentment against Japanese rule.[25]

[24] Only the airfield at Dededo was not operational at the time of the American landing. American surveys had shown that Guam had terrain suitable for a minimum of six long-range bomber strips, 11 medium bomber runways, six fighter, and four emergency airfields. *ONI–99.*

[25] The story of Japanese rule on Guam is taken from Maj F. O. Hough, *The Island War,* (Philadelphia, 1947), 282–284, hereinafter cited as *The Island War;*

THE JAPANESE WERE READY [26]

Heavy air strikes against the Gilbert Islands in September 1943 alerted Japanese Imperial Headquarters to a possible American advance through the Central Pacific. In an attempt to strengthen the island barrier against the advancing enemy, a veteran division, the 13th, was tapped for duty in the Marianas. In October an advance detachment, 300 strong, left Central China with the strongest element slated for the island of Guam. The division itself, which had been fighting in China since 1937, did not follow its advance guard to the Pacific outposts, but remained to take part in the Hengyang-Kweilin (South China) campaign of late 1944. Instead, a substitute division from the formidable Kwantung Army in Manchuria was selected to take its place. This unit, the 29th Division (Lieutenant General Takeshi Takashina), was reorganized early in February 1944 into an RCT-type (Regimental Combat Team) division [27] for immediate duty in the Central Pacific.

PFC S. Fink, "Co-Prosperity on Guam," *MC Gazette,* October 1944, 43–47; interrogations of Guamanians contained in IIIAC C–2 Jnl.

[26] In preparing the story of the Japanese buildup on Guam American intelligence journals, reports, and operation plan annexes of IIIAC units have been consulted. In addition, several important Japanese documents have been used extensively to check American findings and insure an accurate narrative. Among them is a study from the files of the OCMH, USA written by officers from Imperial General Headquarters giving the Tokyo view of the Guam campaign, hereinafter cited as *Japanese Defense of Guam.* The former operations officer of the Japanese 29th Division, LtCol Hideyuki Takeda, who came out of the Guam jungle to surrender following the end of the war, wrote an outline in October 1946 of the Japanese defense plan and operations on the island which is hereinafter cited as *Takeda.* In February 1952 Col Takeda answered a series of questions from the DirMCHistory that sought to clear up many important disputed points of Japanese strategy and tactics during the defense of the island. This document, probably the most important single enemy source on the Guam operation, will be hereinafter cited as *Takeda Letter.*

[27] The 29th had been a standard triangular division in Manchuria, and upon reorganization dropped its engineer, cavalry, and transport regiments and gained a tank unit. Each of its infantry regiments was assigned an artillery battalion and an engineer company. Transportation was now handled by a motor transport company and a sea transport unit. *OB for Japanese,* 71–72.

MAJOR GENERAL TOMITARA HORI, commander of the South Seas Detached Force, the main Japanese Army assault unit during the capture of Guam on 10 December 1941.

Men from the Nagoya District of Honshu Island, most of whom had been in service since 1941, formed the unit's combat teams, the 18th, 38th, and 50th. On 19 February, units of the 29th cleared their training areas near Liaoyang and entrained for Pusan, Korea on the first leg of their journey to Guam.

Even as the 29th left Manchuria, Imperial Headquarters ordered additional troops readied to reinforce the division. Elements of the 1st (Tokyo District) and 11th (Shikoku Island District) Divisions, also of the Kwantung Army, were formed into the 6th Expeditionary Force and sailed from Pusan early in March. They had an uneventful voyage, but such was not the case for their predecessors. Watchdog American submarines caught the 29th's convoy about 48 hours out of Saipan and torpedoed two of the transports, sinking one. This ship, the *Sakito Maru*, transporting the 18th RCT and

eight of the division's tanks, carried to the bottom almost 1,400 men and all of the regiment's equipment. Accompanying destroyers picked up survivors and brought them into Saipan, where the unit was reorganized and partially re-equipped. The ship carrying the 50th RCT received orders to stop at Tinian where the regiment disembarked and took over the island's garrison. The rest of the convoy, carrying division headquarters and the 38th, continued on to Guam, reaching there on 4 March.

On landing, the division joined the 54th Keibitai, a naval guard unit which had garrisoned the island since its seizure by the Japanese on 10 December 1941. Until July 1944 additional naval antiaircraft (AA) and guard units moved to Guam to serve under the 54th's command, so that the total of naval combat troops had reached nearly 3,000 by the time of the American landing. In addition, two naval construction battalions, the 217th and 218th Setsueitai, came in during the occupation to work on Guam's airfields, and their 1,800 men were available as untrained combat troops. Ground remnants of the air groups that had been stationed on the island rounded out the total of available naval forces. Their planes were gone, some lost in attacks on carrier task forces, others shot down over Western New Guinea. To oppose General Douglas MacArthur's landing at Biak on 27 May approximately half of the available naval land-based aircraft had been shuttled down from the Palaus and Marianas.

Consequently, by the time the American assault force appeared off Saipan in June, the Japanese no longer possessed effective shore-based naval air in the Marianas. Tokyo watched intently the progress of the battle for Saipan, and loss of the island led to the decision of enemy Combined Fleet Headquarters that it "had no intention of trying to carry out large-scale attacks, having assumed that Guam and Tinian [also] would be lost."[28]

---

[28] USSBS(Pac), NavAnalysisDiv, *Interrogations of Japanese Officials*, (Washington, 1946), Interrogation No. 448 of Capt Mitsuo Fushida, IJN: Senior Staff Officer, 1st Air Fleet, Sept43–Apr44; Air Staff Officer to CinC, Combined Fleet, Apr44–Sept45. This work will be cited hereinafter by USSBS(Pac) interrogation numbers and descriptions.

With the arrival of the 29th Division head-quarters on Guam, command of Guam and Rota passed to an area group headquarters under General Takashina. At this time orders placed all Navy as well as Army forces under his operational control in case the island should be assaulted. On 20 March, the 5,100 men of the 6th Expeditionary Force (six infantry battalions, two artillery battalions, and two engineer companies), commanded by Major General Kiyoshi Shigematsu, arrived and completed the roster of major units charged with the defense of Guam. By 4 June, the depleted 18th Regiment,[29] less the 1st Battalion left on Saipan, had rejoined the division, bringing with it two companies of the 9th Tank Regiment. This brought the military strength on the island to approximately 18,500. (See Appendix VII)

Shortly thereafter, Takashina reorganized the 6th Expeditionary Force into two tactical units for greater efficiency. The three infantry battalions of the 11th Division formed four battalions (319th to 322d) of the 48th Independent Mixed Brigade (IMB), while battal-

---

[29] Infantry battalions of the 18th Regt were under-strength because of the sinking of the *Sakito Maru*, and their organization on Guam included only a head-quarters, three rifle companies, and a trench mortar company (seven 90mm's).

20CM COAST DEFENSE GUN position located on Bangi Point illustrates the half-finished condition of many Japanese defensive installations at the time of the III Amphibious Corps landing. (Navy Photograph.)

ions from the 1st Division made up the 10th Independent Mixed Regiment (IMR).[30] On 23 June 1/10 with an artillery battery and an engineer platoon attached moved to Rota to garrison that island. A few days later, a task force composed of the 3d Battalion, 18th Regiment plus supporting engineers and amphibious transport units followed. According to Lieutenant Colonel Hideyuki Takeda (Operations Officer of the 29th Division) the mission of the force:

. . . was to move to Rota for the purpose of conducting a counter-landing on Saipan, upon suitable opportunity, in order to reinforce the Saipan defense forces. . . . [However,] since the condition of the sea made the plan impossible, it returned to Guam on 29 June. In the course of the amphibious movement a boat accident occurred and two boats and 100 men were lost.[31]

---

[30] Infantry battalions of the 48th IMB and 10th IMR were organized into a headquarters, three rifle companies, a machine-gun company, and an infantry gun company (two 47mm AT guns and either two or four howitzers). The 38th RCT's battalions had the same organization, except the gun company had four 37mm AT guns and two howitzers.

[31] *Takeda Letter.*

LIEUTENANT GENERAL TAKESHI TAKASHINA (right), Commanding General, 29th Infantry Division, inspects defenses along Agat Beach with Colonel Tsunetaro Suenaga, Commanding Officer, 38th Infantry. (Army Photograph)

Surviving troops were immediately assigned defensive positions and started to strengthen their areas as rapidly as possible. Although the remainder of the 29th Division had made intensive efforts to build up beach and airfield defenses, time began to run out. When Japanese commanders found they could not complete all the work that had been planned, they concentrated on strengthening the high ground inland and to the flanks of the most likely landing beaches. From Tumon Bay to Facpi Point obstacles and mines studded the fringing reef, while machine guns, mortars, artillery, and coast defense guns were laid to cover the obstacles and beaches. Small but adequate dumps containing ammunition, rations, and medical supplies were scattered at points throughout the island where area defense forces might make a stand. That the build-up was progressing at a rapid pace is borne out by the fact that late in May American photo reconnaissance planes added 70 new targets to the III Amphibious Corps intelligence maps. On 6 June pilots reported 51 more enemy positions.[32]

With the capture of 31st Army Headquarters on Saipan, a vast quantity of documents dealing with unit dispositions and strengths throughout the Central Pacific islands fell into American hands. Using this information, intelligence officers drastically revised their estimate of Japanese strength on Guam. An indication of the value of this find is shown in the revisions in order of battle: 8 May, 6,900–9,300 troops; 27 May, 10,100–11,800; 9 July, 27,618–28,118; 18 July, 18,657 (plus aviation ground troops).[33] This last figure, accompanied by a detailed breakdown of units present on the island, agreed with very few exceptions with the final order of battle compiled by III Amphibious Corps after contact had been made with the defending forces.[34] One item of information not available to corps was the fact that the 31st Army's commander, Lieutenant General Hideyoshi Obata, was on Guam. He had been forced to stop there when the American landing at Saipan caught him returning from an inspection tour of the Palau Islands. From an improvised headquarters, he supervised the defense of the Marianas, leaving the immediate defense of Guam, however, to General Takashina.[35]

With the help of Saipan information, IIIAC plotted Takashina's main defensive dispositions and distributed a sketch map to units showing the enemy situation at the end of June. Guam had been divided into two major defense sectors: the area from Facpi Point to Agat Bay, including Orote Peninsula, was under the commanding officer of the 38th RCT, Colonel Tsunetaro Suenaga, who had his headquarters in the vicinity of Mt. Alifan; the rest of the island came under the 48th IMB's general, Shigematsu, with local sectors under the commanders of the 10th IMR and the 18th Regiment. (See Map 3) In the Agat sector, 1/38 and 2/38 defended the area from Bangi Point to Agat Village. Naval infantry, antiaircraft, and coast defense[36] units mainly from the 54th Keibitai covered Orote Peninsula with its airfield. A battery of mountain artillery[37] and the 1st Company, 9th Tank Regiment supported the 38th Infantry.

General Shigematsu's dispositions included the 2d and 3d Battalions of the 10th IMR spread out from Umatac to Yona in southern Guam, with the regimental headquarters at Inarajan. The extreme northern portion of the island was assigned to 2/18 while the headquarters of the regiment was near Mt. Chachao

---

[32] IIIAC OpPlan 1–44, 11May44.

[33] *Ibid.*, and TF 56 G–2 Rpt, Appendix H.

[34] See Appendix VII, Japanese Order of Battle on Guam. The remarkably accurate order of battle compiled by IIIAC was principally the work of Capt R. H. Beckwith according to the former C–2. Ltr Col W. F. Coleman to author, 23Sept52.

[35] *Takeda; Japanese Defense of Guam.*

[36] A tabulation by IIIAC on 10Aug44 showed that 19 8-inch, eight 6-inch, 22 5-inch, and six 3-inch coast defense guns had been destroyed or captured on Guam. IIIAC C–2 Periodic Rpt 21.

[37] A document captured on Saipan lists the following Army artillery pieces as being on Guam on 1Jun44:

14	105mm Howitzers
18	75mm Guns
40	75mm Pack Howitzers
8	75mm AA Guns
9	70mm Pack Howitzers
9	57mm AT Guns
30	47mm AT Guns
47	37mm AT Guns
6	20mm AA Guns

TF 56 G–2 Rpt, Appendix H.

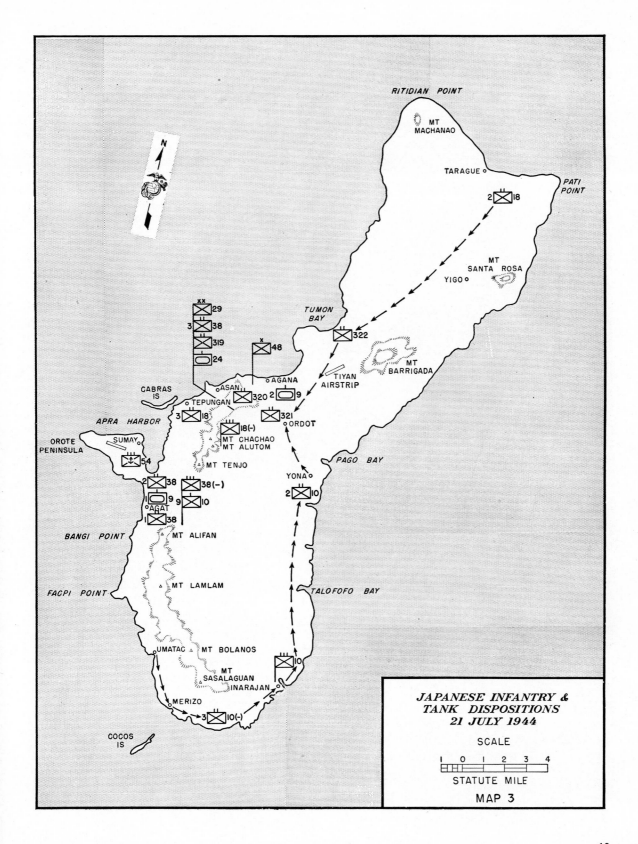

RITIDIAN POINT

MT
MACHANAO

TARAGUE

PATI
POINT

2 ⊠ 18

MT
SANTA ROSA

YIGO

TUMON
BAY

322

MT
BARRIGADA

TIYAN
AIRSTRIP

xx
29

3 ⊠ 38

319

24

x 48

AGANA

ASAN

TEPUNGAN

320 2 9

321

ORDOT

CABRAS
IS

APRA HARBOR

3 ⊠ 18

18(-)

MT CHACHAO
MT ALUTOM

MT TENJO

OROTE
PENINSULA

SUMAY

54

PAGO BAY

2 ⊠ 38

38(-)

YONA

9 9 ⊠ 10

1 ⊠ 38

AGAT

2 ⊠ 10

BANGI POINT

MT ALIFAN

FACPI POINT

MT LAMLAM

TALOFOFO BAY

MT BOLANOS

UMATAC

10

MT
SASALAGUAN

INARAJAN

MERIZO

3 ⊠ 10(-)

COCOS
IS

JAPANESE INFANTRY &
TANK DISPOSITIONS
21 JULY 1944

SCALE

1 0 1 2 3 4

STATUTE MILE

MAP 3

13

SIX-INCH GUN, part of a three-gun battery on Chonito Cliff, whose fortification was halted by the preliminary bombardment of the Southern Attack Force. Notice the commanding field of fire this gun had over the Asan beachhead. (Navy Photograph.)

and the 3d Battalion in the vicinity of Tepungan. The infantry battalions of the 48th IMB were located as follows: the 320th behind the Asan beaches, the 321st spread out from Agana to the Tiyan airfield, and the 322d at Tumon Bay in the vicinity of the incomplete Dededo airstrip. Two battalions of artillery and the 2d Company, 9th Tank Regiment backed up the beach defenses.

In addition to its headquarters troops, the 29th Division held a substantial mobile reserve in the hills behind Agana. Included in it were the 3d Battalion of the 38th RCT, the 319th Battalion of the 48th IMB, and the 24th Tank Company. Located at the airfields and along the beaches were scattered elements of naval ground and air units manning AA and coast defense gun positions under control of local Army sector commanders.

The preliminary bombardment in June and the long prelanding preparation in July opened the eyes of the Japanese to the beaches selected by the Americans for their landing.[38] An artillery officer of the 38th RCT noted the impact area of the "all-day bombings and bombardment" and logically concluded that the landings would take place near Gaan Point.[39] Even the privates had the right idea: one from 2/10 noted in his diary on 11 July that "the chances seem to be that the enemy main force plans to

[38] CruDiv-6 (RAdm C. T. Joy) of the preliminary bombardment group of TF 53 commanded by RAdm W. L. Ainsworth started working over the beaches on Guam as scheduled at 0815, 16 June (W-minus 2). This shelling continued for two hours before Adm Spruance ordered cancellation of 18 June as W-Day because of an imminent fleet engagement. This preliminary bombardment was a clear tip-off to the Japanese as to the exact landing beaches to be used by the Americans. ComFifthFlt WD, June 1944, 12; ltr VAdm W. L. Ainsworth to author, 3Oct52.

[39] CinCPac-CinCPOA Item 11,943—Diary of 2dLt Kanemitsu Kurukowa.

land in the Agana-Piti area." [40] Division headquarters acted on the tell-tale information furnished by American bombs and shells and began maneuvering the outlying elements of its command into positions to repulse the expected landings.

Starting on 8 July, the 10th IMR began withdrawing from southern Guam to an assembly area near Yona where it could back up the Asan beaches. The 9th Company of the 10th IMR was assigned on 11 July to reserve positions near Mt. Alifan directly supporting the 38th RCT. Infantry units in the north started moving later in July to the Ordot area to reinforce the 320th Battalion at Asan. Repeated Japanese diary entries for this period indicate that fire from American ships and planes severely handicapped all these movements. One engineer squad leader summed up the general feeling when he wrote, "On this island no matter where one goes the shells follow." [41]

Even while Japanese units moved into position to cut off the landing areas, the 29th Division maintained effective communication with them by wire [42] or radio. The disruptive effect of the continual American pounding slowed, but did not stop the concentration of the enemy. Moving mostly at night, the battalions gradually assembled in their assigned areas. An order signed by General Shigematsu on 15 July indicated he was moving to his battle command post in the Fonte hill mass overlooking the Asan Beach. With final preparations made, the defending Japanese were ordered to "seek certain victory at the beginning of the battle . . . to utterly destroy the landing enemy at the water's edge." [43] The Japanese were ready.

---

[40] CinCPac-CinCPOA Item 10,996—Diary of Leading Pvt Murano Kaki.

[41] CinCPac-CinCPOA Item 10,410—Diary of unidentified soldier.

[42] Wire lines from division to sector defense headquarters were always laid in two and sometimes three separate routes through defiladed areas. Within the sectors, since the Japanese knew the landing areas, they were able to lay their lines in ring shape through protected ravines and gullies on the flanks of the beaches. *Takeda Letter*.

[43] CinCPac-CinCPOA Item 10,377—Agana Sector Garrison Order A–127, 15Jul44.

CHAPTER II Planning and Preparing

Throughout a series of high-level international military conferences in 1943 various ideas for speeding up the Pacific war were presented and discussed. Admiral Ernest J. King, Commander-in-Chief, United States Fleet, championed a plan to throw the power of the Navy behind a drive through the Central Pacific. Consistently, he presented the Marianas to the Combined Chiefs of Staff (CCS) of the Allies and to the Joint Chiefs of Staff (JCS) as a key objective. He felt it was necessary to have these islands to control the Central Pacific routes of advance to the Philippines and the Japanese home islands. Just as consistently, his concept was challenged by those feeling that a powerful thrust up from the Southwest Pacific would better achieve, and with fewer casualties, the same end result. It became apparent by late 1943 that a decision must be made to assign priority to one or the other of these conflicting strategies.

During JCS conferences in mid-November, the admiral's plan gained a powerful advocate, General Henry H. Arnold, Commanding General, Army Air Forces. Air Force planners felt the B–29 fields that existed in China would not be adequate for the projected air war of attrition against Japan. Proposed bases at Chengtu and Chungking would require the big planes either to refuel at supplemental bases or carry a reduced bomb load. Airstrips closer to the China coast could not be considered because the Japanese either had captured them or were threatening them. General Arnold felt that the Marianas would offer base security, and at the same time reduce the round trip flight to Japan by 1,200 miles.[1] These factors, added to Admiral King's concept, tipped the scale in favor of the Central Pacific route.

The Combined Chiefs gave their approval of the JCS agreements at a conference in Cairo in early December 1943. President Roosevelt and Prime Minister Churchill indorsed a plan for specific operations to defeat Japan, which included the campaign to seize Guam and the Japanese Marianas. Concurrent operations in both the Central and Southwest Pacific theaters were approved. However, should there be an unavoidable contest for troops, ships, or supplies the Central Pacific would be favored.[2]

JOINT PLANNING[3]

With the go-ahead signal given by top Allied leaders, Admiral Chester W. Nimitz, acting in his dual capacity as Commander-in-Chief, Pacific Fleet (CinCPac) and Pacific Ocean Areas

[1] General of the Air Force H. H. Arnold, *Global Mission*, (New York, 1949), 476–480, 536, hereinafter cited as *Global Mission*.

[2] For a detailed account of the highest level conferences and decisions leading up to the Marianas campaign see *Saipan*, 13–22.

[3] The principal sources used in the preparation of this section were the planning reports of TF 51, TF 56, TF 53, IIIAC, and the operation reports of the 3d MarDiv and the 1st ProvMarBrig.

(CinCPOA),[4] could issue his plan for Central Pacific operations during 1944. This campaign plan, GRANITE, published 27 December 1943, contained a tentative schedule of targets for the coming year. In it the Marianas were listed for mid-November as the 1944 finale for CinCPOA's forces. Seventeen days later, 13 January 1944, another issue of GRANITE set the time for the first phase of the Marianas campaign, capture of Saipan and Tinian, as 1 November. The attack on Guam, the second phase, was scheduled to be launched by 15 December.

Soon, however, planners revised their original estimates. Marine and Army troops smashed ashore on the islands of Kwajalein Atoll and scored a speedy victory at surprisingly little cost. As a result, Admiral Nimitz advanced the date for the Eniwetok assault from 1 May to 17 February. Five days after the initial landing this atoll was in American hands.[5] During the same period, on 16–17 February, Vice Admiral Marc A. Mitscher's Fast Carrier Task Force's (TF 58) covering strike against Truk revealed the vaunted Japanese naval base much weaker than had been supposed.[6] It now became obvious that air strikes could contain the Japanese remaining on Truk,[7] thus removing the threat to the flank of the Central Pacific drive. Seizure of the Admiralties in the spring of 1944 assured neutralization of the Japanese strong point by land-based aircraft and cleared the path for the capture of the Southern Marianas.

As a result of re-evaluation of the progress of the Pacific war in light of the early 1944 successes, JCS had issued a directive on 12 March 1944 covering future Pacific operations. With it came a definite end of any debate on the inevitability of the Marianas campaign. In the Southwest Pacific, in order to expedite the development of the Admiralties as a forward base, General MacArthur (CinCSWPA)[8] had been ordered to advance the date of his attack on Hollandia, New Guinea. He also had received directions to cancel the proposed operations against Kavieng[9] and after seizing bases in the Admiralties to isolate that Japanese base and the one at Rabaul. All ships of the Pacific Fleet allotted for Kavieng were to be returned to CinCPac's control by 5 May.

Under terms of the same directive, Admiral Nimitz received instructions to step up carrier strikes against the Marianas, Palaus, and Carolines. The order also called for the seizure of the Southern Marianas for purposes of developing B–29 bases and secondary naval bases and set 15 June as the target date for the operation (FORAGER). Both major Pacific commanders were directed to coordinate their future plans to provide mutual support in all forthcoming operations.[10]

---

[4] Adm Nimitz as senior naval officer in the Pacific was in command of all ships of the Pacific Fleet (CinCPac). At the same time, he and Gen MacArthur divided American command of Pacific areas. MacArthur exercised control of all Army, Navy, and Marine forces in the Southwest Pacific (CinCSWPA) while Nimitz had the same role in the South, Central, and North Pacific, jointly titled Pacific Ocean Areas (CinCPOA).

[5] For the story of American operations against the Japanese in the Marshalls see the MC historical monograph by LtCol J. A. Crown due for publication in 1954.

[6] Adm Mineichi Koga, CinC, ComFlt, ordered the evacuation of Truk as advanced fleet base on 10Feb44 to avoid expected American attacks there. He met his death as a result of another American assault, that of Gen MacArthur's forces on Hollandia. On 31 March his plane was lost at sea while he was flying from the Palaus to Davao to direct operations against the landing forces. *Campaigns*, 205–207.

[7] According to the Japanese they were alerted to the threat of a landing on Truk by this first carrier strike. By mid-April a division and a half of Army troops had

been brought in to augment the small Navy garrison. For the duration of the war over 30,000 men were immobilized on the by-passed island. USSBS(Pac) Interrogation No. 503 of VAdm Shigeru Fukudome; CofS, Combined Fleet, 1940–Apr41; Chief 1st Section, Naval General Staff, Apr41–May43; Commander, 2d Air Fleet, Jul44–15Jan45; Commander, 10th Area Fleet, 15Jan45–Dec45, hereinafter cited as *Fukudome*.

[8] CinCSoWesPac was the abbreviation used mostly by Navy documents. However, the abbreviation CinCSWPA appears in JCS documents and will be used throughout this monograph.

[9] One of the Marine units later employed in the Guam assault, the 3d MarDiv, was originally scheduled for this operation. The 4th Mar, also originally slated for Kavieng, was sent against Emirau instead and later participated in the Guam operation as part of the 1st ProvMarBrig.

[10] JCS 713/4, 12Mar44.

In keeping with his orders, CinCPOA sent a secret dispatch to major units on 13 March assigning highest priority to preparations for the Marianas campaign. A week later, 20 March, his Joint Staff at Pearl Harbor issued a study to guide commanders in their advance planning. It called for employment of the V Amphibious Corps (VAC), consisting of the 2d and 4th Marine Divisions, and the Army's XXIV Corps Artillery. These units would be charged with responsibility of seizing Saipan and Tinian and mount out from the Hawaiian area. In addition, another Marine amphibious corps, IIIAC,[11] would mount for the operation from Guadalcanal and recapture Guam. Integral parts of the corps included the 3d Marine Division, the 1st Provisional Marine Brigade, and IIIAC Artillery. The Army's 27th Infantry Division, although under operational control of VAC, was to be Expeditionary Troops Reserve. Loading from the Hawaiian area, the 27th had the mission of being prepared to support either corps. Assigned as area reserve for FORAGER and alerted for movement to the target 20 days after D-Day at Saipan was the 77th Infantry Division, scheduled to arrive soon in the Hawaiian Islands from the United States. For the important assignment of Commander, Expeditionary Troops (TF 56) CinCPOA named Lieutenant General Holland M. Smith, Commanding General, VAC.[12]

Since FORAGER, as well as all other Central Pacific operations came under naval jurisdiction, Admiral Nimitz assigned Admiral Raymond A. Spruance to over-all command. (See Organization Chart, Map Section) Spruance, as Commander Fifth Fleet and Central Pacific Task Forces, designated Vice Admiral Richmond K. Turner to control the Joint Expeditionary Force (TF 51) assigned to the Marianas assault. The forces under Turner were further divided into two task forces: one, the Northern Attack Force (TF 52), to land the assault and garrison troops under VAC on the islands of Saipan and Tinian; the other, TF 53, the South-

IIIAC LEADERS examine a plaster relief map of Guam on board the *Appalachian*. Left to right: Major General Geiger, Corps Commander; Colonel Silverthorn, Corps Chief of Staff; Brigadier General del Valle, Corps Artillery Commander.

ern Attack Force (Rear Admiral Richard L. Conolly) to land and protect the troops of the IIIAC on Guam. Admiral Turner would exercise a dual command over TF 51 and 52, just as General Smith would serve concurrently as Expeditionary Troops Commander and Commanding General of the Northern Troops and Landing Force.

Pursuant to directives from higher headquarters, staff planners from Admiral Conolly's Amphibious Group Three met at Pearl Harbor with those from Major General Roy S. Geiger's IIIAC. Also present were representatives of TF 51 and TF 56 with their preliminary drafts to furnish a guide for lower echelon conferees. Work started on the basic plan to recapture STEVEDORE (code name assigned Guam) on 30 March. Four days later (3 April) General Holland Smith approved a tentative operation plan presented by General Geiger, and the following day its provisions were tentatively accepted in turn by Admirals Turner and Spruance.

The plan called for the IIIAC, designated Southern Troops and Landing Force (STLF), to make simultaneous landings at two points on the west coast of Guam. To accomplish this, Admiral Conolly divided TF 53 into Northern and Southern Attack Groups, the former under his own command and the latter under Rear

---

[11] On 15Apr44, the I Marine Amphibious Corps was redesignated III Amphibious Corps. For purposes of continuity this unit has been referred to as IIIAC or III Corps throughout the monograph.

[12] TF 56 G–3 Rpt, 1–2.

Admiral Lawrence F. Reifsnider. In the north, the 3d Marine Division would land on beaches between Adelup Point and the Tatgua River; in the south, the 1st Provisional Marine Brigade, followed by III Corps Artillery, would land on beaches between Agat Village and Bangi Point. Both units were then to advance inland and establish the Force Beachhead Line (FBL) along the commanding ground, Adelup–Alutom–Tenjo–Alifan–Facpi Point. Control over the important Orote Peninsula-Apra Harbor area was to be gained as rapidly as possible, and then further operations conducted to seize the remainder of Guam. In addition, the plan provided that the corps reinforce the Saipan landing if the situation required it.[13]

One of the major units of III Corps committed to STEVEDORE was in the process of formation at this time. The 1st Provisional Marine Brigade had been activated on 22 March with its skeleton headquarters located at Pearl Harbor. The troop strength of the brigade was not immediately available; the 4th Marines had just occupied Emirau (20 March) and the 22d Marines was still engaged taking the Lesser

Marshalls. Both units would be transferred to Guadalcanal upon being released from their respective assignments. A few senior members of the brigade staff, however, were working on the myriad problems entailed in the formation of such a large unit. Along with this gigantic task, a tentative operation plan for STEVEDORE had to be formulated. Despite the short time allotted, the staff submitted a plan and had it approved before General Geiger returned to Guadalcanal on 7 April. Brigadier General Lemuel C. Shepherd, Jr. assumed command of the brigade on 16 April, replacing Colonel John T. Walker who remained as Chief of Staff.[14]

Eight days after the departure of the corps staff from Pearl Harbor, Admiral Conolly also flew to Guadalcanal in order to facilitate joint planning between the naval support vessels and the corps troops. He and his staff established a temporary CP near the 3d Marine Division at IIIAC Headquarters at Tetere, and detailed planning got under way. Until 27 April the naval officers got an unaccustomed taste of "camping out," at which time CTF 53's flag-

---

[13] IIIAC SAR, Planning Rpt, 1–2.

[14] BrigGen Thomas E. Watson who took command of the 1st ProvMarBrig when it was activated on 22Mar44 had been assigned as CG, 2d MarDiv on 10Apr44.

REAR ADMIRAL CONOLLY, Southern Attack Force Commander, confers with top leaders of the Northern Attack Group on Guadalcanal. Left to right: Brigadier General Noble, ADC, 3d Marine Division; Commander Buchanan, Commander, Northern Transport Group; Admiral Conolly; Major General Turnage, Commanding General, 3d Marine Division.

USS APPALACHIAN, flagship of Admiral Conolly, command vessel and communication center of the Southern Attack Force. (Navy Photograph.)

ship, USS *Appalachian* (AGC–1),[15] arrived to take the staff on board. The time was profitably spent, however, in smoothing the rough edges of operation plans and annexes. Also the officers took advantage of the opportunity presented for opposite numbers of staffs to become better acquainted with each other and the specialties of the respective services. With the opening of the 1st Brigade's CP at Tassafaronga, Guadalcanal on 2 May,[16] all major landing force units committed to STEVEDORE had elements in the area.

Most of the ships assigned TF 53 had been engaged in transporting and supporting General MacArthur's troops at Hollandia and had not yet arrived in the Guadalcanal area. Drawn largely from the South Pacific Forces of Admiral William F. Halsey, the ships were dispatched to nearby bases in the Solomons for servicing as they returned from the Southwest Pacific Area. This avoided overtaxing the fa-

cilities at Guadalcanal and Tulagi. The majority of the ships had returned by 10 May, and the work of replenishing expended supplies and repairing operational damage progressed satisfactorily thereafter.

On 7 May, III Corps received the final operation and administrative plan from Expeditionary Troops Headquarters. Five days later Admiral Turner's operation plan arrived on board the *Appalachian*. Both planning groups immediately started work on final drafts of orders to be distributed to subordinate units. A good portion of this task was already completed and had been accomplished through the constant efforts of staffs at all levels to coordinate directives from higher headquarters. Perhaps the greatest aid to speedy completion of the planning process was the standard practice followed of making tentative or rough drafts of plans available to lower echelons. This enabled work to proceed concurrently at attack force-corps and attack group-division levels. Corps completed STLF Operation Plan 1–44 with its accompanying administrative order on 11 May, and two days later the 3d Marine Division finished its plan. Both publications, however, lacked annexes giving particulars of air and naval gunfire (NGF) support. But Admiral Conolly's operation plan for the task force, distributed on 17 May, included not only air and NGF support details but also a tentative landing date (W-Day) of 18 June. By the end of the month, brigade had completed its plan, and the missing air and NGF annexes had been added to the division's document.[17]

---

[15] The AGC is an especially designed amphibious command ship for the use of the attack force and landing force staffs. It is equipped with extra communication gear, a photo lab, sound recording devices, and has large conference rooms to facilitate coordination of staff actions. Initially designated an auxiliary general communications vessel, AGC, it is now officially listed by the Navy as an amphibious force flagship.

[16] BrigGen Shepherd and a nucleus of his staff had arrived by air from Pearl Harbor on 22Apr44 to take part in the planning for STEVEDORE prior to the formal opening of the brigade CP. Ltr LtCol W. R. Norton to CMC, 26Nov52, hereinafter cited as *Norton.*

[17] Two alternate operation plans were subsequently made in case later information disclosed that either of the designated beaches in the preferred plan was too heavily defended or otherwise unsuitable for a landing. OpPlan 3–44 (Alternate plan-FORAGER) was issued on 30 May. This plan provided for landing the entire force in echelon on the beaches between Agat and Facpi Pt, seizing Orote Peninsula and Apra Harbor, and being prepared to conduct further operations to complete the seizure of Guam. OpPlan 4–44 (Second Alternate plan-FORAGER) was issued on 9 June. This plan envisaged the 3d MarDiv landing as per OpPlan 1–44, with the brigade landing on beaches between Bangi Pt and Facpi Pt, followed by an attack to the north to seize Orote Peninsula and Apra Harbor as per the preferred plan. IIIAC SAR, Planning Rpt, 2.

LOGISTICS

From a logistical as well as a tactical standpoint, the Marianas presented some new problems to amphibious planners in the Central Pacific. The campaigns to secure the tiny atolls of the Marshalls and the restricted beachheads of the Solomons had been successfully concluded. Now, a war of maneuver on a limited land mass was contemplated and requirements for supply and resupply,[18] evacuation and hospitalization, transportation, and the mission of service troops had to be reevaluated. With lives at stake, the absolute necessity of being right the first time imposed a terrific responsibility on the men mapping out the service functions of the operation.

Although the allotment of shipping for STEVEDORE was adequate to lift the units originally assigned, revisions and additions to the troop list forced a drastic reduction in cargo space available.[19] The number of organic vehicles to be brought along was especially limited, and commanders carefully scanned equipment requirements at all levels to eliminate anything that might be classed as "excess baggage." Unexpected orders on 4 May placed an additional burden on TF 53 and IIIAC by giving them responsibility for embarking the entire first garrison echelon. This included 84 officers and 498 enlisted men of Major General Henry L. Larsen's Island Command Headquarters group.[20] Thereafter, in view of the shipping available, constant adjustments were necessary to meet combat and service requirements of assault and garrison units. The personnel

and equipment additions further curtailed cargo space and acted to limit the capabilities of some units assigned to the assault echelon.[21] Close personal cooperation at the higher staff level continued between the various ship commanders and commanding officers of the units to be transported to the target.[22] Continual coordination by respective transport quartermasters (TQM's) insured effective loading arrangements best suited to the needs of the embarked units.

Sanitation for troops on board ship, details of casualty treatment and evacuation at Guam, and provisions for adequate medical care at all times were the subject of numerous conferences between landing and attack force medical officers. The plan, as it finally evolved, called for all units to embark with their full medical strength, plus a three to five percent increase over table of organization allowances for corpsmen.[23] Levels of medical supply were set so that they would be adequate for both the assault and garrison units. But the shortage of shipping space caused higher headquarters to disapprove the request of the corps surgeon to embark medical supplies for the civilian population.[24] Fortunately, the order limiting organic transportation to be lifted to Guam did not include ambulance jeeps, and consequently medical units could take along their full allowance of vehicles.

The transportation picture for amphibious vehicles was also quite a bit better than for most motor transport. The 3d Amphibian Tractor Battalion (180 tractors) had been assigned to the 3d Marine Division, and the 4th with its 178 tractors had been attached to the 1st Pro-

---

[18] In order to conserve shipping space on resupply vessels after the campaign was over, the 1st ProvMarBrig was ordered to leave most of its organizational equipment on Guam. After repair and servicing by 5th FldDep the gear was to be issued to the 3d MarDiv which was slated for island garrison. The brigade, on its return to Guadalcanal, would receive replacements from SoPac supply depots. TF 56 G–4 Rpt, 13.

[19] IIIAC SAR, SupRpt, 3.

[20] IsCom WD, 15Apr–15Aug44, 2–5. MajGen H. L. Larsen, prospective Island Commander of Guam, and 11 members of his staff arrived at IIIAC Headquarters on 29 May and immediately started coordinating their preliminary plans with the assault elements of the corps. This early coordination proved to be of mutual benefit. Ltr MajGen M. H. Silverthorn to CMC, 16Oct-52, hereinafter cited as *Silverthorn*.

[21] IIIAC SAR, SupRpt, 1–4.

[22] More than one officer has commented on the close cooperation between Adm Conolly, his staff, and the assault ground forces. The Corps C–2 recalls hearing Adm Conolly tell General Geiger that "my aim is to get the troops ashore standing up. You tell me what you want done to accomplish this and we'll do it." Ltr Col W. F. Coleman to CMC, 5Sep52, hereinafter cited as *Coleman 1952*.

[23] IIIAC SAR, MedRpt, 1.

[24] After the landing on Guam, sufficient supplies to care for the Guamanians were furnished from existing Marine stocks, captured Japanese dumps, and material sent in from transports by Adm Conolly. *Ibid.*, 2.

visional Marine Brigade.[25]   After these LVT's landed the initial assault waves, they would be available for transshipment of cargo and troops over the reef barriers to the beach.   In this task they would be assisted by the amphibian trucks (DUKW's) of the IIIAC Motor Transport Battalion.   This unit had been converted recently to a DUKW organization for the STEVEDORE operation, and its drivers had been hurriedly trained by civilian technicians and Army personnel furnished by the Commanding General, Forward Area South Pacific. During the landing of the assault waves, the DUKW's would carry in artillery pieces and radio jeeps and then be used for resupply.   Of the battalion's 100 DUKW's 60 were assigned to the 3d Division[26] while the remainder, one company (C), with 40 DUKW's, supported the brigade.

To assist the amphibious vehicles in their role as cargo carriers and to help bridge the reef-filled gap between deep water and the beach,

[25] For STEVEDORE both battalions were reinforced. Co A of the 10th AmphTracBn was assigned to the 3d AmphTracBn and Co A, 11th AmphTracBn to the 4th.

[26] The 60 DUKW's attached to the 3d MarDiv were distributed as follows: six sections of five vehicles each to lift in the 105mm howitzers of 3/12 and 4/12; three sections of eight DUKW's each to bring in radio jeeps; six to serve as mobile CP's for division, combat teams, and DUKW headquarters. The remaining capacity of the radio DUKW's was loaded with 37mm antitank guns and/or infantry ammunition. In each section of DUKW's one vehicle was fitted with an "A" frame to assist in unloading. 3d MarDiv OpPlan 2–44, 13May44.

PONTOON-LADEN LST prepares to discharge assault troops on W-Day before moving in to unload its temporary piers at the reef's edge.

TF 53 made provisions to take pontoon barges and piers to the target.   Their bulk presented a grave transportation problem to already harassed transport quartermasters.   It was solved, however, by having them mounted and side-carried to the target by LST's (landing ship, tank).   In the Northern Attack Group, seven LST's were assigned to carry four self-propelled pontoon barges each, and the Southern Attack Group had four similarly assigned. Twelve pontoon causeways, each with two sections 14 x 100 feet, also were sent along by means of LST carrier, eight to the northern beaches and four to the southern.   Once established off the reef at Guam, the pontoons could be used as floating docks, temporary storage points for high-priority gear, and as refueling stations for amphibious vehicles.   As a further aid to conquering the fringing reefs, and to provide traction for wheeled vehicles moving ashore, each LST of the attack force carried three reinforced wire mats, 240 square feet in area, to be laid on the coral by men of the shore party.[27]

In order to coordinate supply activities ashore, corps formed a service group using as a nucleus officers and men from the staffs of the corps engineer and corps quartermaster. Under Lieutenant Colonel Francis M. McAlister, the group would control the corps shore party, engineer, medical, supply, and transport facilities.   In addition, it would operate the port to be established in Apra Harbor and the airfields to be built until such time as units of the garrison forces took over.   It was contemplated that upon completion of the unloading of assault shipping, those units temporarily attached to the brigade and division as shore party personnel for the landing would revert to group control.

Moreover, the brigade's and division's pioneer and naval construction units were to come under group control as soon as possible after W-Day to assist in the enormous task of converting Guam into an advance base.   This centralized control of logistical activity ashore after troops secured the beachhead would have two advantages.   It would insure adequate support of

[27] CTF 53 OpPlan A162–44, 17May44.

units fighting the Japanese, and at the same time expedite the groundwork in base development. The service group could not hold training exercises since the units to be assigned to it on Guam were tactically attached to assault elements for the landing. Staffs, however, held conferences and all interested unit commanders had a hand in deciding policies.[28]

INTELLIGENCE

The information available regarding Guam and the enemy troops defending it affected all considerations of Naval and Marine planning. Studies which had been prepared periodically for Marine Corps Schools at Quantico, Virginia, which examined the island with a view toward its eventual development as a major base, furnished some intelligence.[29] More current knowledge was obtained from officers who had been stationed on Guam and natives who were away serving in the Navy at the time of their homeland's capture.

Considering the length of time the Navy had controlled the island, available topographic maps were surprisingly poor in detail on road nets and ground contours. Hydrographic charts, however, gave an excellent picture of the lay of reefs offshore. In June 1943 the Military Intelligence Service of the War Department gathered all available information and issued a preliminary intelligence guide for planners. After Pacific Ocean Area forces were definitely committeed to FORAGER, the Office of Naval Intelligence compiled a strategic study of Guam. Issued in February 1944, this exhaustive 345-page evaluation, labeled ONI–99, proved to be the prime source of information regarding the island.

The unknown factor to intelligence officers was the Japanese defensive situation. All indications showed the enemy rushing reinforcements to the Marianas, although the exact number of men and the extent of the build-up was indefinite. In the preliminary estimate of the enemy situation, issued in May with the final corps operation plan, an informed guess indicated that units of the Japanese 29th Infantry Division might be on Guam. It was not thought, however, that the entire unit had reached there.[30] The estimate turned out to be inaccurate. The division and its reinforcing units had reached the island and had begun the process of building up its defenses. In an attempt to shed some light on the enemy situation and changes in terrain wrought by the Japanese, commanders requested an up-to-date aerial photographic coverage. In this particular, intelligence agencies fell short of expected performance.

Cloud cover lessened the value of pictures taken on the first photo mission on 25 April. Repeated flights, however, in May and June did obtain an adequate coverage of most of the island and the invasion beaches. Even with these better photos, some commanders never did get a clear picture of the ground assigned them to capture.[31] Not until the invasion force embarked could a good one-to-five-thousand mosaic be assembled for study. At the same time, stereo-pairs were received and furnished the best analysis of the enemy's beachhead defenses.[32]

The submarine USS *Greenling* returned to base on 29 April after 27 days of reconnaissance operations in the Marianas and provided III Corps with its "best obliques" of Guam's beach terrain. Taken during periodic periscope exposures, the photographs gave a clear, close view of the proposed landing beaches and terrain inland. In addition to the photos, the sub had taken depth soundings, checked pre-

---

[28] IIIAC SAR, SerGruRpt, 1 and 1A–6A.

[29] The "Guam Problem" was given as part of a course at Marine Corps Schools as far back as 1936. Many of the officers serving with the 3d MarDiv and 1st ProvMarBrig during the planning for the invasion of the island had spent many days studying the problem of the defense and capture of Guam. One regimental commander commented, "In my own case my experience with the Guam Problem served me well and as a result I had a clear picture in my mind of the terrain and natural obstacles, which facilitated my planning, and later, control of troops." Ltr LtGen E. A. Craig to CMC, 19Nov52, hereinafter cited as *Craig Nov52*.

[30] IIIAC OpPlan 1–44, 11May44.

[31] The battalion commander of 1st Bn, 3d Mar noted that, "BLT 1/3 never had a photo showing the terrain in its zone of action between the reservoir and the Tenjo Road. There was always a big white spot marked 'cloud'." Ltr Maj H. Aplington, II to CMC, 9Apr47, hereinafter cited as *Aplington*.

[32] IIIAC SAR, IntelRpt, 3.

vailing tides and currents, and observed the air traffic from the fields on the island so that planners now had this intelligence available.

This added coverage helped the photographic situation at higher levels, but sufficient pictures were still not available to lower echelons until after the landings. This was not the case with maps, however, as adequate quantities of a

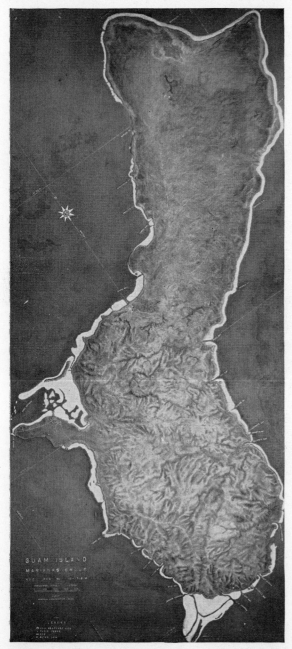

ISLAND OF GUAM as it appears on the rubber terrain map used to familiarize assault troops with their objective.

1:20,000 special air and gunnery target map (11 sheets) with a superimposed grid system had been distributed to lower troop levels. Corps used a 1:62,500 for control purposes, while units of the attack force used charts of one or two inches to the nautical mile during preparation and bombardment phases. The 1:20,000 map was a Marine Corps Schools draft based on Corps of Engineer surveys and revised through April 1944. For military purposes, it had several glaring faults. Vast areas of the ground actually covered by dense vegetation appeared as bare terrain. In many cases, broken ground contour lines indicated the interior had not been thoroughly surveyed. Finally, as troop commanders would soon discover, the map location of roads and trails in northern Guam often turned out to be inaccurate by hundreds of yards. Ironically, the Japanese defenders of the island, improving on the base survey used by the Americans, had furnished their troops with a much more accurate picture of Guam's terrain.[33] However, despite its obvious defects from an infantryman's point of view, the map used by III Corps units proved to be sufficiently accurate in most sectors to furnish good artillery data.[34]

Since good aerial photos were lacking, the 1:20,000 map had to be used as basic control for plaster relief maps of the island. Briefing sessions and planning conferences both used these models to obtain a clearer picture of terrain. Corps distributed sufficient quantities to provide one for every infantry and artillery battalion. In addition, the relief map section prepared 1:5000 plaster copies with a two to

[33] The former commanding officer of 3/21 furnished the Historical Branch with a copy of this enemy map for reference. Commenting on the map supplied to IIIAC units he said, "I have been waiting almost eight years to put in my two cents on this score. Ground forms were inaccurately shown all over the map that we used. It is deplorable that we had owned this island approximately forty years and still did not have an accurate map." Ltr Col W. H. Duplantis to author, 20Jan52, hereinafter cited as *Duplantis*.
[34] 12th Mar SAR, 1–2. Col E. C. Ferguson, commanding the brigade's artillery group, later commented that the map was extremely accurate on Orote Peninsula. On the other hand, the 12th Mar remarked on the inaccuracy of the map in northern Guam.

one exaggeration of the immediate beach area to aid assault elements.[35]

Responsible for the accuracy of these large scale models was Commander R. F. Armknecht (CEC) who had been public works officer on Guam prior to the war. He personally modeled most of this map, which impressed Admiral Conolly so much that he ordered five copies made for distribution to fire support ships. The many rubber terrain maps sent out from the United States, based on the Marine Corps Schools map, proved "inherently inaccurate." Nevertheless, because of their portability, the troops had only these models available on board the invasion transports.[36]

TACTICAL PLANNING

The tactical concept of the operation formulated by planning groups at Pearl Harbor in early April stood the test of prolonged scrutiny. Measured against available forces for landing, follow-up, and support, it seemed the plan most assured of success. Throughout April, corps attached the necessary reinforcing units to the brigade and division. Even though some of these units, such as the forward echelons of the 5th Field Depot and the 9th and 14th Defense Battalions, were slated for garrison duty on Guam they also received assignments for the assault phase. Other units, like the 1st Armored Amphibian Battalion, were committed only for the operation to provide added fire power during the landing. By the time the STLF received all attachments necessary for the landing the aggregate strength reached 39,080 men. This figure included both the assault elements and those garrison forces to be taken in the first echelon.[37]

Because initial enemy opposition might be fierce enough to contain the beachheads and prevent the planned link-up on the FBL, successful employment of corps artillery presented a problem. The minimum effective range of the powerful 155mm guns and howitzers was so great that they might be limited to deep support missions should the assault move slowly. To meet this contingency, Brigadier General Pedro A. del Valle and his newly-formed artillery staff[38] planned to land two 155mm battalions in the south behind the brigade. This would permit the heavier guns of the 7th 155mm Gun Battalion, with only long range capabilities, to reinforce the fires of the 12th Marines in support of the 3d Division. At the same time, the plan would allow the howitzers of the 1st Battalion, with their shorter range capabilities, to add their fire to those of the brigade artillery and protect the corps south flank.

In addition to approving del Valle's plan for using his 155mm units, General Geiger gave the artillery commander control over all artillery and antiaircraft units in the Southern Landing Force.[39] In this manner, coordination of fires with air and naval gunfire could be achieved as soon as corps artillery established its fire direction center ashore. Also, the plan would ensure the massing of fires on a single target if it required the full impact of all artillery on the island.

Naval planners handling their big guns supporting Southern Attack Force paralleled corps artillery in developing an effective fire control concept. Restrictive fire plans were laid for naval gunfire and aerial bombardment to be conducted simultaneously on the same coastal area during the prelanding preparation.[40] Although designed primarily as a safety precaution, the system also made substantial improvement in over-all bombardment volume possible. As outlined in the directive, when one area received fire from both agencies, ship's guns would limit their maximum ordinates of shell trajectory to 1,200 feet. At the same time pilots would be required to pull out of their bombing runs at 1,500 feet. The resulting coordination of air and NGF would ensure the

[35] "The 21st Marines also constructed a very large terrain model of their zone of action and adjacent areas. This model was studied extensively to familiarize all hands with the terrain to be encountered." Ltr LtCol J. H. Tinsley to author, 8Jan52, hereinafter cited as *Tinsley*.

[36] IIIAC SAR, IntelRpt, 4–5.

[37] *Silverthorn*.

[38] Corps artillery was activated on 13Apr44 as IMAC Artillery, and its designation was changed on 15 April to III Corps Artillery. The headquarters was forming at the same time it was planning and training for STEVEDORE.

[39] IIIAC OpPlan 1–14, 11May44.

[40] Ltr LtCol W. M. Gilliam to author, 11Feb52, hereinafter cited as *Gilliam*.

BRIGADE COMMANDERS check the Orote Peninsula-Apra Harbor area on a relief map of Guam. Left to right: General Shepherd, Commanding General; Colonel Walker, Chief of Staff; Lieutenant Colonel Shapley, Commanding Officer, 4th Marines; Colonel Schneider, Commanding Officer, 22d Marines.

landing force of maximum support for their assault.[41]

TRAINING AND REHEARSAL

Life for the ground units and the sailors on board attack ships was anything but tranquil during the planning period. Commanders stepped up the normal intensive training of Marine units as embarkation dates approached. Most of the ships of TF 53 had to face the big task of refitting from their last operation and at the same time load for STEVEDORE. There seemed little need to remind the experienced troops and crewmen that continual practice was the key to a successful amphibious assault.

With landings over wide reefs a possibility in the future, and to add to techniques employed at Bougainville, the 3d Marine Division [42] had conducted experiments involving transfers of troops and 75mm pack howitzers from LCVP's to LVT's. In addition, tests were made loading 105mm howitzers into DUKW's, studies of the approaches of LVT's and DUKW's to various types of beaches carried on, and checks made on landing tanks

from LCM's onto reefs.[43] Up to the moment of loading out for final rehearsals, the 105mm battalions of the 12th Marines worked with their newly-assigned DUKW's, planning and investigating the best way to employ the vehicles assigned for the landing.[44] In addition to amphibious exercises, the division's men became familiar with the small-unit combat-training areas in the jungle and kunai grass plains surrounding their camp at Coconut Grove, Tetere.

At Tassafaronga, where the 1st Provisional Marine Brigade camped, the training cycle was considerably shortened. The final echelons of the 4th and 22d Marines did not arrive at Guadalcanal from Emirau and Kwajalein, respectively, until late April. Each unit remained heavily reinforced with support and service elements that stayed under regimental control for ease of handling.[45] However, the 75mm pack howitzer battalions, which had been under regimental control, were detached and placed under a provisional brigade artillery group commanded by Lieutenant Colonel Edwin C. Ferguson to facilitate the massing of supporting fires.[46]

The newly formed brigade spent part of its training time ironing out the kinks inevitable in the formation of any large or small unit. Fortunately, the recent combat experience of these Marines made the training task easier. On the other hand, the 22d's recent activities proved detrimental in some respects. As training progressed some of the men began to show the effects of their sojourn on Samoa and their physical efforts in helping capture the Mar-

---

[41] CTF 53 OpRpt, Air Support Comments, 5C.

[42] For the story of the division's activities at Bougainville, see Maj J. N. Rentz, *Bougainville and the Northern Solomons*, MC Historical Monograph, (Washington, 1948).

[43] 3d MarDiv SAR, OpComments, 1. The Army's 7th InfDiv originated the method of using DUKW's to carry artillery ashore at Kwajalein. Ltr Adm R. K. Turner to CMC, 27Jan53, hereinafter cited as *Turner*.

[44] Ltr Col A. L. Bowser, Jr. to author, 25Feb52, hereinafter cited as *Bowser*.

[45] Besides the regular H&S Co and Wpns Co of a Marine regiment, each unit had its own engineer, pioneer, medical, tank, and motor transport companies.

[46] The brigade artillery group grew beyond its original planned proportions. At the time of the landing on Guam Col Ferguson had under his tactical control both 75mm pack howitzer battalions, a battery of 155mm howitzers assigned by corps artillery, and a 105mm battalion from the Army's 77th InfDiv after that unit was committed to STEVEDORE. Ltr Col E. C. Ferguson to author, 20Feb52.

shalls. In Samoa many troops had become infected with filariasis [47] and the exertions of combat and training induced a severe reaction in a considerable number of cases. In a short period of time it became necessary to replace 1,800 men of the 22d Marines because of this disease, casualties resulting from battle, transfers, and rotation. This was acomplished by transferring 500 men from the 3d Marine Division overage and filling out the remainder with replacements.[48] With the injection of these unseasoned Marines into the brigade, training officers had to put more emphasis on small unit tactics.

Both the division and brigade devoted a portion of their combat training to developing an efficient tank-infantry team whose mutual supporting fires could crack the expected strong Japanese defenses. In addition, artillery units trained tankmen in the techniques of forward observation so that fire missions could be directed from as far forward as possible.[49]

The size and configuration of the maneuver area assigned the brigade considerably hampered training activities. With elements of the brigade, Army, and IIIAC all near Tassafaronga there seemed a "never ending problem of coordination in the use of training areas."[50] Despite the difficulties encountered and the element of haste present in its preparation for STEVEDORE, the brigade met the stepped-up schedule.

Final pre-rehearsal training of sea and land elements of the attack force commenced on 12 May. In an area near Cape Esperance on Guadalcanal, allotted to TF 53 by the Commanding General, Forward Areas South Pacific, activities got under way. Six days of

ship-to-shore exercises (three for each attack group) gave each combat team and its supporting transport division an opportunity to practice landing techniques. Next followed two days of air support activities in conjunction with regimental landings. And finally, two days of combined air and NGF operations, using live bombs and ammunition, permitted the flagship of each attack group to gain experience in controlling the power of its naval support.[51]

On 22 May, with the preliminary exercises completed, all major unit commanders reported on board the *Appalachian* for a conference on the rehearsal and the operation. At the same time, ship captains and gunnery officers received a thorough briefing on their roles in both the practice and actual landing. With the Cape Esperance area suitable for landing only one division at a time, Admiral Conolly decided to spread the final landing drill over a five-day

---

[51] CTF 53 OpRpt, 3.

REAR ADMIRAL REIFSNIDER, Commander of the Southern Attack Group, charged with landing the 1st Provisional Marine Brigade and the 77th Infantry Division. (Navy Photograph.)

---

[47] This disease, known to the Marines as "mumu," was prevalent among troops stationed in Samoa in the early stages of the war. The disease was spread by mosquitos bearing a parasitic larval worm which infected blood and tissue of the victim and caused painful swelling of the lymphatics.

[48] Ltr BrigGen W. J. Scheyer to CMC, 26Sept52, hereinafter cited as *Scheyer.*

[49] The former CO, PkHowBn, 22d Mar in commenting on this tank-artillery team stated that "the tanker's armored OP often sees more than an FO who has to duck bullets." Ltr LtCol A. M. Mahoney to author, 25Feb52.

[50] *Norton.*

period. This allowed both attack groups to complete approach, landing, and follow-up phases.

In the evening of 22 May, TG 53.1 with the 3d Division embarked, sortied from Guadalcanal and Tulagi. Using planned approach formations during the night, the group arrived off the landing beach at 0600 and started to disembark troops. LVT's loaded with men and equipment of assault platoons crawled down LST ramps into the water and started toward the beach. NGF and air worked over the landing area, duplicating procedures planned for Guam. After first waves moved ashore, tractors returned to a pre-determined transfer point and transshipped troops and equipment from landing boats. The absence of a fringing reef, such as the one blocking both assault beaches at Guam, was compensated for in so far as possible by imitating the exact technique to be used in the operation. Ashore, the regiments maneuvered according to the operation plan, supported by token unloadings of heavy equipment. Because of the possibility of malarial conditions in the rehearsal area, troops reembarked before nightfall. In the morning, 24 May, the division reloaded the equipment left ashore and the convoy proceeded to Tetere. Here, over controlled and marked beaches, units of the shore party practiced unloading reserve equipment and supplies.

TECHNIQUES OF TRANSFERRING from LCVP to LVT were practiced during Cape Esperance rehearsals to familiarize troops with the method (as shown above) used at Guam.

During the second phase of the rehearsal starting 25 May, the Southern Attack Group, with the brigade and corps artillery embarked, made its "dry run." Once again Marines assaulted the Esperance beach, but this time troops followed the Agat landing plan. When ships returned to Tassafaronga, the brigade shore party unloaded supplies and set up dumps as they would on Guam. Without a barrier reef to contend with, unloading proceeded smoothly. There was little indication of the trouble that would arise at the target when both corps artillery and the brigade had to be supplied using the same men and vehicles.[52]

All units of TF 53 participated in the dress rehearsals except two—Cruiser Division 6 (CruDiv-6) remained at Majuro for servicing, and Carrier Division 24 (CarDiv-24) stayed at Espiritu Santo for repairs. CruDiv-12, however, substituted for the missing cruiser division in its fire support role, and the pilots of the air groups of CarDiv-24 flew to Guadalcanal to support the operation from bases ashore. Gunnery officers and ship captains of CruDiv-6 received briefing from TF 53's air and gunnery officers who flew to Majuro. At the same time pilots from carriers of TF 58, who had been working as a striking force for Fifth Fleet and were now present at the atoll anchorage, heard of their role in the STEVEDORE operation. As the day for mounting out the assault approached, Admiral Conolly's task force set about making final arrangements to lift, land, and support the Marines of III Corps.[53]

NAVAL LIFT

After the rehearsal, support units left Guadalcanal for other bases in the Solomons to replenish ammunition and make other logistical preparations for departure. Loading of units in the Guadalcanal area proceeded smoothly

---

[52] The corps artillery had requested that sufficient DUKW's be assigned to land all its ammunition direct from ships to firing areas. Brigade opposed this and said that their shore party could handle the situation. Corps accepted the brigade plan, but on Guam the shore party was unable to bring in adequate amounts of 155mm shells and powder during the first few days of the operation. Ltr Col F. P. Henderson to author, 25Feb52, hereinafter cited as *Henderson*.

[53] CTF 53 OpRpt, 3–4.

CROWDED LST moves toward Guam showing the makeshift living arrangements made by assault troops that led one observer to compare the sight to that of a "tenement district."

and on 1 June the LST tractor groups left for the staging area at Kwajalein Atoll. The faster transport and support groups, which included the *Appalachian* with IIIAC Headquarters on board, followed on 4 June, joining the LST group at Kwajalein on 8 June. Fuel, water, and provisions were taken on board at the anchorage as scheduled, and the first LST's cleared the atoll late in the afternoon of 9 June. Three days later, the rest of TF 53 departed from the Marshalls, moving in convoy formation to an assembly area east of Saipan.

Planes from TF 58 had struck Guam on 11 June in the first of a series of preparatory raids on all the Marianas leading up to the landing on Saipan. Four days later, 15 June, while guns and planes of TF 52 pounded the island, assault divisions of VAC landed on Saipain.

That evening (1931), Admiral Spruance sent a dispatch to Admiral Conolly confirming W-Day for STEVEDORE as 18 June. At midnight the task force commenced retiring to the eastward preparatory to making the final approach run on 17 June.

In the meantime, submarine sightings had indicated that the Japanese planned to leap at the proffered bait and that their fleet had left the Philippines to attack the American expeditionary force. Consequently, in the face of an imminent fleet engagement, Admiral Spruance cancelled W-Day as 18 June. He stated that the landing date would be redesignated and directed that the preinvasion strikes on Guam by TF 58 be discontinued until further notice.[54]

[54] CTF 51 OpRpt, 25–26.

29

Ships of TF 53 spent the period from 16–25 June advancing and retiring in an area 150–300 miles to the eastward of Saipan. Once the threat of the enemy fleet had been eliminated by TF 58, the reason for the delay in assaulting Guam became, not the Japanese surface forces, but the determined defenders of Saipan. Following the commitment of the Expeditionary Troops Reserve (16–20 June), the IIIAC was maintained afloat in case a need arose to reinforce Marines and soldiers battling on that island.

When, on 25 June, Admirals Spruance and Turner decided the 3d Marine Division was no longer needed as a floating reserve, it and most units of corps received orders to return to a restaging area at Eniwetok. Ships loaded with men of the 1st Provisional Marine Brigade, however, remained in the Saipan area pending an improvement in the situation ashore. On 30 June, with VAC's position more secure, the Southern Attack Group was released and directed to proceed to Eniwetok.[55]

For men on board the transports and landing ships the reef-islands of the atoll were a welcome sight. Already the troops had spent a month in their "temporary" quarters, and the voyage had lost any novelty appeal it might once have had. Only one incident had broken the dull routine of seemingly endless days. A formation of enemy torpedo bombers attacked TG 53.16, the Northern Tractor Group, on 18 June but the curtain of fire raised by the LST's and LCI's drove the attackers off after downing three of the Japanese planes. LCI(G) 468, the only casualty to the assault force, received a torpedo hit, and after being towed for awhile finally sank.[56] Aside from this mishap, the monotonous days at sea followed one after the other with little prospect of anything but more monotony.

At Eniwetok commanders set up a regular schedule of landings which enabled troops to move ashore and regain their land legs. Some units employed debarkation arrangements which would be used at Guam, and the men always disembarked and came back on board over cargo nets. On the many sandspits in the lagoon, troops participated in small-unit tactics and engaged in various forms of athletics. In the evening, back on board the ships, boxing matches and movies helped the men to relax.

LST's in the atoll lagoon presented a weird sight. Tents, tarpaulins, in fact every conceivable type of cover had been rigged on the weather deck to provide some protection from the broiling sun. To one officer it looked like a ". . . tenement district with Marine's bedding strewn everywhere in an effort to find a flat place to lie down."[57] At that, the men on the landing ships had it better than those on the transports where quarters were in crowded holds. The tropical sun beating down on the steel decks turned the troop compartments into infernos. Sleeping proved difficult if not impossible, and a much sought after privilege was bedding "topside" under the night sky. Heat rash prevailed but the opportunity to eat good food, including fresh meat, offset the discomfort caused by the skin irritation. A few ships began running low on some supplies but on others the Marines still enjoyed the ice cream that came with life on board most ships.[58] All-in-all, the good food, rest, plenty of hard physical exercise by calisthenics each day, and the training and recreation ashore kept the men in comparatively good physical condition.

Nevertheless, the Marines began to get bored with "ship-board" life and all individuals were ready for action. Assault troops had been briefed on their target until "Guam was coming out of their ears."[59] One naval officer with the assault force noted that, so familiar had the men become with the landing beaches, they spoke of them "as though they were Coney Island, Old Orchard, Daytona, or a California Beach."[60] Probably, there never was a group of Marines more eager to leave the ships of the fleet for an amphibious assault.

[55] CTF 53 OpRpt, 5–6.

[56] CTF 51 OpRpt, OpNarrative, Annex 1; CTG 53.2 OpRpt, 4.

[57] Ltr LtCol C. W. Kunz, Jr. to author, 27Feb52, hereinafter cited as *Kunz*.

[58] In one transport division, TransDiv-2, the commander, Capt H. D. Baker, ordered that ice cream be served only to Marines because the mix started to run out. *Craig Nov52*.

[59] *Aplington*.

[60] Cdr H. E. Smith (CEC), "I Saw the Morning Break," *USNI Proceedings*, March 1946, 406.

RE-EVALUATION OF THE SITUATION

While troops sweltered on board their transports in Eniwetok's lagoon, their commanders were busily implementing plans for STEVEDORE. Admiral Conolly, Generals Geiger and del Valle, plus key staff officers left by air for Saipan on 29 June. After arrival on the island, still the scene of heavy fighting, the entire group made a front line tour to examine the effect of naval gunfire, air bombardment, and artillery support against targets almost identical with those expected to be encountered on Guam. Then Admirals Turner and Spruance held a series of conferences on board their flagships, the USS *Rocky Mount* and the USS *Indianapolis*.[61] New intelligence gained from interrogations and captured documents on this first island assaulted in the Marianas indicated that Guam was even more formidably defended than Saipan.[62]

---

[61] Ltr Capt I. E. McMillian, USN, to CMC, 28Oct52.
[62] TF 56 G–3 Rpt, Annex D.

The determined resistance expected at the beaches and the sharp rise in Japanese strength known to be on the island were the chief concerns of the conferees. High-level commanders now considered the forces assigned to IIIAC insufficient for the speedy capture of Guam. Accordingly, the planners decided to add the 77th Infantry Division (Reinforced) with its 19,245 men [63] as floating reserve.[64] The III Corps Artillery gained more fire power with

---

[63] CominCh P–007, *Amphibious Operations—Invasion of the Marianas*, Chap 1, 1, hereinafter cited as *CominCh P–007*. The 77th InfDiv, activated on 25Mar42, was composed mostly of selectees and reserves and had yet to experience combat in WW II. The unit, however, had completed extensive training and maneuvers in infantry, desert, mountain, and amphibious warfare tactics at various camps in the U. S. After reaching the Pacific in March-April 1944, the division had been stationed at the Jungle Training Center on Oahu.

[64] On 22 July, in accordance with a directive from CinCPOA, the 26th Marines departed San Diego and passed to control of CG ExTrps to serve as ExTrps Reserve for Guam. ExTrps G–3 Rpt, Annex D, 7.

ARTILLERYMEN of the 22d Marines Pack Howitzer Battalion are briefed on their part in the assault by their intelligence officer, Captain Philip P. Santon.

the assigning of the 2d 155mm Howitzer Battalion to the operation. In addition, the scope of the preliminary bombardment was increased tremendously and the decision made to conduct further reconnaissance of the beaches and reefs prior to W-Day.[65]

On 6 July, CTF 56 formally released the 77th Infantry Division to General Geiger's control. By this time, the first elements of the division had started toward the restaging area. Reinforced by the 305th Field Artillery Battalion, the 305th RCT, and an advance division command group had sailed from Pearl Harbor on 1 July under command of Brigadier General Edwin H. Randle, Assistant Division Commander (ADC).[66] The remainder of the division with its commander, Major General

Andrew D. Bruce, awaited the arrival of transport divisions from Saipan, and embarked on 8 July to join TF 53.

The new tactical plan called for the employment of the 305th RCT as part of the 1st Provisional Marine Brigade. The rest of the Army division would remain afloat in corps reserve ready to land on either the northern or southern beaches. In the event the 3d Division did not require the weight of the 77th, the plan envisaged landing the Army troops on the same beaches used by the brigade and then relieving General Shepherd's men on the FBL. The brigade could then concentrate its forces to capture Orote Peninsula and upon accomplishing this task, again take over defense of the FBL. The two divisions, with their rear protected by the brigade, could then join, drive north, and secure the rest of the island. At a conference held on board the *Appalachian* on 10 July, General Geiger gave major unit commanders, including the newly-arrived ADC of the 77th, the new plan.[67]

As soon as it was definitely known when the Army reinforcements would be available, Admiral Spruance set the date for the assault.

[65] *Ibid.*, 4–5.

[66] "All that General Randle and his staff knew was that they were to receive instructions at Eniwetok. So enroute they worked on plans for landing on Tinian because the assault on Saipan and Guam had already been planned in detail. All that the men of the 305th Regimental Combat Team knew was that there was a nasty war on and they were sailing right into the midst of it." *Ours to Hold it High: The History of the 77th Infantry Division in World War II*, (Washington, 1947), 43, hereinafter cited as *77th InfDiv History*.

[67] IIIAC SAR, Planning Rpt, 3.

OROTE PENINSULA AIRFIELD erupts with the smoke of bombs dropped by planes of Admiral Mitscher's Fast Carrier Task Force during a preinvasion strike in early July. (Navy Photograph.)

He sent a message to Admiral Conolly on 8 July fixing 21 July 1944 as W-Day on Guam.[68]

ATTACK PREPARATIONS

For the Japanese on Guam the period following the Saipan landing was a continuous nightmare. Stabbing raids by planes from TF 58 occurred with ever-increasing frequency as the month of June wore on. Even during the height of the Japanese fleet's attack on TF 58 the weary defenders had no respite. Reinforcement flights from Iwo Jima and Japan being sent to aid the Imperial Navy in its effort to stop the Saipan landing, found Admiral Mitscher's flyers ready to halt such attempts. Enemy pilots seeking to stage their attacks through Guam's airfields found their landing plans interrupted by American interceptor planes.

Battleships, cruisers, and destroyers from the fast carrier task force began a series of harassing raids on 27 June, concentrating their fire on Orote Peninsula installations, that increased the damage wrought by bombing.[69] Guam was now cut off effectively from all hopes of relief. The heckling attacks of TF 58 lifted the curtain on the most thorough pre-landing preparation seen thus far in the Pacific.

The bombardment pace was stepped up on 4 July. One carrier group (TG 58.3) lay to off the island sending its planes in during daylight hours to strafe and bomb the Japanese and smash defensive installations. The destroyers of the group threw their 5-inch shells into Agana, Asan, and Agat during the night. As TG 58.3 left for Eniwetok to refuel on 6 July, two more carrier groups arrived off Guam and continued the round-the-clock bombardment. On alternate days each carrier group hit the Rota airfield to render it inoperable and further isolate the embattled garrison on Guam.[70]

Following the plan as outlined at the commander's conference on Saipan, elements of TF 53 entered the picture on 8 July when CruDiv-6

USS PENNSYLVANIA is wreathed in smoke as its 14-inch rifles shell the area south of Orote Peninsula. (Navy Photograph.)

and CarDiv-24 took station off Guam to add their power to the preparation. The scope of the bombardment grew as additional supporting units, some from TF 52, arrived in the area. A continual procession of ships shuttled back and forth between ammunition and fueling rendezvous at Saipan and Eniwetok, making a lethal pause to spread devastation on Guam. From 11 July onward at least one battleship division was always present to lend the massive broadsides of its rifles to NGF salvos.[71] The umbrella of carrier planes that blanketed the island neutralized effectively any remaining air opposition still present at Guam's crater-pocked airstrips. These naval pilots received the first evidence that the defenders were keyed to a fighting pitch. Antiaircraft fire brought down 16 planes before assault troops hit on W-Day.[72]

Admiral Conolly, embarked in the *Appalachian*, arrived off Guam to assume personal control of the bombardment program on 14 July. The admiral ordered the flagship to take position approximately 3,500 yards off the coast, and much to the surprise of everyone on board directed gun crews to commence firing at designated targets. That night Conolly sent a message to CinCPac to the effect that, "the *Appalachian*, ably supported by other elements of the fleet, this day bombarded Guam." A second dispatch went to the bombarding ships and directed all vessels to move in close and deliver point-blank fire.[73]

[68] CTF 53 OpRpt, 6.

[69] CinCPac WD, June 1944.

[70] CinCPac WD, July 1944. These carrier groups, TG 58.1 and 58.2, had just returned from a two-day raid on Chichi and Iwo Jima, part of a series of strikes on these islands designed to prevent enemy air reinforcements from reaching the Marianas.

[71] CTF 53 OpRpt, OpLog, 16A–23A.

[72] CinCPac WD, July 1944.

[73] *Scheyer.*

UNDERWATER DEMOLITION MEN of UDT–4 paddle their rubber boat toward the reef off Agat on 19 July to continue their work of destroying enemy obstacles. (Navy Photograph.)

The presence of General Geiger in the command ship, "as the individual most interested in the reduction of beach defenses, had the effect of placing naval gunfire where it would do the most damage." [74] Close coordination of air and NGF support was achieved by setting up a board of officers to evaluate the effect of the continual pounding the island received. The attack force air, gunnery, and intelligence officers worked with representatives of General Geiger to carry out a systematic plan for destroying enemy defenses. Daily the board prepared a target list to guide ships and carrier planes in their bombardment missions. After a target had been thoroughly worked over, it was checked off the list, but occasionally re-examined to make certain it would cause no trouble on W-Day. Observation planes that hovered over the island discovered new targets, and the board added them to the list. For a good portion of this preliminary bombardment period, the island was divided into two zones with air and NGF alternating morning and afternoon in striking these. This eliminated all restrictions on minimum plane pull-out and support ship's ranges. [75]

During the softening-up process planned for Guam Navy Underwater Demolition Teams (UDT's) received the important task of removing obstacles from Asan and Agat beaches and improving the reef approaches for landing craft. Three UDT's were made available to TF 53 for the operation: UDT's 3 and 4 joined the attack force at Guadalcanal while UDT 6 reported at Eniwetok on 9 July after participating in the Saipan campaign. For three nights and two days beginning on 14 July, UDT 3 carried on reconnaissance of assault beaches and made diversionary checks of possible landing points all along the west coast. At night swimmers crossed the reef and examined the actual shore line, while LCI gunboats,[76] destroyers, cruisers, and battleships provided protective cover. Any enemy fire on the team's scouts drew an instant reaction from guns of all calibers. This cover proved so effective that only one member of the team was killed during the entire reconnaissance operation.

When Teams 4 and 6 arrived from Eniwetok on 17 July the second phase of the UDT work started. Protected by LCI(G)'s operating close to shore and screened by smoke laid on beach areas by planes from TF 53, all three teams began four days of clearing barriers from reefs in front of assault beaches. Off Agat the obstacles consisted mostly of palm log cribs

[74] Ltr BrigGen M. H. Silverthorn to CMC, 1May47.

[75] CTF 53 OpRpt, Air Support Comments, 12C.

[76] The close support provided UDT 3 by the LCI (G)'s proved so effective that on 16 July CTF 51 was requested to send eight more gunboats from Saipan to reinforce those already available. Within 24 hours the craft were at Guam where they helped cover beach demolition operations until 20 July. CTF 53 OpRpt, 8–9.

filled with coral, joined together by wire cable. On the northern reef, teams found wire cages four feet square and three to four feet high filled with cemented coral.[77] Very little barbed wire and no underwater mines were located. By midnight of W-minus 1, hand-placed demolition charges had blown 640 obstacles off Asan and 300 off Agat. The value of the UDT's work is clear. Admiral Conolly stated that, "positively, landings could not have been made on either Agat or Asan beaches nor any other suitable beaches without these elaborate but successfully prosecuted clearance operations." [78]

During the course of covering operations for the UDT's, LCI(G) 348 grounded on the reef 400–500 yards from Asan at about 2000, 17 July. Admiral Conolly immediately requested a tug be sent from Saipan to rescue the vessel. Throughout the night, destroyers covered the stranded gunboat and at daylight cruisers from fire support units moved in and successfully neutralized enemy fire. The tug, *Apache*, arrived at 1415, took position to seaward of the 348, and at 1730 with the help of a rising tide pulled the grounded LCI(G) free. With the gunboat in tow, the *Apache* returned to Saipan.[79]

The promptness with which the request for help was answered by Admiral Turner demonstrated a unique feature of the naval support at Guam. Because W-Day had been delayed until after the end of the Saipan campaign, unprecedented numbers of ships from TF 52 and TF 58 could be allocated to reinforce the Southern Attack Force. Unquestionably, these additional planes and ship's guns contributed heavily to the effectiveness of the prelanding preparation.

While supporting units smashed Guam's defenses, the transport and tractor groups of TF 53 made ready to depart from Eniwetok for the objective. Screened by a host of destroyers, gunboats, mine sweepers, patrol craft, and submarine chasers, the LST's left the anchorage on 15 July. Two days later, transports got under way, accompanied by covering units of the attack force escort carrier group. Just a few hours prior to the departure of these ships, transports carrying the 77th Infantry Division (less the 305th RCT) entered the lagoon. Refueling lines were taken on board and preparations made to bring the floating reserve to the Guam area at sunrise on W-plus 1.[80]

At Guam, as W-Day drew nearer, the destructive rain of shells and bombs increased. Early on 20 July the *Indianapolis*, with the Fifth Fleet commander on board, arrived and joined the fire support vessels. By afternoon of W-minus 1, all forces connected with STEVEDORE were in position or approaching on schedule. All known major defensive installations covering the landing beaches had been silenced, and demolition teams were completing

---

[80] CTG 53.2 OpRpt, OpNarrative, 7.

SIX-INCH GUN from the main battery of the USS *Honolulu* fires on Guam while in the background one of the UDT destroyer transports moves in to cover demolition operations. (Navy Photograph.)

---

[77] A POW captured on W-Day revealed he had been a member of an antiboat gun crew that watched the UDT's destroy these beach barricades. Although almost close enough to throw rocks at the teams the gun crew had done nothing to interfere. When asked why his section did not open fire on the Americans the POW replied that "No one gave us orders to shoot." *Coleman 1952.*

[78] CTF 53 OpRpt, **10.**

[79] *Ibid.*, 9.

RELIGIOUS SERVICES are held on board one of the transports as Marines of IIIAC move closer to combat on Guam.

their task of clearing reef obstructions. Favorable weather had been predicted for 21 July, and Admiral Conolly confirmed that date as W-Day, setting H-Hour for 0830.[81]

At dusk major NGF support vessels retired for the night, ready to return at first light and place fire on areas assigned them in the operation plan. On board the fifteen carriers of TF 58 and the five escort carriers of the attack force, ordnance men armed planes for their lethal strikes. In the seas immediately surrounding the island lay a vast armada: six battleships, nine cruisers, and fifty-seven destroyers.[82] From this number four battleships, three cruisers, and four destroyers had been allotted close-in support missions off Asan, and two battleships, three cruisers, and three destroyers had drawn the same role at the Agat landing beaches. (See Map 4, Map Section.) In addition, a host of smaller ships and landing craft were available to cover the landing teams with a protective curtain of fire.

At 0530, 21 July 1944, NGF support vessels moved into assigned firing areas and commenced prearranged bombardment schedules. The assault to recapture Guam was underway.

---

[81] CTF 53 OpRpt, 11.

[82] *Ibid.,* OpLog, 25A–26A; CTG 53.2 OpRpt, Op-Narrative, 8–10.

CHAPTER III   W-Day to Landing of the Reserve

Under cover of darkness on 21 July, troop ships of TF 53 moved into the transport area and took their positions. Preparations began for the simultaneous assault on the northern and southern beaches. By 0600 all assault units of the task force had reached their assigned areas. Against the background of naval gunfire, officers gave final words of advice as troops made last-minute readjustments of equipment.

LST's carrying the assault LVT's and DUKW's moved into launching areas and lowered their ramps. Most assault waves were waterborne in time to see strikes by planes from the USS *Wasp* on Cabras Island and a destructive attack by USS *Yorktown* planes on Blue and Green beaches. Circles made by the rendezvousing LVT's began to disintegrate as waves formed behind LCI(G)'s and LVT(A)'s. By 0740 troops had started toward the shore accompanied by an increasing din of naval gunfire.

LCI(G)'s opened up with a tremendous rocket barrage on all beaches and as the gunboats neared the reef they added the fire from their 20mm and 40mm guns.[1] In a few minutes the once clear, bright day became hazy from smoke and dust. Landing beaches were completely blacked out as assault waves moved across the line of departure.

All the while a steady stream of naval shells screamed overhead as the softening-up process continued, but at 0822 the real show started. Naval gunfire loosened a devastating barrage on the immediate beach areas and continued until landing waves were 1,200 yards from shore. Large caliber fire then lifted and moved inland. Five-inch fire continued until LVT(A)'s started across the reef.

Eighty-four fighters and 16 torpedo bombers added their H-Hour contribution to beaches, then shifted their attack 1,000 yards inland. LCI(G)'s led assault waves and continued firing until they turned to take station on the flanks. There they resumed fire to hinder movement of the enemy. LVT(A)'s now became responsible for fire on the beach area until troops came ashore. The armored amphibians leading the 3d Division landed at 0829. In the south, LVT(A)'s of the brigade first touched down at 0832.[2] Assault troops scrambled ashore on all beaches one minute later.

Men making their first landing felt in their own minds that nothing could live through such a pulverizing barrage as they had just seen. This illusion lasted only until mortar fire started to fall among approaching LVT's. The Japanese made a quick recovery from the bom-

[1] Each of the 18 LCI(G)'s assigned to support the landing, nine to each attack group, had been fitted prior to departure from Guadalcanal with 42 rocket launchers. It was possible, therefore, for each LCI(G) to fire a total of 504 rockets in a very short period of time. A total of 4,536 rockets exploded on each beach just prior to touch down of the first waves. CTF 53 OpRpt, NGF Support Comments, 5B.

[2] CTF 53 OpRpt, OpLog, 28A; CTG 53.2 OpRpt, OpNarrative, 11.

TORPEDO BOMBERS OF TASK FORCE 53'S escort carrier group fly over circling landing craft on the way toward the beach to give support on W-Day. (Navy Photograph.)

bardment and opened up on all beaches. Small-arms fire grew more intense and mortars, antiboat guns, and artillery scored direct hits on LVT's.[3]

ASAN-ADELUP BEACHHEAD

The 3d Marine Division operation order called for the three regiments to land abreast, capture the high ground immediately inland, and prepare for further operations to the east and southeast. (See Map 5, Map Section) Division did not provide for a floating reserve, but each combat team designated one of its battalions as a regimental reserve afloat. The division itself would have to depend on the corps reserve (77th Infantry Division less the 305th RCT).

The 3d Marines (Colonel W. Carvel Hall), landing on the left was to secure Chonito Cliff, Adelup Point, and the commanding terrain extending to the right of the cliff area. This

would protect the left flank of the division. On the right, the 9th (Colonel Edward A. Craig) would land one battalion (3d) in assault to seize and hold the low ridges off of the beach; after the other two battalions landed and passed through the assault unit on order, the 3d Battalion would assemble in regimental reserve and be prepared to capture Cabras Island by an amphibious landing. The 21st Marines, commanded by Colonel Arthur H. Butler, going ashore in the center, would drive inland to secure a line of cliffs and defend until the division was ready to expand the beachhead. On reaching the cliff objective the regiment would assign one battalion as division reserve.[4]

The 2,500 yards of beaches used by the division lay between a pair of "devil's horns." Beaches Red 1 and Red 2, used by the 3d Marines, rested almost against the left horn, Adelup Point. Beach Green, in the center, was assigned to the 21st Marines and from the right horn, Asan Point, stretched the 9th Marines' Beach Blue.[5] (See Map 6)

The 9th Marines moved ashore in a column

---

[3] The leading waves of the brigade suffered 10 LVT and LVT(A) casualties. 1st ProvMarBrig WD, 1Jul–10Aug44, 4. The division reported nine LVT's and LVT(A)'s destroyed by enemy fire during the landing. 3d MarDiv WD, July 1944, 6.

[4] 3d MarDiv OpPlan 2–44, 13May44.
[5] 3d MarDiv SAR, OpNarrative, 1.

of battalion landing teams: 3d in assault, followed by the 2d, with the 1st in reserve. Under fire from the front and right flank (Asan Point) the right assault company (I) of the 3d Battalion (Lieutenant Colonel Walter Asmuth, Jr.)[6] made very little progress, and the reserve company (L) had to be committed to give added strength. But still the attack remained stalled. Asmuth called for tanks, which had landed at H-plus 40 minutes, and with the armor supplying overhead fire, the units advanced slowly. On the other hand, the left company (K) swept across the rice paddies and took the ridge to the front (the first objective) with astonishing rapidity. The swift advance threw the enemy off balance and the follow-up units of the 9th mopped up the Japanese defenders not killed by the assault. This cleared the all-important rice paddy area behind Blue Beach where the division's artillery regiment planned to set up.[7]

The 3d Battalion reached the D–1 line [8] (See Map 7, Map Section) and the regimental re-

[6] Wounded in the W-Day action and evacuated.

[7] Ltr Col E. A. Craig to CMC, 15Apr47, hereinafter cited as *Craig*; ltr Col W. Asmuth, Jr. to CMC, 11Sept52.

[8] On the operation overlay issued for the landing, III Corps designated phase lines, usually terrain features extending across the zone of action, which would aid coordination and control during the attack. The division and regiments, in turn, set up intermediate objectives to govern the actions of subordinate units. These lines are labeled for uniformity in the monograph D–1; D–2, etc.; D–1a, D–2b, etc., in the division actions and O–1, O–2, etc.; O–a, O–b, etc., in corps advances.

serve (1/9) had moved ashore by 1345. Colonel Craig made preparations to continue the attack with the 1st and 2d Battalions passing through the 3d. Eight minutes after receiving a message from the commanding general to advance beyond D–1 by 1700, Craig ordered the 1st and 2d to move out. As the 2d crossed the bridge over the Nidual River, machine guns from cleverly camouflaged positions along the west face of Asan Point opened up, forcing the Marines to fight to the rear for a short distance. Near these positions Colonel Craig's men found a three-gun battery of Japanese 8-inch naval howitzers in concrete emplacements. These big weapons covered the beaches and seaward to the west of Asan Point but they had been abandoned. Against moderate small-arms fire the advance continued, but increased resistance from enemy-occupied caves stopped the drive 400 yards short of the D–2 line.[9] All units began digging in, and by 1830 the 9th had tied-in with the 21st on the left. W-Day activities had been a success for the 9th Marines but the regiment had 231 casualties, including a comparatively high toll of officers: 20 killed or wounded.[10]

In the center, between the devil's horns, the 21st Marines hit on schedule. Receiving little

[9] Ltr LtGen E. A. Craig to CMC, 30Sept52, hereinafter cited as *Craig 1952*.

[10] 9th Mar SAR, 1; 9th Mar Unit Rpts. The regimental executive officer, LtCol J. Sabater was one of the officers wounded, and as a result the 9th Marines did not have an executive officer until 30 July when LtCol R. M. King joined the regiment.

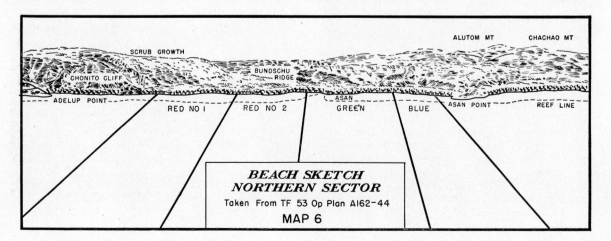

BEACH SKETCH
NORTHERN SECTOR
Taken From TF 53 Op Plan A162-44
MAP 6

GREEN AND BLUE BEACH, with Asan Point in the right foreground, as seen from the air show area assaulted by the 9th and 21st Marines on W-Day. (Navy Photograph.)

fire initially, the regiment landed in a column of battalions: 3d, 2d, and 1st. The men soon learned that terrain, rather than the enemy would be their worst obstacle the first day ashore. After securing the immediate high ground overlooking the beach, the 3d Battalion halted to reorganize at the foot of the "almost impossible" cliffs.[11]

Colonel Butler had made his plans with the

"almost impossible" in mind. As soon as the LVT's had returned to the transfer line and brought the reserve battalion (1st) ashore, the 2d would be released from its assembly area and move abreast of the 3d. The 2d Battalion (Lieutenant Colonel Eustace R. Smoak) would then attack up a defile in the left of the zone. Lieutenant Colonel Wendell H. Duplantis with his 3d Battalion would move up the Asan River valley in the right of the regimental zone. Both units, after establishing a foothold on the cliffs, would extend to right and left respectively and establish a line.[12]

The Japanese knew nothing of Colonel Butler's plan, but as soon as it began to unfold the

[11] "Commanders and their staffs had been told on Guadalcanal by officers familiar with the terrain on Guam that it would be almost impossible to scale the cliffs immediately beyond the beaches, particularly in the zone of the 3d and 21st Marines." 1stLt R. A. Arthur and 1stLt K Cohlmia, *The Third Marine Division*, (Washington, 1948), 147, hereinafter cited as *3d MarDiv History*.

[12] 21st Mar SAR, 1–2.

enemy made a determined effort to stop its execution. The 1st Battalion (Lieutenant Colonel Marlowe C. Williams) met increasing mortar and artillery fire as it came ashore and moved into an assembly area near the Asan River at the foot of the high ground overlooking the beach. The unit could not set up its CP in the assigned area because of the enemy interference and the resultant relocation caused a slight delay in the establishment of wire and messenger communications with regiment.[13]

As the 2d Battalion maneuvered into position the Japanese offered only light opposition, but the terrain was not so obliging. As Marines inched up the rough, bare rock, the day grew hotter, and the long shipboard confinement began to take its toll as men fell by the wayside. By sheer physical stamina the remainder reached the top of the cliff, but the Japanese did not let the attackers relax. They started to spray machine-gun bullets from a ridge not 50 yards away, and as the 2d Battalion began to dig in, a heavy mortar concentration fell on its newly-won position.[14]

On the right the 3d Battalion encountered stiff resistance immediately. As the unit started to move up the valley, mortar shells caused numerous casualties. An enemy reinforced machine-gun platoon defending a defile along the river began to fire and stopped the advance. With naval gunfire neutralizing the mortar positions and 1/9 laying down a base of fire, Lieutenant Colonel Duplantis' units launched a coordinated attack and overpowered the strong point. Approximately 14 machine guns, heavy and light, six mortars, considerable ammunition, and what is believed to be the first prisoners taken on Guam were seized during the action.[15] But the enemy was not the only problem as the advance continued. Men began to run out of water, and many fell from exhaus-

tion. The capture of the cliff at this point seemed "almost impossible," but through concerted efforts and the urging of officers and NCO's the men went forward. One officer, Captain Rodney L. Heinze, Company I commander, walked along the front lines of his company, lifted individual Marines who had fallen, and helped them forward.[16]

The 3d Battalion finally reached the top of the cliff and began the important mission of making contact with the 2d on the left and the 9th Marines on the right. The tangled mass of vines and scrub growth made physical or visual contact difficult. To complicate further the job at hand, heavy mortar and small-arms fire harassed the troops as they began to dig in.

The Japanese had not forgotten the 1st Battalion in its assembly area at the foot of the cliff. Intense mortar fire during the day caused many casualties and disrupted work at hand.[17] Nevertheless, on order from the regimental commander, the 1st swept the zone behind the D–1 line, encountering few enemy. After completing the mopping-up assignment, the battalion returned to its assembly area and reverted to division reserve.[18]

On top of the cliff in the 21st's zone, the two attacking battalions prepared for the night. Contact had been made with the 9th Marines on the right, but repeated attempts by patrols had failed to find the 3d Marines on the left. A deep, jungle-filled ravine stretched between the two regiments, making contact, visual or otherwise, virtually impossible. So 2/21 was ordered to refuse its left flank to the very edge of the cliff. The remaining gap was well neutralized since the enemy and the 2d Battalion both used their mortars to cover the area.

After the 21st dug in, Japanese mortar shells began to fall more often. During the night, repeated small-scale attacks of about platoon strength failed to penetrate the lines. However, the 2d Battalion, which received the brunt

[13] Ltr Maj L. A. Gilson, Jr. to CMC, 13Oct52.

[14] The battalion had no 81mm mortar support for about an hour of the afternoon's activities. One mortar blew up about 1415 killing or wounding the entire crew and disrupting the fire of its section. The other section of the battalion mortar platoon was in the process of displacing forward at this time. Ltr LtCol A. Hedesh to CMC, 26Sept52.

[15] Ltr Col W. H. Duplantis to CMC, 30Oct52, hereinafter cited as *Duplantis 1952.*

[16] Ltr Maj P. M. Jones to CMC, 8Apr47, hereinafter cited as *Jones.*

[17] The battalion executive officer placed the casualty figure at approximately 10% of the battalion before it went into the line on 22 July. Ltr LtCol R. R. Van Stockum to author, 7Jan52, hereinafter cited as *Van Stockum.*

[18] 21st Mar SAR, 2.

JAPANESE CAVE POSITION on the reverse slope of Chonito Cliff furnished excellent protection for the enemy from the prelanding bombardment and enabled them to reoccupy prepared positions to oppose the 3d Marines advance. Adelup Point is in the background.

of this action, withdrew its right flank slightly to block the enemy's approach into the position.[19]

Early in the afternoon (1330), Brigadier General Alfred H. Noble, assistant division commander, had come ashore over the 21st Marines' beaches. And after that regiment had cleared the area, advance division command post set up in a gully on the left bank of the Asan River.[20] By the time General Turnage

had moved to the beach, communications had been established with all combat teams, and at 1715 Turnage assumed command ashore.[21]

The 3d Marines, landing on the left flank of the division, soon found that the devil's left horn, Adelup Point, held plenty of the enemy. Support from Chonito Cliff,[22] the high ground immediately off of the beach, added to the effectiveness of the Point's defenses. The Japanese

[19] 1stLt A. A. Frances, "The Battle for Banzai Ridge," *MC Gazette*, June 1945, 13–18.

[20] This CP location was not the original area selected prior to the landing, mortar and small-arms fire having made that impossible to occupy at this time. HqBn, 3d MarDiv SAR, 1–2.

[21] 3d MarDiv D–3 Jnl.

[22] Available sources indicate a difference of opinion as to the extent of this very important terrain feature. To avoid confusion Chonito Cliff as used in this monograph refers only to the nose of high ground immediately inland from the seawall and northeast of Beach Red 1.

had survived the tremendous pre-invasion bombardment by holing up in a complex cave system in and behind the cliff. From their perfect observation posts on the height, the enemy directed mortar and artillery fire on beaches being used by the 3d Marines.

First waves landed on Beaches Red 1 and Red 2 on schedule despite this intense fire. Fifteen minutes after H-Hour, assault waves reported heavy casualties on both beaches. Mortar shells scored direct hits on LVT waves as they moved toward the shore. But a job had to be done, and Colonel Hall's 3d Marines took its losses, reorganized, and prepared for the attack on the O–a line, the first high ground inland.

Two battalions landed in assault, the 1st on the right. Despite many losses, the 3d Battalion (Lieutenant Colonel Ralph L. Houser), on the left, moved slowly ahead. The 3d's plan had called for Companies I and K to land abreast, hit the beach with a rush, and dash to the initial objective (Chonito Cliff) before the Japanese could recover from the pre-invasion bombardment. Company I, on the right, tried to move up the draw south of Chonito but the enemy stopped the attempt. Houser pressed flame-thrower operators into service immediately, and they performed invaluable service in neutralizing many of the caves in the face of the cliff. Company K succeeded in crossing the beach road and pivoted to flank the cliff area on the left, but enemy machine guns halted the drive before it gained momentum.[23] Tanks of Company C, 3d Tank Battalion took position along the road running parallel to the sea and commenced pouring shells directly into the caves. Colonel Houser committed his reserve (Company L) and by noon, Chonito Cliff had been cleared and the Marines had advanced to the O–a line. Tanks then shifted their fire to Adelup Point to join that from destroyers and LCI(G)'s which had been working over the area since early morning. But this continuous pounding had failed to knock out several enemy guns that harassed the flank of the division.[24]

Adelup Point was not the only source of trouble that plagued the 3d Marines on W-Day. As

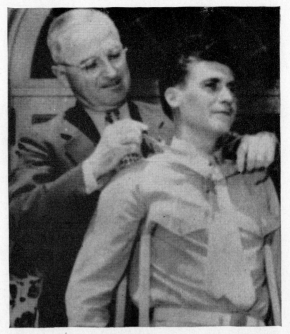

PRIVATE FIRST CLASS LUTHER SKAGGS, JR., 3d Battalion, 3d Marines, is presented the Medal of Honor by President Truman for action during the first day and night ashore on Guam. Private Skaggs assumed command and effectively directed the fire of a mortar section supporting his unit's attack and despite critical wounds led his men in repulsing several strong enemy counterattacks.

the 1st Battalion landed and started across rice paddies toward Bundschu Ridge, a nose of land running down toward the beach,[25] enemy machine guns began to fire from the woods bordering the open ground. Company B, in assault on the right, quickly cleared these woods and made good progress until it ran into jungle and rock.

The Japanese did not give Company A, on the left, time to organize for an assault, but opened fire on LVT's as they moved ashore and stopped to unload troops. Casualties mounted as reorganization got under way. Enemy opposition, plus the fact that terrain bore little resemblance to that studied on maps and models, added to the normal confusion which

[23] Ltr LtCol R. R. Bastian, Jr. to CMC, 23Aug52.
[24] 3d Mar Jnl.

[25] Referred to as Bundschu Ridge in most sources and hereinafter so called. This ridge was named on board ship for Capt Geary R. Bundschu, Company A commander, whose unit was assigned the mission of taking this terrain feature. Ironically, it was the fighting on this ridge that took his life.

follows any assault landing.[26] But cool thinking and the training under adverse conditions on Guadalcanal paid off. Captain Geary R. Bundschu quickly organized his company and made preparations for the assault on the ridge that already bore his name.   (See Map 13)

The attack started with two platoons in assault and one in support, but the going was slow and rough. The support platoon had to be committed in short order. This added strength enabled Bundschu to get within 100 yards of the top by 1045, but he reported he needed corpsmen and stretchers badly. This message gave just a hint of things to come. Moving that last 100 yards proved to be a lengthy and costly business. Only one officer, Lieutenant James A. Gallo, Jr., and a few men of the company survived the action that followed.

It is doubtful if Captain Bundschu realized until after 1200 what he was up against.[27] The initial assault on the ridge had been driven back by two machine guns emplaced to deliver enfilade fire on advancing troops. A platoon tried to flank one position by going up a heavily wooded gully but the waiting Japanese forced it to withdraw. About 1400 Bundschu asked his battalion commander, Major Henry Aplington, II, for permission to disengage. But Aplington felt this could not be done because of the unit being so involved. However, the right platoon (1st) succeeded in disengaging. Lieutenant Gallo, its leader, reorganized the remnants of his unit and those of the 3d Platoon and awaited orders from his company commander.[28]

After a conference between the regimental commander and Captain Bundschu, Colonel Hall ordered a second frontal assault on the ridge. Bundschu and Gallo organized the re-maining men of Company A into two forces for the attempt. The company commander requested that an 81mm mortar barrage be placed on the hill,[29] and just before sundown the attack started. Bundschu and his men inched forward but the same machine gun that had caused them trouble earlier in the day soon stopped the advance. Repeated attempts to take the position failed. Finally, covered by fire from every available weapon, the Marines silenced the gun with grenades. An assault reached the top of the hill, but by this time the remaining handful of Marines found it impossible to reorganize and defend this crest.[30]

On the right, Lieutenant Gallo and his men fared no better. Under cover of the 81mm barrage, they crawled up the ridge and reached a position under the machine gun in their sector. But the Japanese, by rolling hand grenades down on the advancing troops, made the position untenable and halted the attack. Little had been accomplished. The company was back where it had been earlier in the day, but this time with fewer men.[31]

During the course of the Bundschu Ridge action, the regimental commander had decided to commit his reserve, Lieutenant Colonel Hector de Zayas' 2d Battalion. When it became apparent that the enemy offered the most resistance in the center of the zone of action, Hall alerted de Zayas' unit for a move into the line between the two assault battalions. Shortly thereafter, at 1300, Colonel Hall assembled his battalion commanders on top of Chonito Cliff and issued his fragmentary order:

The enemy resistance on Adelup Point is light. Resistance is strong in the center and on the right. He continues to prevent the 1st Battalion from seizing the high ground behind Red 2. We continue the attack with three battalions abreast at 1500. 2d Bat-

---

[26] Maps were deficient in several respects. They lacked detail of small hills, defiles, and secondary road nets. Omission of vegetation detail, except in isolated instances, hindered planning and locating positions. Photos received prior to the embarkation of troops were incomplete because of excessive cloud cover. Excellent photos were received later but not in sufficient quantity. 3d MarDiv SAR, IntelRpt, 1; 1st ProvMar-Brig OpRpt, 4–6.

[27] *Aplington.*

[28] Interview with Capt J. A. Gallo, Jr., 15Nov51, hereinafter cited as *Gallo.*

[29] Little effect was achieved by the requested barrage because the Japanese made good use of the caves and other prepared positions. The enemy waited under cover until the firing stopped, then moved back to their weapons before the Marines could reach the ridge crest.

[30] *Gallo.* Capt Bundschu was killed during this action.

[31] *Ibid.* The next morning, after hanging on tenaciously during the night, Gallo could only muster 20 men. Most of the losses were suffered in the afternoon attack.

COMPANY A of the 3d Marines held up on the forward slope of Bundschu Ridge. Mortar and machine-gun fire inflicted very heavy casualties and prevented the unit from advancing beyond this point on W-Day.

talion move to O–a and take position as center battalion. 3d Battalion attack on left and seize Adelup Point. 81mm mortars revert to battalion controls.[32]

[32] 3d Mar SAR, 1. The regimental operation plan for the landing called for the 81mm mortar platoons from HqCo of each of the battalions to land with their parent units and then set up a mortar group near

Preparations for the attack got under way. Meanwhile, the Japanese made a few plans of their own. They moved reserves from the

the boundary of Red Beach 1 and 2 where regiment could mass fires on Adelup Point. 3d Mar OpPlan 3–44, 27May44.

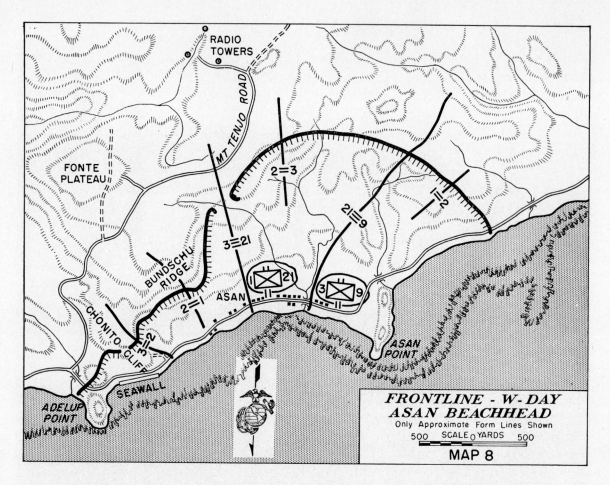

FONTE PLATEAU

RADIO TOWERS

MT TENJO ROAD

2≡3

2≡9

2≡21

3≡21

BUNDSCHU RIDGE

ASAN

2≡1

3≡9

CHONITO CLIFF

3≡21

3≡2

SEAWALL

ASAN POINT

ADELUP POINT

FRONTLINE - W - DAY
ASAN BEACHHEAD
Only Approximate Form Lines Shown
500 SCALE 0 YARDS 500

MAP 8

Fonte area, the next high ground inland, and manned all available weapons in an effort to contain the 3d Marine Division in its small beachhead. Despite constant air strikes and naval gunfire bombardment, the enemy continued moving men to strategic positions.[33]

Utilizing every supporting arm available to the regiment, the 3d Marines (less the 1st Battalion busily engaged on Bundschu Ridge) attacked at 1500. All units met stiff resistance immediately after jumping off. The only battalion to make progress was the 3d, which moved along the coast to get into position for an attack on Adelup Point. Following a heavy preparation by tanks, destroyers, and

LCI(G)'s, the assault was successful but sustained substantial losses.

Having suffered a considerable number of casualties while coming ashore and moving into the assembly area, the 2d Battalion had some idea of the fire it would encounter. However, the unit's baptism had been from snipers and sporadic mortars and did not compare with the volume received when the battalion tried to move from the O–a line. The murderous fire continued the rest of the day, and when the 2d received orders to dig in for the night it found itself short of the D–1 line. It had, nevertheless, taken the immediate high ground in its sector.[34]

Less than 1,000 yards behind front lines, other units supporting the division made ready for the night. Enemy mortar and artillery fire had been heavy, and snipers harassed men

[33] Behind this bristling defensive line, Gen Takashina assembled "the troops which had been located in the Tumon area, Agana area, and the southern part of the Pago area of Sinajana [to] let them participate in the battle of Fonte area at the right moment of driving the Americans from Fonte." *Takeda.*

[34] 3d Mar Jnl.

as they went about their jobs. But this did not keep work from progressing on schedule.

Careful planning and the new techniques developed on Guadalcanal, discussed earlier, enabled artillery to move ashore soon after H-Hour. By 1215 one battery of Lieutenant Colonel Alpha L. Bowser, Jr.'s 3d Battalion, 12th Marines was in position and firing.[35] Shortly thereafter the 4th Battalion came ashore and started into its position where it found two enemy machine guns still active. Fortunately Colonel Craig had his command post in this area and, upon request, he directed a tank to take out these emplacements so the 4th could go into action.[36] Other units quickly set up and by 1640 all division artillery was ashore. Howitzer sections hurriedly made preparations to fire, but at first, the infantry could get little or no fire close to its own front lines. Minimum range and lack of observation by forward observers curtailed close-in firing. However, by using air spot, the artillery furnished beneficial support by harassing enemy troop concentrations and suspected and known enemy mortar and artillery positions. Both 75mm and 105mm howitzers quickly took enemy reserves moving to the front under fire, and there is no question that the artillery played an important role in helping establish the beachhead on W-Day.

Doing double duty in the beachhead, the 19th Marines (engineers) furnished shore party details and boat riders,[37] as well as supplying the infantry regiments with engineer support. A road was cut to provide the 21st Marines with a supply route. Demolition work on caves and the removal of mines from the beach area required time and patience, for the Japanese harassed the engineers constantly with mortar and sniper fire.

Equipment and supplies moved ashore with proficiency. As LVT's and DUKW's loaded with ammunition and supplies arrived on the beach, shore party personnel sent the vehicles directly to dumps that had been established. Heavy mortar fire fell all during the day, causing no end of trouble to parties working on the beach; yet things kept moving. Men from the 3d Service Battalion [38] and the 3d Motor Transport Battalion formed a combination hard to beat in the expeditious handling and movement of supplies.

At the end of the first day the 3d Marine Division, Reinforced, working as an efficient fighting team, had a foothold on Guam, (See Map 8) The day's operations had been costly (105 KIA, 536 WIA, and 56 MIA), but had troop leaders been less aggressive in moving their units off the beach, casualties would have been much heavier. Hundreds of rounds of enemy mortar and artillery shells had been observed exploding harmlessly in areas just previously occupied by advancing Marines.[39]

THE SOUTHERN ASSAULT

The brigade operation plan called for landing Lieutenant Colonel Alan Shapley's 4th Marines and Colonel Merlin F. Schneider's 22d Marines as the assault units and holding the Army's 305th RCT (77th Division), commanded by Colonel Vincent J. Tanzola, as brigade floating reserve. (See Map 9, Map Section)

The 4th, on the right, was to establish a beachhead and protect the flank of the brigade. The 22d, after landing on the left, and securing Agat Village, would drive north and cut off Orote Peninsula. When committed, the 305th had the mission of being prepared to make a passage of lines of the 4th and protect that sector of the beachhead. The brigade would then make preparations for further offensive operations.[40]

Beaches Yellow and White, target of General Shepherd's command, lay between Agat Village and Bangi Point. (See Map 10) As in the 3d

[35] 3d MarDiv SAR, OpNarrative, 2. Actually, Btry H reported its registration piece in position and ready to fire at 1145.

[36] Ltr LtCol T. R. Belzer to CMC, 9Sept52, hereinafter cited as *Belzer*.

[37] One element of the shore party was made up of landing craft working party detachments consisting of a minimum of two men. These men were assigned permanently to each landing craft as boat riders to assist in the discharge of cargo from ships to boats in the transport area and from boats to landing vehicles at the reef. 3d MarDiv AdmPlan 2–44, Shore Party Annex, 13May44.

[38] 3d SerBn SAR, 1. Attached to 3d SerBn for the landing were the 2d AmmoCo and Co B, 5th FldDep.

[39] 3d MarDiv WD, July 1944, 6.

[40] 1st ProvMarBrig OpPlan 7–44, 11Jul44.

ASSAULT WAVES of the 1st Provisional Marine Brigade move toward the beach at Agat as the final rounds of the naval gunfire preparation explode ashore. (Navy Photograph.)

Division's sector, a wide reef protected the shore. Knowing this to be a natural obstacle, the Japanese had prepared to exploit it. Brutal mortar and artillery fire fell on approaching waves of LVT's as they crawled across the reef.

The enemy had his defenses ashore, consisting of numerous pillboxes built in coral outcroppings, well-organized. Concrete blockhouses, located on Gaan Point, held a 75mm [41] and a 37mm gun which enfiladed the beaches. One 75mm field piece on Yona Island had not been knocked out. The emplacements did not show through the scattered clouds on aerial photographs available prior to the landing. The blockhouses formed large sand covered mounds, and the many palm trees made detection difficult.[42]

These guns raked Beaches Yellow 1 and 2 as men of the 22d started to cross them. The regiment landed with the 1st and 2d Battalions in assault. The 3d, boated in LCVP's, remained at the line of departure in reserve. The loss of men and equipment at the water's edge made organization for the attack inland difficult.[43] But, as quickly as possible, units moved

---

[41] This gun is constantly reported in war diaries and action reports as a 77mm field piece. Guns of the same caliber were supposedly encountered later in the campaign. However, an exhaustive search of records of captured and destroyed ordnance and of intelligence information of the Japanese armed forces reveals no such weapon. The probable explanation is that troops in heat of battle mistook the improved 75mm Model 94 with muzzle brake for a gun of larger caliber.

[42] Ltr LtCol R. W. Shaw to CMC, 29Sept52.

[43] Later, on Yellow Beach 2 alone, the bodies of 75 Marines were counted. B. G. Cass, ed., *History of the Sixth Marine Division*, (Washington, 1946), 14, hereinafter cited as *6th MarDiv History*.

off the beaches and started toward their first objective.

On the right, the 2d (Lieutenant Colonel Donn C. Hart) advanced rapidly inland, overcame scattered resistance, and reorganized about 400 yards from the beach.[44] When the advance continued, a Japanese strong point in Company G's zone of action held up the battalion. However, the direct fire of regimental tanks,[45] fresh from the beach, helped eliminate this trouble. The companies then moved forward and secured the high ground about 1,000 yards inland.

After landing, the 1st Battalion, commanded by Lieutenant Colonel Walfried H. Fromhold, wheeled left and commenced the drive toward Agat. As Company B, on the left flank next to the sea, reached the outskirts of the village, it met stiffened opposition. Naval bombardment had leveled the buildings, but the rubble furnished good protection for the Japanese defenders who had filtered back to the town.

[44] Initially, Japanese fires appear to have been concentrated on the beaches. Once units were 200–300 yards inland they were able to move more freely.

[45] These tanks had eliminated the troublesome emplacement on Gaan Point, taking the position from the rear and blasting the surprised enemy gunners before they could offer effective resistance. TkCo, 22d Mar SAR, 3.

Colonel Fromhold committed his reserve, Company C, and the momentum of the attack carried the battalion to Harmon Road by 1130. About the same time regimental headquarters attached Company I (3/22), which had landed on Yellow Beach at 1010, to 1/22 as reserve.[46]

Fifteen minutes later General Shepherd, with his forward command echelon, disembarked and started toward the beach. After they arrived ashore brigade set up its command post in a coconut grove about 200 yards southeast of Gaan Point, and at 1350 Shepherd assumed control of all troops in his zone of action.[47]

Other problems besides fighting the enemy confronted 1/22. Front line units started to run low on ammunition, and a message sent to the beach requesting a resupply brought an answer at 1350 of "Nothing on beach yet. Sent LVT's. Will have supplies when they return."[48] Evacuation of casualties also proved difficult. As it landed, an aid station party had received a direct hit from a 75mm field gun. Many medical supplies were destroyed and only one member of the medical team escaped uninjured. As a result, the battalion had no doctor until

[46] Ltr Maj S. A. Todd to CMC, 30Oct52.
[47] 1st ProvMarBrig WD, 1Jul–10Aug44, 4.
[48] 1/22 Jnl.

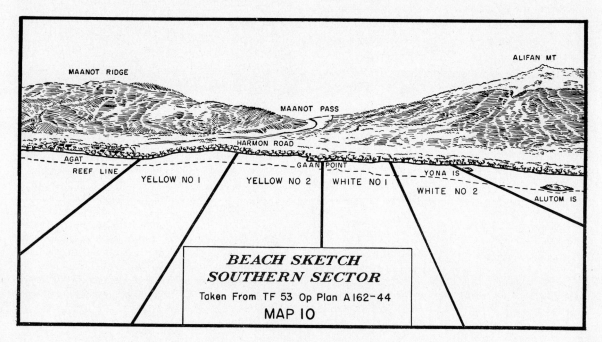

MAANOT RIDGE

ALIFAN MT

MAANOT PASS

HARMON ROAD

AGAT

REEF LINE

YELLOW NO 1   YELLOW NO 2   WHITE NO 1

GAAN POINT

YONA IS

WHITE NO 2

ALUTOM IS

BEACH SKETCH SOUTHERN SECTOR

Taken From TF 53 Op Plan A162-44

MAP 10

GAAN POINT PILLBOX shows the scars of repeated shellings which failed to knock out this 75mm gun and a companion 37mm that accounted for many tractors and men in the first waves of the 22d Marines. (Navy Photograph.)

afternoon. In spite of such difficulties, Fromhold made plans to continue the attack when ordered.[49]

Regimental headquarters had its problems, too. Because of a radio failure, communications could not be established with the remainder of the reserve battalion (3d) and consequently its commander, Lieutenant Colonel Clair W. Shisler, did not receive orders to come ashore until 1236. This prevented the unit from landing in time to participate in the remainder of the day's action,[50] but did not delay the attack on the O–1 [51] (See Map 11, Map Section) line by the rest of the regiment.

The 1st Battalion jumped off at 1245 and met stiff but spotty resistance. As the attack progressed the unit started across gently sloping terrain that was ideal tank country. Lieutenant Colonel Fromhold requested armor, but the tanks did not arrive until the middle of

the afternoon.[52] After joining the infantry, they assisted in the advance through Agat, knocking out strong points which held up the advance.

Captain Charles F. Widdecke's Company C, on the left flank of the brigade, made good progress until stopped by machine-gun fire from a hill northeast of Agat. This insignificant-looking mound held up the advance, and the fighting there was indicative of the action of W-Day. Widdecke's men attempted to flank the position about 1500, but deadly fire forced a withdrawal. For over an hour the enemy kept Company C pinned down in a series of narrow trenches at the base of the hill. When reinforcements arrived, another attack brought no better results. Concealed machine guns swept the open area and forced the Marines back to the trenches. Troops began to improve their position for the night. But the day's work had been costly. At 1455, Captain Widdecke reported, "Company C committed all platoons, no reserve, weak, could not hold counterattack." [53] At 1715 the battalion commander sent a platoon of reserves to help strengthen the position. Three hours later all companies had sent word they were set for the night.

After reorganizing on the high ground secured in the morning, Lieutenant Colonel Hart's 2d Battalion made preparations for the 1250 attack on O–1. Even before the assault got under way, enemy artillery fire began to fall on the unit, growing in intensity as Hart's men jumped off. The assault elements inched ahead against stubborn resistance until a dual-purpose gun stopped Company E. A called air strike produced unsatisfactory results as the strafing hit the front lines and ten bombs fell in the area of Company F. By the time casualties had been removed and a reorganization

---

[49] *Ibid.*

[50] 1st ProvMarBrig Jnl.

[51] Brigade designated its phase lines within the FBL O–1, O–2, etc. The regiments in many of their attacks set up CT objectives labeled R–1, R–2, etc. During the latter part of the campaign when the brigade moved to the north, most orders used corps objectives, which were designated O–1, O–2, etc.

[52] Although tanks landed on the reef off White 1 at 0834 they had trouble getting to shore. Shell holes, mines, mortar fire, and mis-direction by the beachmaster were some of the difficulties encountered. By the time the confusion had been resolved it was 0946. Then the tanks reported to the 2d Bn, as ordered, but lack of opposition and unsuitable terrain dictated a move to the 1st Bn's zone of action. TkCo, 22dMar SAR, 3–4.

[53] 1/22 Jnl.

MOUNT ALIFAN looms above men of the 4th Marines as they move through its foothills to the attack. In the background a plane being used for observation keeps track of the front lines for fire control agencies.

effected the battalion had received orders to dig in for the night.[54]

The day had been a difficult one for Lieutenant Colonel Shapley's 4th Marines also. Assault elements met opposition immediately after crossing the reef. Plans calling for LVT's to move 1,000 yards inland before discharging troops had to be abandoned.[55]

The regiment landed with two battalions in assault and one in reserve. The scheme of maneuver called for the 1st and 2d to land abreast and drive inland. As the advance moved ahead, extending the zone of action, the 3d Battalion (less one company) would work in on the right, next to the beach.

On landing, the 2d Battalion (Major John S. Messer), on the left, hit a low but strongly defended hill less than 100 yards from the shoreline. Maps had not disclosed this 10–20-foot elevation whose reverse slope offered the enemy excellent protection.[56] Major Messer's men made slow progress, but by noon the pocket of resistance had been reduced and the 2d started toward Mt. Alifan.

Major Bernard W. Green's 1st Battalion came ashore with two companies in assault. Company A, on the right, met stiff opposition from pillboxes but reduced their effectiveness and started across the open fields at the foot of Mt. Alifan. Company B met only token resist-

[54] 2/22 Jnl.

[55] 1st ProvMarBrig WD, 1Jul–10Aug44, 4. Two LVT's carrying a platoon of Co B were able to carry out original plans. However, this caused some anxious moments for the platoon leader, Lt Willard C. Hofer, who for two hours found himself 1,000 yards ahead of any other assault unit. Interview with Capt. L. E. Fribourg, 5Dec51.

[56] Interview with Capt C. O. Diliberto, 16Dec51.

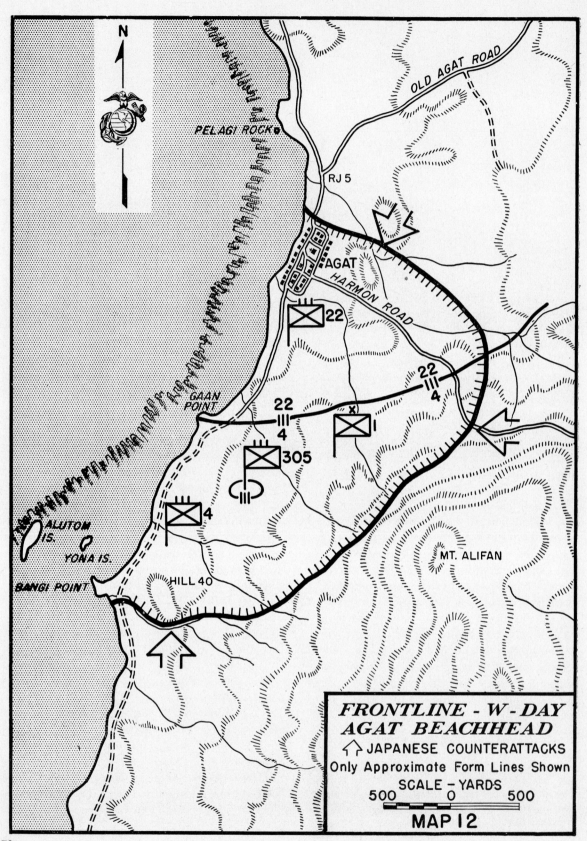

N

PELAGI ROCK

OLD AGAT ROAD

RJ 5

AGAT

HARMON ROAD

22

22
4

GAAN
POINT

22
4

X
1

305

4

ALUTOM
IS.

YONA IS.

MT. ALIFAN

BANGI POINT

HILL 40

**FRONTLINE - W - DAY
AGAT BEACHHEAD**
⬆ JAPANESE COUNTERATTACKS
Only Approximate Form Lines Shown
SCALE - YARDS
500   0   500

MAP 12

CONTROL BOATS direct the confused but orderly traffic of men and supplies in a variety of landing craft at the transfer line.

ance and advanced rapidly inland. The discovery of a drainage ditch in its zone of action gave the company good cover and enabled it to move 1,000–2,000 yards by 1030.

When the attack had progressed 700 yards, Company C, initially in reserve, landed and swung right to hit Hill 40 and Bangi Point. The hill, dominating the road that paralleled the beach, proved to be strongly defended. Men from Company C crept ahead until a deadly stream of machine-gun bullets halted the attack. Major Green called for two tanks when Company A also came under fire from the well-concealed guns. This added support supplied the necessary impetus to the attack that followed. This time the Marines captured the hill.[57]

When two companies of the reserve battalion (3d) arrived ashore, they started to relieve the 1st Battalion. Company K took over Hill 40 and Bangi Point while Company I moved up on the left flank in the battalion's zone. One platoon of the reserve company (L/3) occupied Alutom Island but found no Japanese defenders. The remainder of the reserve moved into an assembly area about 300 yards inland from White 2.

Lieutenant Colonel Shapley had all units of the 4th Marines in position at 1345 to resume the attack to seize O–1. Scattered resistance met the assault elements as they jumped off,

but the regiment made satisfactory progress. Company B had established a road block on Harmon Road by 1730 and could see the 2d Battalion, 22d Marines on its left. A deep gully prevented physical contact. From the road the lines bent back around the lower slopes of Mt. Alifan to Hill 40 on the beach. Shapley could only establish strong points across the wide front; supporting arms covered all possible avenues of approach into the regiment's position.[58] (See Map 12)

The situation at the end of the brigade's first day ashore is best summed up by the message General Shepherd sent to General Geiger at 1830:

Own casualties about 350. Enemy unknown. Critical shortages fuel and ammunition all types. Think we can handle it. Will continue as planned tomorrow.[59]

Several factors delayed the movement of supplies ashore the first morning. Inner edges of reefs, heavy with silt, made it difficult to locate suitable places to beach landing vehicles. In addition, the loss of 24 LVT's on W-Day seriously hampered the work of transshipment. Landing craft moved supplies to the transfer area on schedule, but the lack of sufficient amphibious vehicles caused a serious backlog at this point. Numerous expedients, such as rubber boat causeways, rafts, and floating fuel drums manhandled by wading Marines relieved

---

[57] 1/4 WD, 30May–9Sept44, 2.

[58] 1st ProvMarBrig Jnl.
[59] *Ibid.*

75MM PACK HOWITZER carried ashore in a DUKW is unloaded by an A-frame attached to another DUKW.

the situation somewhat. Nevertheless, the Navy decided to continue unloading throughout the night in an effort to get more gear ashore, and General Shepherd requested that ammunition and water be placed on the priority list.[60]

In anticipation of the expected violent Japanese reaction, Shepherd issued his instructions for night defenses. He ordered particular attention be paid to organization in depth and the maintaining of local reserves for a counterattack.[61] To comply with this decision and to block the only armor approach route into the center of the brigade's position, the 4th Marines parked five tanks in a little hollow just off Harmon Road. Artillery registered in normal barrages, and front line observers requested illumination from the Navy. Other preparations of the 4th included sending the Reconnaissance Platoon and a detachment of engineers to strengthen the defensive line. And finally, Company C went into reserve near the regimental CP with orders to be prepared to

move out during the night. In the 22d's zone assault platoons consolidated their positions, and 3/22 stood by to bar any attempted enemy infiltration. The brigade's defense was now ready and alert.

At 2330 units reported Japanese operating all along the front. A half-hour later the enemy made his first attempt to penetrate the lines of the brigade. A mortar barrage came down on the right flank of the 4th Marines. Tossing demolition charges and small land mines like hand grenades, the Japanese threw themselves against the front lines. Before the attack could be repulsed six Marines had been bayoneted in their fox holes.[62]

The enemy chose Hill 40 as the target for the next attack. A platoon of Company K was hit hard about 0100 and forced to withdraw. Reorganizing at the foot of the hill, the men counterattacked and recaptured the ground, only to be driven off a second time. When two squads, led by Lieutenant Marvin C. Plock, arrived as reinforcements, a third try again carried the hill. This time the determined Marines could not be dislodged.

This was not the last attack against Major Hamilton M. Hoyler's 3d Battalion, however. The enemy regrouped in an unusual silence. Hoyler's men watched the proceedings and made their own preparations. Hand grenades were lined up along the edges of fox holes, weapons checked and sighted to give the best fields of fire, and artillery alerted.

About 0330 the assault started. Company K received the brunt. Lieutenant Martin J. Sexton's men stopped the main thrust,[63] but front line units ran low on ammunition, and small groups of Japanese infiltrated into the pack howitzer positions. The executive officer of Battery A, Pack Howitzer Battalion, 4th Marines described the action this way:

At 2330, I challenged two figures edging along the side of the crater, but they turned out to be communicators checking a wire line. About 30 minutes later, I saw four figures creeping along the same line, but

[60] Ltr LtCol A. Larson to CMC, 10May47.
[61] 1st ProvMarBrig OpOrder 9, 21Jul44.

[62] *6th MarDiv History*, 15.
[63] The next morning 390 enemy bodies gave mute testimony to the effectiveness of the Marines' fire. Forty-five were counted on Hill 40 and the remainder lay in front of the lines toward the beach. 3/4 WD, 21Jul–30Aug44, 1.

when I challenged them, they hit the ground and rolled away from the hole, muttering in Japanese. The "Gunny" in the hole with me threw a grenade, killing one and the other three were picked off by the gun sections. After this, reports of crawling figures started coming in from gun sections and outposts all around the battery. Simultaneously with these reports, fire missions started pouring in. By about 0130, we were up to our necks in fire missions and infiltrating Japanese. Every so often, I had to call a section out for a short time so it could take care of the intruders with carbines and then I would send it back into action again. Somehow, one Japanese nambu machine gunner managed to get between our guns and the front lines and all night harassed us with fire.[64]

But the most serious threat to the brigade's beachhead took place at Company B's road block. Four enemy tanks came lumbering up Harmon Road about 0230, followed by guns mounted on trucks. This tank-infantry attack might cause serious trouble, indeed. If a breakthrough could be accomplished, the enemy would have a clear road to Agat Village, where guns could be placed to enfilade the entire beachhead. But a bazooka man of the 4th Marines, Private First Class Bruno Oribiletti, met the column head-on. This was the first time the men of the regiment employed the rocket launcher,[65] and as an antitank weapon it soon demonstrated its value. Oribiletti knocked out the first two tanks before enemy fire killed him. A platoon of General Sherman tanks led by Lieutenant James R. Williams destroyed the remaining Japanese armor.[66] This was the same platoon that had been so strategically parked earlier that night. The loss of their armor discouraged the enemy foot soldiers, and they retreated behind Mt. Alifan.

What is thought to have been a coordinated part of the same attack hit the 1st Battalion, 4th Marines on its right flank. Under cover of a heavy mortar barrage, and supported by machine guns, the enemy surged through a draw toward Company A's lines. Led by an officer carrying a flag on a bamboo pole, shouting men swung Samurai swords and threw hand grenades with good results. The momentum of the assault carried some of the enemy almost

JAPANESE LIGHT TANK destroyed at the Company B, 4th Marines roadblock during the enemy counterattack on the night of 21–22 July. (Army Photograph.)

to the artillery positions, only 400 yards from the beach, where artillerymen halted the attackers. The fierce fighting in this sector was costly to both sides. Marines counted over 200 Japanese dead in the morning, but one platoon of Company A had been reduced to four men. Regiment did not have replacements available, and the company participated in the remainder of the Guam campaign with only two platoons.[67]

The enemy did not limit his counterattacks to the 4th Marines sector. On the north flank of the brigade, the 22d Marines also went through a sleepless night with small infiltration groups intent on reaching the Marines' rear areas responsible for most of the activity. One such unit, of about company size, made it to the vicinity of the regimental CP. Clerks, runners, and other headquarters personnel helped to clear the region. Six Marines were wounded, but by daybreak three Japanese officers and 66 soldiers had been killed.

---

[64] Ltr Capt B. S. Read to author, 3Jan52.

[65] Ltr Maj O. V. Bergren to CMC, 6Jun47, hereinafter cited as *Bergren.*

[66] TkCo, 4th Mar SAR, 13.

[67] *Bergren.*

Company C (1/22) that night witnessed one of those enemy tactical moves that only the Japanese themselves can explain. Down the hill—the hill that had held up the company most of the afternoon—marched 12 enemy soldiers. The men of Nippon carried one light and three heavy machine guns and walked steadily toward the center of the position. If their mission was to die for the Emperor, the Marines helped them accomplish it. Machine-gun fire riddled the oncoming Japanese who made no attempt to set up their weapons and defend themselves, and most of the group never reached the front lines.

About 0515 a platoon of Ammunition Company, 5th Field Depot, repelled an enemy demolition group headed for the brigade ammunition dump. The raiders left 14 dead behind.

Much of the credit for repelling the night-long enemy attacks must go to artillery and naval gunfire. In addition, ship's 5-inch guns and the infantry's 60mm mortars furnished constant illumination, which increased the effectiveness of defensive fires as well as permitting good observation of the enemy's movements.[68]

The last of the counterattacks designed to destroy the southern beachhead ceased at dawn. The enemy had thrown the 38th Infantry Regiment (less 3d Battalion) against the Marines in the night effort. One battalion had hit each of the brigade flanks, and the reinforcing units of the regiment had made the frontal assault against the 4th Marines. According to Japanese accounts, Colonel Suenaga, the regimental commander, was killed while leading the center attack.

Following the night's activities that had destroyed the 38th Regiment as a fighting force,[69] the brigade quickly restored its front lines by employing local reserves, and preparations got under way to resume the advance.

LANDING OF THE 305th RCT

The brigade operation plan called for one landing team (LT) of the Army's 305th Regimental Combat Team to be boated and at the line of departure by 1030 on W-Day. Colonel Tanzola assigned this mission to the 2d Battalion (Lieutenant Colonel Robert D. Adair). Shortly after the Marine assault waves cleared the line of departure, Colonel Adair ordered his men into their landing craft. A liaison team from the 305th Field Artillery Battalion also embarked into small boats to accompany the LT to shore.

After arriving at the control boat on schedule, the commander found brigade headquarters had no immediate need for his troops. Then began the monotony of waiting for orders. The artillery liaison party went ashore to select positions, but the 2d Battalion continued circling at the LD. After seemingly endless hours, 2/305 received a message at 1405 to land and assemble in an area 400 yards inland from Gaan Point.[70]

With no LVT's allotted or available, troops waded ashore through waist-deep water over a reef full of pot holes and shell craters. Weapons and equipment got water-soaked when men stumbled over submerged coral heads. If someone found good footing, everyone tended to move toward that sector of the reef. As a result, units became intermingled and forgot about dispersion. Fortunately, the Marines kept the Japanese too busy to fire on the beach or reef. After quickly reorganizing on Beach White 1, the battalion moved into its assembly area where it set up defensive positions for the night and immediately started to make preparations for the next day's mission.

Trouble seemed to be following the 305th. About 1430 General Shepherd ordered the rest of Colonel Tanzola's combat team to land. But communication difficulties delayed the message until 1530;[71] then the regiment only had enough craft available to land one battalion. The 1st (Lieutenant Colonel James E. Landrum) embarked in its landing craft and proceeded to the control boat for clearance to the beach. Naval officers refused to dispatch the boats because of lack of landing instructions. By the time the brigade had verified the movement the hour was 1730.[72]

[68] Ibid.
[69] Takeda.

[70] 1st ProvMarBrig WD, 1Jul–10Aug44, 4.
[71] 305th Inf Jnl.
[72] 305th Inf Action Rpt, 1.

In the meantime, Colonel Tanzola, becoming quite concerned about the fast-approaching darkness, sent a message to brigade headquarters:

Order to 305th Infantry conflicting. Was ordered to land entire CT. Cannot complete unloading of team before dark. Instructions received by TD 38 [Transport Division 38] differ. Suggest suspension of unloading. Request clear order be issued. Expedite reply.[73]

The reply came promptly, "Land your CT at once in accordance with previous instructions." [74]

Lieutenant Colonel Landrum and his men found conditions very similar to those which had faced the 2d Battalion. The RCT still had no LVT's, and upon starting across the reef the troops encountered the same holes, shell craters, and coral heads. Incoming tide raised the water chest-high, and men had to swim out of the deeper holes. Darkness added to their difficulties; they swerved south, landing dangerously near enemy-held territory. The battalion commander had planned to be in the center of his leading waves to keep control. However, because of the coral and depth of the water he landed on the left of the first wave, complicating the problem. Troops groped in search of their units, causing further disorder. But swift and decisive action by officers and NCO's resolved the confusion. Colonel Landrum located his assembly area and with his staff and guides moved approximately 60 percent of the battalion to it.

By 2130 the work of digging in for the night was well along. In the meantime, military police had stopped the remainder of the battalion on the beach fearing the movement forward during darkness might bring about unnecessary casualties. Consequently Landrum could not assemble his entire unit until after daylight the next day.[75]

The 3d Battalion, commanded by Lieutenant Colonel Edward Chalgren, Jr., was delayed even more. While waiting for the return of landing craft, the unit's transport (USS *Alpine*) suddenly received orders to get under way. A report of an enemy submarine in the area kept the ship at sea until 2120.[76] Darkness slowed debarkation and a shortage of boats (over half of the ship's boats had not been recovered when the *Alpine* put to sea) delayed unloading. Shortly after midnight the first wave started toward the beach, but failure of boat compasses caused crews much difficulty in maintaining the correct direction in proceeding the 12,000 yards from ship to shore. About 0200 the leading waves hit the reef that was concealed by high tide and darkness. After several boats nearly capsized in an attempt to cross the reef approximately 800 yards off White Beach 2 the battalion commander ordered the ramps lowered and troops began to wade ashore. Battalion and company guides, previously dispatched in daylight, met the men of 3/305 as they trudged through the shoulder-deep water and led them to assembly areas where they remained for the night.

To reduce confusion and danger for later waves, Lieutenant Colonel Chalgren and his staff borrowed five LVT's from the Marines and stationed the vehicles at the reef line. One LVT acted as control boat to direct incoming traffic while the remaining four amphibious tractors ferried troops across the treacherous coral. By dawn most of the battalion had landed, but some elements did not hit dry land until 0600. Men were seasick, wet, and tired, and harrassed by occasional mortar rounds landing in or near the beach assembly area where congestion and coral rock generally prevented digging even shallow trenches. By 0700 all men had been accounted for and companies had reorganized.[77]

Colonel Tanzola and his staff had their troubles too. They disembarked about 2330 and upon reaching the reef found no transportation. As they waded and swam to the beach, a rubber raft drifted near. The regimental commander immediately put the raft to use and floated to shore on it.

[73] 1st ProvMarBrig Jnl.

[74] 305th Inf Jnl.

[75] Ltr Col J. E. Landrum, Jr. to CMC, 22Oct52, hereinafter cited as *Landrum.*

[76] 305th Inf Jnl.

[77] Ltr Col E. A. Chalgren, Jr. to author, 23Jan53, hereinafter cited as *Chalgren.*

During the night the only serious enemy interference came in the 1st Battalion's zone. Early in the morning a small probing attack hit Companies A and B. Seven soldiers were killed and ten wounded, some of them by friendly troops confused by their first taste of battle. When daylight came, men of the 1st counted 20 Japanese bodies in and around their positions.

During this first restless night ashore and subsequent days, mutually cordial relations were established and maintained with the Marines. The men of the brigade nicknamed the 305th Infantry, "the 305th Marines." Marines, most of whom had never voted, affectionately referred to the 77th's fast-slogging oldsters as "the old bastards," and gained respect for the fighting ability of this previously untried division.[78]

TROUBLE ON THE LEFT FLANK

Japanese activities in the 3d Division's zone during the night of 21–22 July were not quite so vigorous as those carried on against the brigade. However, troublesome mortar and artillery fire on the beaches forced unloading to a halt at about 0230. Small-scale counterattacks hit all along the lines, but with naval

[78] The 77th Division was composed mostly of selectees taken from the 3d Draft. The average age of the initial complement was 32, but many of the troops were approaching 38 years old. *77th InfDiv History*, 13, 65–67.

20MM CANNON of Battery I, 14th Defense Battalion emplaced atop Chonito Cliff ready to support the advance of the 3d Marines. In the background is the shell-cratered outline of Adelup Point.

gunfire and artillery playing a leading role the Marines stopped the enemy thrusts.

The most serious encounter took place in front of the 3d Marines. With enemy contact reported as close as ten yards, Colonel Hall committed his reserve to bolster the thinning lines. This added strength repulsed the attack, but the situation became so critical that division headquarters alerted the shore party to occupy defensive positions on order.[79]

The immediate effect of the enemy action was to delay the jump-off time of the division's attack. A coordinated effort was set for 0700, but the commanding general authorized the 21st to hold up until contact could be made with the 3d Marines. During the night the Japanese successfully infiltrated through the gully between the two regiments and established a block therein, further complicating the problem of contact. By 0830, however, the 3d had cleared up all infiltration parties, including the one holding the ravine, and Colonel Hall reported his right flank intact.[80]

About the time the division CP received this message, headquarters was recovering from a heavy shelling. The message center suffered a direct hit that killed Lieutenant Colonel Chevey S. White (D–1) and wounded 20 other Marines.[81]

Although the entire 3d Regiment ran into stiff opposition all along the front, the area around Bundschu Ridge seemed to offer the most resistance at the moment. Badly battered Company A could move neither forward nor backward. The 1st Battalion's executive officer, Major John A. Ptak, who had spent the night with the men of Company A, recommended a plan to break the deadlock. The 21st Marines would extend its front to the left to take over the ground now held by Company C (1/3). The relieved company would then execute a flanking maneuver in an attempt to extricate the pinned-down unit.[82]

The regimental commander ordered the 2d Battalion to assist by having one company try to flank the ridge from the left. (See Map 13)

PRIVATE FIRST CLASS LEONARD F. MASON, 2d Battalion, 3d Marines, posthumously awarded the Medal of Honor for action on 22 July when he attacked and destroyed, although mortally wounded, two enemy machine-gun positions which had stopped his unit's advance.

Company E was assigned this mission and started to move toward the hill. At about 1000, Company C started across the rice paddies to flank the Japanese on the right. Trying to move into position for the coordinated attack with Companies A and E, the men got lost in the tangled mass of undergrowth. Nevertheless, the planned 20-minute preparation went ahead on schedule. Half-tracks, 20mm, 40mm,[83] and all organic weapons let loose with a tremendous barrage. Assault units followed the fire as closely as possible. A few Marines reached the top of the ridge, but shells from a 90mm mortar forced them to withdraw. Although they did not know it at this time, their presence caused the Japanese to abandon the position. The next day when

[79] 3d MarDiv D–3 Jnl.

[80] 3d Mar Jnl.

[81] 3d MarDiv D–1 Jnl.

[82] 1/3 Jnl.

[83] Btry I, 14th DefBn first brought its automatic cannon to bear on enemy targets in direct support missions for the 3d Mar early in the afternoon of W-Day. 14th DefBn SAR, 5.

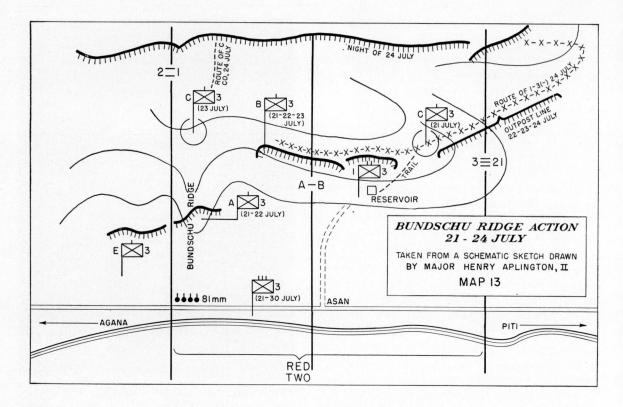

BUNDSCHU RIDGE ACTION
21 - 24 JULY

TAKEN FROM A SCHEMATIC SKETCH DRAWN
BY MAJOR HENRY APLINGTON, II

MAP 13

men of the 3d Marines walked up the hill they found trenches and foxholes littered with enemy dead.

The two days' fighting hit the 3d Marines hard. Colonel Hall reported that he had lost 615 men, killed, wounded, and missing.[84] Some companies could muster only 30–40 men. Company A was practically non-existent.

The 21st Marines remained on the same line most of W-plus 1, reorganizing, sending out patrols, and waiting until the 3d Marines could move ahead. Lines were extended dangerously thin, and any further advance would only have made the situation worse. The 2d Battalion, in position on an open ridge, received brutal mortar fire all day and suffered severely. In order to have a fresh unit on line for the next day's anticipated attack, Colonel Butler requested that division permit him to replace the 1st Battalion, now in division reserve, with the 2d.[85] General Turnage agreed. Late in the afternoon the relief began under cover of

artillery and naval gunfire, being completed about 2000.

On the right flank, the 9th Marines moved ahead against light opposition when it jumped off at 0715. Colonel Craig's units overran many excellent positions, including a bivouac area large enough to accommodate a regiment. Only sporadic resistance was encountered from small groups of Japanese left behind.[86] About noon Craig alerted the 3d Battalion for the attack on Cabras Island. (See Map 16, Map Section)

In view of the complete lack of intelligence as to the strength and disposition of the enemy on that island, a shore-to-shore amphibious assault had been planned, to be carried out as soon as the 2d Battalion occupied Piti Navy Yard.[87]

Following a full-scale naval gunfire and air bombardment, LVT's led by LVT(A)'s churned

[84] 3d Mar SAR, 2.

[85] 21st Mar SAR, 2.

[86] These were undoubtably the rear guard elements of 3/18 which were moving from this area towards Mt. Chachao and a union with 2/18 coming down from the north. This was part of the assembly of forces directed by the 29th Div in preparation for an all-out counterattack. *Takeda*; 3d MarDiv D-2 Periodic Rpt 69

[87] *Craig.*

ashore on the only beach on the island at 1425. Scaling ladders had been given the men to enable them to get up the high ground back of the narrow landing area. One LVT hit a land mine, but no enemy gunfire met the men as they scrambled ashore. Heavy brambles and hundreds of mines, however, made the going slow and tedious. The absence of any organized resistance indicated little danger of enemy counterattacks, and the approach of dusk brought the inland advance to a halt after 400 yards.

The evening of W-plus 1 found the division in better defensive positions than the night before, but General Turnage was concerned about the next day's fighting. He felt he needed another combat team to strengthen his division and sent a message to corps requesting one:

Enemy resistance increased considerably today on Div left and center. All Bn's of 3rd CT have been committed in continuous attack since landing. 21st CT less 1 Bn in Div Res has been committed continuously with all units in assault. One of the assault Bn's of 21st CT is being relieved on line by Div Res Bn today. Former is approx 40% depleted. Since further advance will continue to thin our lines it is now apparent that an additional combat team is needed. 9th CT is fully committed to capture of Piti & Cabras. Accordingly it is urgently recommended that an additional CT be attached this Div at the earliest practicable date.[88]

The night was relatively quiet with the only heavy enemy action reported by the 21st Marines. About midnight an intense mortar barrage hit the front lines of the 1st Battalion. The attack followed closely and culminated with a bayonet charge, which 1/21 repulsed with crippling losses to the enemy. Harassing fire fell throughout the division area, but few casualties were reported.

Early in the morning of the 23d, the division received a message from Headquarters Southern Landing Force which read:

Essential that close contact between adjacent units be established late afternoon and maintained throughout the night. Take action to insure this daily.[89]

This was to be the basis for most of the activity on W-plus 2. The 3d Marines and the 21st had never been able to make contact since land-

AMPHIBIAN TANKS cross the reef toward Cabras Island as they lead the shore-to-shore assault of the 3d Battalion, 9th Marines. (Navy Photograph.)

ing. Many futile attempts to join up had been made, but the tangled undergrowth had made this impossible.

Under the cover of dense vegetation, outcroppings of jagged coral and heaped boulders barred movement. Each of the innumerable gullies, small valleys, and ridges crisscrossing the sector added to the difficulties of tying in the units. This particular area the Commandant of the Marine Corps, Lieutenant General Alexander A. Vandegrift, later described as, "Some of the most rugged country I have ever seen."[90]

Yet one patrol from the 1st Battalion, 3d Marines, did make contact with the 21st on W-plus 1 by skirting this entire area. However, in trying to return to their own headquarters across the ground where the tie-in was required, the men lost their way and had to turn back to the 21st's lines for the night. Although on the map only a few hundred yards separated the regiments, and the patrol had radio contact with the 3d Marines all the way, it still could not locate its own lines.[91]

---

[88] 3d MarDiv D-3 Jnl.
[89] Ibid.

[90] 3d MarDiv SAR, 4.
[91] 3d Mar Jnl.

81MM MORTAR CREW MEMBERS duck away from the blast of their weapon as they fire in support of troops pushing up the rugged slopes of the Asan beachhead. (Navy Photograph.)

Colonel Hall made plans to renew the attack at daylight, but he was none too optimistic about its success as evidenced by the message he sent to division:

My left flank is quite secure so I am taking Weapons Company and attaching them to Aplington [1st Bn]. They will give Aplington the men to make contact with 21st. I am going to try and advance up that mess in front of me. What I really need is a battalion whereas I have only 160 men to use on that 500-yard slope. They might move to the top but they couldn't advance on. Company A is down to about 30–40 men with an air liaison officer in charge, Company E is down to half strength. They have no strength to push on.[92]

In the morning, every available weapon—air, naval gunfire, artillery, 20mm's, 40mm's, and guns from half-tracks and tanks—threw shells into the ridges and gullies in front of the 3d Marines. Lieutenant Colonel Houser's 3d Battalion, on the left flank of the division, attacked at 0900 and met opposition of the most stubborn and furious kind. Shortly after noon the ex-

ecutive officer, Major Royal R. Bastian, Jr., who had taken over when Colonel Houser was wounded and evacuated at 1100, called for reserves to meet an enemy counterattack hitting all along his front.[93] Meanwhile, he rushed every available man into the line, leaving only skeleton crews with the mortars and machine guns. Excellent support from naval gunfire, air, and artillery broke up the Japanese effort, but the battalion suffered such heavy casualties that it could not renew the attack.

In the center of the 3d Marines' zone, the 2d and 1st Battalions launched a combined drive at 0900 against Bundschu Ridge. The 2d, with Captain William E. Moore, Jr.'s Company E spearheading the drive, moved forward on the left. At the same time Company C (Captain David I. Zeitlin) started to flank the Japanese position on the ridge from the right. Under cover of close support fires,[94] both units hacked their way ahead through the thick vegetation. To the amazement of everyone, no fire came from the position that had held up the 1st Battalion for two days. The enemy had abandoned his defenses. The Marines pushed on, and at 1108 forces finally joined on the crest of the ridge. But further advance was out of the question until troops mopped up the area. Several machine guns, located in the cliffs, continued to cause trouble, and the 1st and 2d Battalions spent the rest of the day ferreting out the Japanese from these cave positions.

In the center of the division's zone, the 21st jumped off at 0900 in an attempt to relieve the pressure on the right flank of the 3d Marines and also to gain contact with that unit. Neither try proved successful. The patrol making the effort to link up turned back when it could not cross the rugged cliffs. Enemy pillboxes prevented the regiment from making any progress in carrying out the other mission. Demolition squads and flame-thrower teams assaulted individual bunkers, but the process was time consuming and by the end of the day the 21st had gained little ground.

---

[92] *Ibid.*

[93] 3/3 Jnl.

[94] During the course of this action, one friendly air strike hit in the lines of Company B which was supporting the attack. Eight Marines were killed and three wounded. 1/3 Jnl.

On Cabras Island, the 3d Battalion, 9th Marines had resumed its advance early in the morning, met no opposition, and at 0900 received orders to turn the island over to the 14th Defense Battalion.[95] Thereupon 3/9 relieved the 2d Battalion, which went into division reserve. During the remainder of W-plus 2 the regiment sent patrols far forward of the front lines. Negative results indicated the enemy had abandoned that area.

For the first time in three days the division could set up a defense for the night on commanding ground. However, the lines were spread very thin. The request for an additional combat team had been denied. Geiger felt that the general situation ashore did not warrant committing the corps reserve at this time.[96]

With front line units reduced by casualties so that only strong points could be established, possible avenues of enemy approach had to be covered with fire. Naval gunfire and artillery again did yeoman work during the night. Artillery alone fired 5,186 rounds of harassing and interdiction fire. There were no strong enemy attacks and few infiltration attempts.

On the morning of 24 July, the division made its first attempt to contact the brigade. A 30-man patrol from the 9th Marines started along the Piti-Sumay Road toward Orote Peninsula. Under cover of LVT(A)'s the small unit made good progress until about 1030 when rifle and machine-gun fire from the high ground flanking the road halted the attempt. On finding itself at the edge of a shelling directed against Orote, the patrol requested permission to return to regiment. Although the 30-man unit did not accomplish the mission of contact, it did gain important intelligence information. This indicated that some Japanese might have withdrawn down the coast toward the south. The enemy left behind huge dumps of ammunition, fuel, supplies, and vehicles but no troops in strength. Neither did the defenders destroy roads or bridges in their haste to withdraw.[97]

In the center of the division line, the 3d and 21st Marines were still trying to make contact. At 0630, 2/21, which had been released from division reserve in the afternoon of 23 July, attacked up the ravine that marked the boundary between the two regiments. A 100-round mortar concentration preceded the jump-off. However, murderous fire from enemy machine guns halted the attack immediately. Mutually supporting caves in the sides of the cliff offered plenty of protection for the Japanese. Company G, moving up on the left of the gully, reached the plateau and offered some fire assistance. But nothing could be done to reduce the effectiveness of the cave positions.

Units in the ravine repulsed two Japanese counterattacks within two hours. Lieutenant Colonel Smoak called for an air strike at 1205. Friendly troops were so close to the enemy that, although the Navy pilots' bombing was nearly perfect, regiment reported 17 Marine casualties.[98] Following the strike, the 2d Battalion advanced 200 yards before fierce resistance forced a halt. Another air strike was put into the area, but this time to no avail. A later count showed that over 100 Imperial soldiers had paid with their lives to retain control of the ravine.

Later in the day, two companies of the 3d Marines went around to the rear of 1/3 and reached the plateau where they tied in with 2/21. Contact was finally established but only by strong points, and a break of 75 yards still existed between the 1st and 2d Battalions of the 3d Marines. Because difficult terrain and dense undergrowth made it impossible to close the gap before dark, Colonel Hall ordered it covered by mortar fire.

By nightfall the left and center of the division defensive lines rested on high ground overlooking the approaches to the Mt. Tenjo Road. On the right, the 9th Marines had improved its positions, advancing a little to take maximum advantage of the terrain. But casualties had mounted, and lack of replacements kept the lines thinned. The division reported 2,034 casualties since the landing, most of them in the infantry regiments.[99]

---

[95] 9th Mar R-2 Jnl.
[96] IIIAC SAR, OpRpt, 2.
[97] 3d MarDiv D-3 Jnl.

---

[98] 21st Mar SAR, 3.
[99] 3d MarDiv D-3 Jnl.

It was up to supporting arms to furnish defensive fires again. Corps now had larger caliber weapons available to help. Two 90mm batteries of the 14th Defense Battalion and the first 155mm guns from corps artillery reported early in the afternoon that they were ready to fire. The Marines needed their added range to harass suspected enemy assembly areas and interdict roads and other avenues of approach. Only a limited number of star shells remained, so Admiral Conolly authorized the use of destroyer searchlights for illumination.[100]

In spite of the division's troublesome left flank, the outlook was somewhat brighter. Supplies were moving ashore in good order. One important item which contributed to this

---

[100] IIIAC C–3 Jnl.

success was the placing of large cranes on the reef and the mounting of others on pontoon barges for the transfer of cargo from boats to LVT's. Also, shore parties had worked expeditiously and tirelessly. TQM's reported some ships completely unloaded, and the over-all average had reached more than 80 percent. The 19th Marines had established water facilities ashore at Asan Spring. This excellent source provided sufficient quantities so that it was no longer necessary to bring fifty gallon drums of water ashore. This lightened the logistical load of the shore party considerably, thereby allowing it to concentrate more on ammunition and other high-priority supplies.[101] The engineers

---

[101] Ltr Col E. M. Williams to CMC, 25Oct52, hereinafter cited as *Williams*.

LONG TOMS of Battery A, 7th 155mm Gun Battalion set up 500 yards from White Beach 2 in the shadow of the mountain range secured by the 4th Marines and the Army's 305th Infantry.

had also built an adequate road net to all units. A pulley system had been improvised to evacuate the wounded and supply the units of the 21st Marines on top of the cliff.[102]

Some valuable intelligence information began to come into the division. Civilians entered the lines near Adelup Point and reported many Japanese in the general area of Fonte-Mt. Tenjo-Ylig Bay-Pago Bay. Strong concentrations located on the Fonte plateau protected an enemy divisional CP. Guamanians said the Japanese moved from the Tumon Bay region at night, staying off the roads, and using stream lines and ravines to get into the Fonte area. These tactics were not new, but the information helped commanders formulate plans to break the defense.

MT. ALIFAN CAPTURED

While units of the 3d Division slowly drove in the outguards of the Fonte defensive position, the Marines in the south forged ahead to the FBL. On W-plus 1 (22 July), the brigade prepared to renew the advance toward Mt. Alifan. The 4th Marines received orders to seize the massif and then extend along the top of the ridge to the vicinity of Mt. Taene, to the south. The 22d would take O–a and be prepared to capture O–2 on order. And for the first time the 305th (less 2d Battalion) would move into the line. It was directed to pass through the left battalion of the 4th Marines and attack in the direction of Maanot Reservoir. When relieved by the 305th, 2/4 would join 2/305 as brigade reserve. Jump-off time was set for 0830.[103]

General Shepherd, however, found it necessary to delay the advance when the 1st and 3d Battalions of the 305th could not get into position in time. Because of the unavoidably confused landing and the loss of needed equipment, Colonel Tanzola's units required two hours to regroup and reorganize. During this period, brigade issued new orders directing 2/305 to

move forward immediately and relieve the 2d Battalion, 4th Marines on the front lines. As soon as the rest of the 305th was ready, it would pass through 2/305 and attack to seize O–2.[104]

At about 0845 the 22d Marines started its advance and pushed ahead steadily against moderate resistance. The hill position northwest of Agat, which had held up the progress of 1/22 the day before, caused little trouble as the Marines walked to its top. Supporting tanks cleared the way to the next high ground, where the attack was temporarily halted. A bridge had been destroyed, and armor could not cross the Ayuja River. A call went out for engineers. None were available, so LVT(A)'s came up for infantry support. They could not cross because of the vertical banks of the river, and the assault units moved ahead without their help.[105]

Company C continued to advance until stopped by machine-gun fire from well-prepared positions. Neutralizing the pillboxes resulted in heavy casualties. Unable to regain the initiative in the remaining daylight hours, the company dug in for the night 250 yards north of RJ 5. Two platoons of Company A, 1/22, crossed Old Agat Road late in the afternoon, but were ordered back to the road for the night.[106] This enabled them to tie in with the 2d Battalion on the right, which had kept pace with the 1st during the day. It had encountered only light, irregular resistance from pillboxes which naval gunfire quickly knocked out.

Having delayed its attack for half an hour, the 4th Marines got under way at 0900. As the regiment started across the foothills toward the steep slopes of Mt. Alifan, it encountered a well-entrenched enemy. From the northern side of the ridge rose numerous little rounded hills

---

[102] The former executive officer of 1/21 recalls that "a forward aid station at the top of this lift was in a most exposed position. Corpsmen here hand-led emergency cases prior to lowering them to the aid station at the base of the lift." *Van Stockum.*

[103] 1st ProvMarBrig OpOrder 10, 21Jul44.

[104] 1st ProvMarBrig Jnl.

[105] The tank company commander reported the bridging of the river as follows: ". . . after engineer assistance had been requested and not received the bulldozer tank and manual labor of tank crews was employed to cross a river holding up our advance. This river, just beyond Agat, with a width of forty feet [most sources indicate this river to be 15–20 feet wide] and a depth of two or three feet, a muddy bottom, and vertical banks was finally crossed on a causeway constructed by the tank company without assistance, after twenty-four hours of work, with a loss of one man killed and three wounded." TkCo, 22d Mar SAR, 4.

[106] 1/22 Jnl.

whose reverse slopes offered the Japanese good positions for enfilade fire. Demolition teams sealed the caves that honeycombed the hills, and hand grenades reduced the coconut log bunkers.

When the advance neared the top of the mountain, the terrain grew worse; even the Japanese could not adequately prepare it for defense. A snarled, thorny undergrowth covered the almost vertical sides of the cliffs. Thick roots from pandanus trees sprawled across the only paths leading upward, making forward progress a Herculean task. The large, entwined vines caught on the men's equipment as they trudged slowly upward. Soon packs and all excess gear were discarded to get some relief.

Fortunately, only scattered resistance met the forward elements as they moved up the narrow trails. Finally a platoon from the 1st Battalion, 4th Marines, led by Lieutenant William A. Kerr, reached the summit. But this position proved indefensible and the patrol returned to its organization and reported no enemy on top of Mt. Alifan.[107]

The Army's 305th Infantry had gone about the business of reorganizing after General Shepherd granted its request for a short delay before the start of the attack. The 2d Battalion completed relief of 2/4 by 1115. Shortly before, at 1030, the 1st and 3d Battalions set out for their first objective. Advancing abreast, they were to capture the high ground over which Harmon Road passed to the east. Eroded and brush-covered hills constituted the biggest obstacles of both battalions as they went forward. Supplies had to be manhandled to front line units, thus slowing the advance. By 1700, however, O–a was reached; the 1st tied-in on the left with the 3d Battalion which had made faster progress over the more favorable terrain in its zone.

By nightfall the brigade line extended from a point several hundred yards north of the Ayuja River along the high ground northeast of Harmon Road to the Alifan massif. Continuing southwest along the ridge line toward Mt. Taene, the defensive line turned to the sea and anchored on Magpo Point.

More support was available for harassing and interdiction fires for the night. Corps artillery now had two-thirds of its 155mm guns and howitzers ashore and ready to fire. This included elements of the 2d 155mm Howitzer Battalion which had been reassigned from V Corps Artillery at Saipan on 14 July.[108] Units of the 9th Defense Battalion had begun disembarking in the morning, and before dark had guns emplaced along the beach between Agat and Bangi Point. Twelve 40mm, twelve 20mm, and twelve .50-caliber machine guns strengthened the beach defenses and the immediate inland perimeter.[109]

The second night ashore for the brigade was quite different from the harrowing first. The enemy tried to infiltrate at various points along the lines, but with little success. No penetration occurred, and the Marines reported only a few casualties. The 22d Marines and units on the beach received harassing fire from mortars and artillery emplaced on Orote. But the expected large-scale counterattacks from Harmon Road and Orote did not materialize.

At daybreak men from the 2d Battalion, 4th Marines observed Japanese troops in the vicinity of Mt. Lamlam moving toward Facpi Point and alerted both air and naval gunfire. The USS *Honolulu* proceeded to a point where she could fire on the area at a moment's notice. Spotter planes were launched, and at about 0930 both air and naval gunfire began to work over the area. The enemy troops quickly dispersed, but observers kept the entire sector under surveillance for the remainder of the day.

Meanwhile, the brigade launched its attack to secure the O–2 line and the FBL. The 22d Marines advanced to the north, with the 305th conforming to that movement but pushing toward Maanot Pass. The 4th Marines made preparations for its relief by the 306th Infantry.

Colonel Tanzola's 305th jumped off on time, advanced rapidly, and reported the O–2 line completely occupied by 1020. In the afternoon the regiment continued advancing north

---

[107] Interview with Capt W. A. Kerr, 10Dec51.

[108] CTF 53 OpRpt, 12.
[109] 9th DefBn WD, July 1944, 3.

MEDIUM TANKS of the 22d Marines aid the infantry in cleaning out enemy machine-gun nests 1,200 yards north of Agat.

from Harmon Road and Maanot Pass. By nightfall units reported all the dominating terrain overlooking Orote Peninsula assigned to the Southern Landing Force in friendly hands.[110] The 1st and 3d Battalions remained on line and the 2d moved to Maanot Pass. This blocked the one good road across the island in the brigade zone and halted any further attempt by the Japanese to penetrate down that avenue of approach.

During the morning of 23 July, the 22d Marines found the enemy falling back and offering only scattered resistance. But in the afternoon when the front lines tried to swing across the neck of Orote Peninsula the situation changed. The assault units received intense enfilade fire from a series of small hills surrounded by rice paddies. Troops trying to get into position for an attack on a hill sank hip-deep in the mushy ground. The Japanese had each small hill organized as a strong point, all of them mutually supporting. Mortars and artillery from both Orote and the Mt. Tenjo area added their weight to the excellent defensive positions.

Marine tanks moved forward to help knock out the opposition, but the soft rice fields hindered their mobility. When the armor tried the road approaches enemy antitank weapons put one tank out of action for the day. Another hit a mine but sustained only minor damage.[111]

One infantry company, hidden by the waist-high grass, skirted the first rice paddy and re-formed its line for the assault. For their efforts the men of the company found another water-soaked, saucer-shaped field covered by deadly automatic-weapons fire. Corps artillery and naval gunfire were called to back up the brigade artillery's efforts to shake the 22d loose. The USS *Pennsylvania* alone fired 53 tons of 14-inch shells in approximately 30 minutes.[112] But with darkness approaching the forward elements had to be withdrawn from their exposed positions. When the word was passed to dig in for the night, the regiment found the terrain unsuitable for defense. All units then pulled back about 400 yards and set up on a line of hills just south of Old Agat Road.

[110] 1st ProvMarBrig Jnl.

[111] TkCo 22d Mar SAR, 4.
[112] 1st ProvMarBrig Jnl.

Earlier in the day bomb-disposal units got their first real workout on Guam. Bombs and mines found in various sectors designated as dump areas were impeding operations. Consequently, at about 1000 a call went out for all available bomb-disposal personnel to report to the shore party commander. Land mines, booby traps, and buried, fused torpedoes and aerial bombs were the most common types encountered. The Japanese had lined the beaches and roads thoroughly, as well as mining likely troop bivouac and supply areas.

The added casualties of the day further reduced the steadily diminishing ranks of the 22d,[113] and it was a thin line that waited for the expected enemy counterattack that night. About midnight a column of enemy troops could be seen coming down Mt. Tenjo but it turned back and went behind the ridge toward Harmon Road. Luckily, the rest of the night passed in comparative quietness except for a few infiltration attempts in front of the regiment. The Marines quickly repulsed all attacks with little loss. Again artillery and naval gunfire gave valuable assistance to the front line troops by not allowing the enemy to concentrate his forces.[114]

Artillery also fired many close support missions during the night. At one time so many scheduled concentrations and targets of opportunity were available that all batteries were engaged. A call from the 22d had to be refused because it would rob other units of needed artillery support. Naval gunfire, however, quickly shelled the targets when informed of the situation.

General Shepherd's plan for the brigade's attack on the 24th went out to units after midnight. To cope with the strong defensive set-up, a different scheme of maneuver had been devised. General Shepherd ordered the 22d Marines to send two battalions in column of companies up the Agat-Sumay Road with the mission of effecting a breakthrough by the employment of force in depth on a narrow front. (See Map 14, Map Section) Upon reaching the northern edge of the rice paddies, the battalions would echelon to the right, attack abreast, and seize the O–2 line from the coast to Apra Harbor. In conjunction with this assault, the other battalion (2/22) was to move from its position astride the Old Agat Road and occupy O–2 in zone. Initially using only a 400-yard front, the unit would capture the dominating high ground near Atantano and then extend to the right to contact the 305th. Shepherd's scheme of maneuver would not only outflank the Japanese strong points covering the rice paddies but would establish a barrier across the neck of Orote and secure the FBL in front of the brigade. Because of the late hour when units received the operation order, jump-off time was set at 0900.[115]

As part of the over-all plan for the assault on Orote, corps had ordered the 77th Division to take over most of the beachhead. At 0800 the boundary for the brigade became the Old Agat Road and the Army took over all the rest of the territory within the FBL. While men of the 22d Marines moved into position air, artillery, and naval gunfire fired a heavy preparation. At 0830 commanders ordered the attack delayed so that naval gunfire could be extended for a half-hour. At the end of that extension the commanding general felt there was still insufficient NGF, so another 30-minute barrage followed.

Finally, at 1000 the simultaneous assault started. The 2d Battalion, 22d Marines, received a counterattack immediately, which knocked it off balance and delayed the advance. Mortars and artillery backed up the enemy attack, causing further complications. To add to the already confused state of affairs, naval gunfire began falling in the front lines.[116] Nevertheless, the NGF plus Marine mortars and artillery did break up the enemy effort, and reorganization began so that the planned attack could get under way.

All companies had left the line of departure (Old Agat Road) by 1300 and the 2d had regained the offensive advantage. Only light opposition met the Marines, and by late afternoon Lieutenant Colonel Hart's men had reached

[113] As of 1600 23 July the 22d Marines reported 63 KIA, 262 WIA, and 93 MIA. *Ibid.*

[114] 1st ProvMarBrig WD, 1Jul–10Aug44, 7.

[115] 1st ProvMarBrig OpOrder 15, 23Jul44; 1st ProvMarBrig WD, 1Jul–10Aug44, 8; interview with Gen L. C. Shepherd, 10Sept52.

[116] 2/22 Jnl.

their objective. On order, they pushed forward to take the commanding ground overlooking the road junctions at Atantano. Although in an advance position, with the enemy putting pressure on its rear and right flank, the battalion held. It organized an all around defense and gained visual contact with the 305th Regiment on the right. Company F of the 4th Marines was sent up to Atantano to reinforce the perimeter for the night.

The main effort of the brigade's two-pronged attack advanced against determined resistance along the Agat-Sumay Road. Lieutenant Colonel Fromhold's 1st Battalion, 22d Marines led the way with the tank company in support. The road was heavily mined with aerial bombs and also covered by preregistered mortar and artillery concentrations. Progress was slow, but with the tanks blasting pillboxes and coconut-log barricades, the infantry inched ahead. Demolition teams closed caves, and artillery and naval gunfire quieted enemy guns on Pelagi Rock. Five enemy tanks challenged the advance, but the Marine Shermans made short work of the lighter Japanese armor and left them burning at the side of the road.[117]

On reaching the R–2 line the 1st fanned out to the right, and Lieutenant Colonel Shisler's 3d Battalion swung farther to the east across the hills, where it quickly overran the strong points around the rice paddies that had caused so much trouble the previous day. (See Map 14, Map Section)

About the middle of the afternoon enemy artillery fire from guns located in the cliffs on Orote increased in intensity. Naval gunfire officers sent a message to the command ship, and soon an LCI(G) and a destroyer opened up on the Japanese weapons. Their fire quickly quieted the troublesome guns. Nevertheless, to make certain the enemy positions remained neutralized, the gunboat and destroyer remained on station to observe.[118]

The 1st Battalion had reached the 0–2 line by darkness but the 3d held up 400 yards short of its objective. A gap existed between the 2d and 3d Battalions, so Major Messer's unit (2/4)

HAND GRENADES are hurled by Marines at Japanese positions on the other side of one of the many rice paddies that slowed the advance toward Orote Peninsula. (Navy Photograph.)

received orders to move into support positions to plug the hole. Although units did not complete the movement until after dark, lines were consolidated for the night. When Japanese reconnaissance patrols made unsuccessful attempts to locate the front lines, the enemy resorted to one of his oldest ruses by screaming, "Help," in English. But the Marines knew their wily enemy and the attempts proved futile against the excellent fire discipline.[119]

At the end of W-plus 3 (24 July) the Southern Landing Force had its beachhead firmly established. After four days of continuous fighting the brigade had the enemy bottled-up on Orote Peninsula. The Army's 77th Division had taken over most of the FBL and was well dug-in. Responsibility for the defense of

[117] 1st ProvMarBrig WD, 1Jul–10Aug44, 8.
[118] CTG 53.2 OpRpt, OpNarrative, 16–17.
[119] *6th MarDiv History*, 23.

MEN AND EQUIPMENT of the 306th Infantry snake through the water over the reef as they come ashore on 23 July. (Army Photograph.)

the beach from Agat Village to Gaan Point rested with the 9th Defense Battalion. The Army's 7th AAA (Automatic Weapons) Battalion guarded the coastline from Gaan to Bangi Point. All corps artillery was ashore and registered, but it had less than one unit of fire around its guns.[120] The supply situation, however, improved by the hour. All in all, conditions in the south could be viewed with optimism.

Still the losses had been considerable in winning the stubbornly defended beachhead. The brigade reported 188 KIA, 728 WIA, and 87 MIA by the evening of W-plus 3;[121] the Army listed 12 KIA and 20 WIA. Nor had the Navy gone unscathed. LCI(G) 365 and SC 1326 (a submarine chaser) had been hit on W-Day with total casualties of nine killed and 22 wounded. A dud shell hit the USS *Ormsby* (APA 49) on W-plus 1 but caused only minor damage. During the morning of 24 July LCI(G)'s 366 and 439 received gunfire that killed six, including the captain and executive officer of the 366. Twenty-eight sailors were wounded in the same engagement as ships cleaned out emplacements in the vicinity of Neye Island.[122]

---

[120] IIIAC Arty SAR, 5.

[121] Casualty figures for the 4th Mar as of 24 July differ in the brigade and regimental reports; the more plausible figure of the lower unit has been included above.

[122] CTG 53.2 OpRpt, OpNarrative, 16.

FLOATING RESERVE WADES ASHORE

In order to carry out the planned relief of the 1st Provisional Marine Brigade by the 77th Infantry Division, General Geiger decided, on 22 July, to commit part of the corps reserve. Accordingly, he sent a message at 1226 ordering the remainder of the 77th Division, less the 307th Infantry, to land on Beaches White 1 and 2.[123]

To accomplish this mission, General Bruce alerted the 306th Infantry for a landing about noon on the 23d. The 305th would revert to division control after the brigade's relief had been affected. The 307th (Colonel Stephen S. Hamilton), less its assigned artillery, would remain afloat as crops reserve.[124]

During the morning Colonel Douglas C. McNair, division chief of staff, headed a group that went ashore to make arrangements for taking over the southern sector of the beachhead. The party included the 306th's commanding officer, Colonel Aubrey D. Smith, and his battalion commanders. They reconnoitered their areas, contacted brigade units to be relieved (4th Marines), and made preparations for the physical relief.

With the division G–4 coordinating the movement from the SC 1319, just off of the reef, the 306th started to land shortly before noon

---

[123] 77th InfDiv G–3 Jul.

[124] IIIAC OpOrder 5–44, 22Jul44.

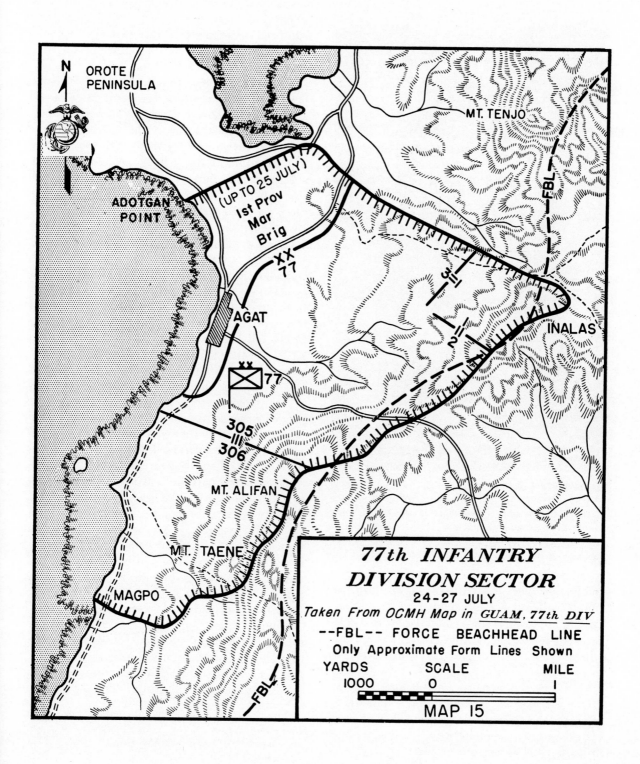

N

OROTE
PENINSULA

MT. TENJO

FBL

(UP TO 25 JULY)
1st Prov
Mar
Brig

ADOTGAN
POINT

XX
77

3

2

AGAT

INALAS

XX
77

305
III
306

MT. ALIFAN

MT. TAENE

MAGPO

FBL

**77th INFANTRY
DIVISION SECTOR**
24-27 JULY
Taken From OCMH Map in *GUAM, 77th DIV*
--FBL-- FORCE BEACHHEAD LINE
Only Approximate Form Lines Shown

YARDS   SCALE   MILE
1000   0   1

MAP 15

MAJOR GENERAL BRUCE (right) confers with his chief of staff, Colonel McNair, on White Beach 2 as men of the 77th Division come ashore in the background. (Army Photograph.)

of the 23d. Getting the unit across what some naval officers have called "the toughest reef in the Pacific War" proved to be a difficult operation. As a reserve division, the 77th had no LVT's. The 60 DUKW's available had to be reserved for cargo and for getting the light artillery ashore. Consequently, plans had to be made to carry troops to the reef in landing craft; from there they waded ashore carrying all their equipment. General Bruce made every effort to land the regiment at low tide, but overloaded ship communications, craft turn arounds, and unforeseen problems delayed the debarkation schedule. As a result, men struggled through waist-high water and most

vehicles drowned out between the reef and beach. Bulldozers dragged the equipment ashore but radio sets in jeeps, even those that had been waterproofed, were ruined. One medium tank dropped into a large pothole and disappeared from sight.[125]

The 3d Battalion, first to land, moved into position between Mt. Alifan and Mt. Taene. Company K, shortly after taking over its sector, was hit by the enemy debouching from a coconut grove just forward of the front lines. The battalion artillery liaison officer contacted a Marine pack howitzer unit and quickly adjusted fire on the advancing enemy. The soldiers repulsed the counterattack immediately. Because of the delay in crossing the reef, the other battalions of the regiment went into assembly areas for the night.[126]

About the same time that the 306th landed, the 77th's Commanding General sent a dispatch to corps asking that not less than two battalions of the 307th be landed by 0530 the next morning. Bruce felt he needed them to permit an anticipated advance to the south and east to occupy the original FBL at Facpi Point. But General Geiger denied the request because it was his opinion that further expansion of the beachhead to the south was neither desirable nor necessary at this time. Also, returning these units to the 77th Division would require committing all of the force reserve, with the exception of one battalion, at a time when additional strength might be needed elsewhere.[127]

Early in the afternoon the 77th Division's advance CP opened for operation ashore,[128] and General Bruce, who had come in for a reconnaissance, issued his operation order for the next day. Plans were made to land Division Special Troops and the 306th Field Artillery Battalion on the 24th. During the night, equipment and supplies continued coming ashore, and by dawn a good percentage of the organic gear had been unloaded.

The relief of the 4th Marines continued during the morning of 24 July. The 306th took

[125] *Guam: Operations of the 77th Division*, American Forces In Action Series, (Washington, 1946), 39, hereinafter cited as *Guam; 77th Div.*

[126] 306th Inf OpRpt, 2.

[127] IIIAC SAR, OpRpt, 3.

[128] 77th InfDiv G–3 Jnl.

over command of the sector at 0800, but not until 1400 were all elements of the regiment in position.[129] Their part of the beachhead now stretched from Mt. Alifan to Magpo Point. On the left, Colonel Tanzola's regiment held a line that joined with the 22d Marines boundary at Old Agat Road. (See Map 15)

Leading waves of the 307th, ordered ashore as corps reserve to positions near the 77th Division's CP, began landing at 1300. A storm at sea raised heavy ground swells which endangered the ship-to-shore movement. One company lost two men when they fell from the nets of the rolling transport.[130] Many became seasick during the several hours that LCVP's circled before being cleared by control boats. As units waded ashore, they moved immediately to an assembly area in the rear of the 305th, from which they could advance either to the north or east. General Geiger made one battalion available to the Commanding General, 77th Division, but General Bruce did not use it.[131]

By 1400 Bruce had moved ashore and established his CP. All units of the brigade had been relieved, and the 305th had reverted to division control; the 307th still remained in force reserve. The brigade's sector was now reduced to just enough area to permit regrouping for the attack on Orote.

[129] 306th Inf OpRpt, 2.
[130] 77th InfDiv History, 69.
[131] IIIAC C-3 Jnl.

CHAPTER IV

Drive to the FBL

The first four days on Guam saw the fighting for the recapture of the island taking on the form of two separate and more or less independent campaigns. Only one attempt had been made to form the two beachheads into a single foothold—that unsuccessful effort by a patrol. Although the situation was not such as to cause alarm, neither did it lend itself to full-blown optimism.

The night of 24 July IIIAC made plans to keep pressure on the Japanese on both fronts. The operation plan for 25 July ordered the 77th Division, less the 307th Infantry in corps reserve, to hold the FBL while the brigade assaulted Orote Peninsula. The 3d Division would resume the attack and take the high ground overlooking Mt. Tenjo Road. Air, corps artillery, and two 90mm batteries of the 14th Defense Battalion would support the effort, with priority of fires to the brigade. To add weight to the peninsular advance, artillery of both the 77th and 3d Divisions would be prepared to fire for the brigade.[1]

General Shepherd had received a warning order for the Orote advance in the afternoon of 24 July. Having visited the assault units of his brigade that morning, he felt his men could do a better job after a day's rest. Accordingly Shepherd sent the following message to General Geiger:

. . . Due to delay in relief of 4th Marines which was

not completed until 1500 today, necessity for moving 4th Marines to assembly areas and relief of 22d Marines in line, reorganization and preparation for attack, strongly recommend assault Orote Peninsula be delayed until 26 July. Troops greatly fatigued by 4 days and nights continuous fighting . . .[2]

Early in the evening, the brigade's commander received word authorizing the delay until 0700, 26 July. Corps directed the 3d Division, however, to press the attack all along the line with the utmost vigor to gain the FBL.[3]

With 1/3 so badly battered that it was ineffective, General Turnage ordered 2/9 (Lieutenant Colonel Robert E. Cushman) attached to the 3d Marines. His plan called for Colonel Cushman's unit to relieve the 1st Battalion, which would then go into division reserve. To allow the relief to be effected, Colonel Hall delayed the regiment's attack until 0930.[4]

While the revitalized 3d Marines made ready to advance, the remainder of the division resumed its drive toward the FBL. The 9th Marines, on the division's right flank, left the LD at 0700 and received artillery fire from the Mt. Chachao area which slowed the assault at first. But counterbattery fire from the 14th Defense Battalion on Cabras Island soon quieted the enemy guns. Units then moved out as rapidly as terrain would permit, and by 0845

[1] IIIAC OpPlan 6–44, 24Jul44.

[2] 1st ProvMarBrig Jnl.
[3] IIIAC C–3 Jnl.
[4] 1/3 Jnl.

the first objective had been taken and many dumps of stores and equipment overrun. Since the advance had been so rapid and the resistance so weak, the 9th was ordered to continue and take the high ground north of Aguada River. This was accomplished by midafternoon, and Craig made plans to continue the advance in an effort to link up with the brigade by nightfall. But at 1400 division headquarters directed the 9th to fall back 1,500 yards to the vicinity of the dominating terrain near the Laguas River in order to shorten the division's front lines. In view of the fact that the regiment had just uncovered a large dump of Japanese beer and soft drinks the men fell back with reluctance. While the units took up their new positions Colonel Craig sent a platoon toward the brigade lines with instructions to make contact and gain information of the enemy activities along the route. The patrol returned about 1800 after completing its mission.[5]

In the center, the 21st Marines started toward the D–2 line with battalions abreast. The 2d Battalion, charged with maintaining contact with the 3d Marines on the left, by-passed resistance in a ravine and went on to the D–2 line. Company E remained behind to mop up and completed its job before noon. Later, over 250 enemy dead were buried in this ravine, many of whom had been killed by the air strikes and the artillery and mortar preparations placed there on the 24th.

The 3d Battalion, on the right of the regimental zone, moved to the O–2 line without meeting any resistance. But the 1st did not have the same good fortune. As it began to advance, the left flank necessarily became exposed because 2/21 and the 3d Marines started their attack well in the rear of D–1. After gaining only 300 yards, point-blank artillery fire enfiladed the left company and stopped forward progress. Lieutenant Colonel Williams requested air support but it could not be obtained as all available aircraft were engaged in missions having a higher priority. Artillery could not take the enemy guns under fire because of a mask created by the cliffs.

The hill could not be by-passed, since the enemy had been launching many night counterattacks from this area. In addition, the Japanese had heavily fortified the reverse slope with machine guns, mortars, and well-emplaced artillery. So, with all supporting weapons giving covering fire, the battalion, with a platoon of tanks attached, launched a limited objective attack. After the assaulting infantry suffered crippling losses, the tanks moved in to hit the position and inflicted considerable damage to enemy installations. Even so, the position proved untenable, and the troops withdrew to high ground just short of the Mt. Tenjo Road where they dug in for the night.[6]

Lieutenant Colonel Duplantis' 3d Battalion with Company I on the left and K on the right, tied in with 1/21. An 800-yard gap, however, existed between 3/21 and the 9th Marines. Duplantis requested that Company L, in regimental reserve, be released to him to protect the exposed flank and give him a maneuvering element in case the Japanese attempted to retake the hill to his rear which dominated the Nidual and Asan River valleys. Colonel Butler agreed and Company L took position on the left bank of the upper reaches of the Asan River overlooking a deep chasm filled with heavy jungle growth. This move gave depth to the battalion's defenses and blocked the defile against enemy infiltration. A detachment from the division reconnaissance company received the mission of patrolling the gap between the two regiments.[7]

On the extreme left of the division line, the 3d Marines had its job cut out. Four days of incessant fighting had gained little terrain for maneuver. The only solution was to continue ferreting the enemy from the caves and holes that infested the Fonte approaches. By 0830 2/9, spearheading the 3d Marines' attack, was in position to pass through 1/3.

Admiral Conolly and General Geiger had come ashore to check on the progress of the division's advance and were in the CP[8] when the final rounds of the ten-minute mortar and

[5] 9th Mar SAR, 2; *Craig 1952.*

[6] 21st Mar SAR, 3–4.
[7] *Duplantis 1952.*
[8] 3d MarDiv D–3 Jnl.

artillery preparation fell. Promptly at 0930 assault companies left the line of departure and executed a spirited passage of lines, giving the unit the initiative it needed. An hour later, after overcoming moderate resistance and encountering heavy mortar fire, 2/9 captured the first objective (Mt. Tenjo Road), giving the Marines control of a much needed route over which tanks could now be brought forward to help in the advance toward Fonte Plateau.

While 2/9 reorganized to renew the attack, one platoon of Company G started to clean up by-passed enemy, but the operation was only partially successful. Small groups of Japanese continued to emerge from caves for three days, harassing battalion and company CP's.

During the morning the remainder of the 3d Marines slugged its way ahead. The effective use of mortars, artillery, tanks, and the basic infantry fire team reduced pockets of resistance. By nightfall units reached the high ground overlooking the lower part of the Mt. Tenjo Road.

In anticipation of the attempt to take the Fonte hill mass, Lieutenant Colonel Cushman requested tank support for his battalion. But the tanks did not arrive early enough to help. About the time that other units of the 3d Marines stopped for the day, 2/9 called for its pre-attack preparation. There is little doubt that the barrage of mortars, artillery, and naval gunfire caused the enemy consternation. However, the same shelling disrupted Company F when short rounds, reportedly from Marine artillery, fell in its area, causing 14 casualties.[9]

The drive toward the Fonte Plateau got under way at 1530. The battalion encountered opposition of the most stubborn and violent kind. Nevertheless, an hour later Marines held a hotly contested foothold on the slopes leading to the objective. Heavy and determined enemy resistance necessitated pulling back the right flank about 200 yards. Cushman narrowed a gap that had opened on the left flank by committing his reserve. By nightfall the unit formed a salient forward of the 3d Marine's lines, but the left flank was still 400 yards short of the plateau and the right 250 yards short.

The four tanks requested earlier arrived just before dark, and the battalion commander parked them near the road in rear of the line, since darkness prohibited employing them elsewhere with any degree of safety. About 1900, Company G, on the left flank, had to be pulled back approximately 150 yards to give better fields of fire. This left Company F, in the center of the salient, holding tenaciously to a rocky mound well forward of the flank units.[10]

The day's advance had stretched the division's lines even farther than before, making over 9,000 yards that had to be controlled. Regiments and battalions had practically no infantry reserves available, and one depleted unit (1/3) constituted the division reserve.[11] On the brighter side, the shore party reported all AKA's and APA's unloaded.[12] But certain types of ammunition were on the scarce side, with the supply of 60mm illuminating shells especially critical since resupply was nonexistent.

Front line units, from their positions on the high ground just captured, could finally observe the country before them. Since W-Day Marines had struggled to take the dominating terrain in this sector, and now they were established on its crest. It was something like coming up out of a hole in the ground. Looking across a stretch of open country, the men could see a mile-long ridge that stretched down toward the rugged cliffs of Mt. Macajna. A trail joining an old Spanish road which elbowed around the south edge of Fonte Ravine and ended in the Agana-Pago Bay Road led down the ridge. Directly in front of the battalions ran the road to Mt. Tenjo, curving past the fallen radio towers and the ruins of the enemy's Fonte defense installations. More than a mile to the right were long grassy ridges. Above them rose the firm peak of Mt. Alutom, the thin outline of Mt. Chachao, and the summit of Mt.

---

[9] 2/9 SAR, 3. Many times when preparations were being fired, the Japanese would time their own artillery so that it would fall in Marine front lines. Commanders, thinking it short rounds, would stop the preparation to check for errors and thus give the enemy time to disperse.

[10] Ibid., 2–3.
[11] 3d MarDiv WD, July 1944, 9.
[12] 3d MarDiv D–4 Jnl.

Tenjo, once planned as the Marines stronghold against invasion, now the boundary between divisions.[13]

With the attack on Orote postponed for one day, General Shepherd had set about getting his brigade into the best possible positions. Front line units took advantage of the time to reorganize, re-equip, and repair worn gear. This did not mean, however, that action was lacking during that day. On the contrary, 1/22 suffered such heavy casualties that 1/4 replaced it at noon. In regard to the condition of the battalion at that time its executive officer wrote:

> . . . I would like to emphasize the point of our heavy casualties by pointing out that by 1300 Companies B and C, which landed with 6 officers each, had no officers left and both companies were below 50% strength in enlisted as a result of casualties. Company A although in better shape also had heavy casualties. We had lost both medical officers, over 50% of the corpsmen and numerous other headquarters personnel.[14]

Following a 15-minute air and artillery preparation the attack to get into position for the Orote assault had gotten under way at 0830, 25 July. The 1st and 3d Battalions of the 22d Marines ran into stiff opposition from the start. The Japanese poured destructive artillery fire on the 1st as it tried to move along the coast road. From positions in the vicinity of Neye Island and others near the airfield on the peninsula, enemy artillerymen effectively protected the strong points around the Dadi Beach area.

The 3d Battalion, driving across the lowlands toward Apra Harbor, ran into a well-entrenched enemy also. Cleverly camouflaged emplacements and numerous machine-gun nests supported concrete pillboxes. Marines had to advance in the face of the withering fire with little cover or concealment, but progress was made.

In addition, both of the assault battalions repulsed tank-led counterattacks during the day. While bazooka teams delayed the enemy armor, Marine Shermans rushed forward. Before the day was over, eight Japanese tanks had been destroyed and four others set afire.[15] Front line units of 3/22 halted for the night just short of the extensive mangrove swamp bordering Apra Harbor while 1/4, after completing the relief of 1/22, dug in on the left, extending the brigade front to Dadi Beach.

While the other two battalions of the regiment slugged it out with the Japanese, 2/22 did extensive patrolling. Combat patrols cleaned out areas in the rear of the assault units and searched the vicinity of Atantano. Other units went out to contact both the Army and the 9th Marines. At noon the first mission had been accomplished when a detachment from the 77th Division came into the battalion's command post. But the other was not completed until late in the afternoon when an outpost contacted a 9th Marine patrol at the bridge across the Big Guatali River. About the same time, with orders to reinforce 3/22, Company E moved forward to go into position on the right flank of the Orote line.[16]

By late afternoon the brigade had secured the area between Agat Bay and Apra Harbor. The main body of Japanese in the south was now confined to the eight square miles of Orote Peninsula. Commander Asaichi Tamai, IJN, 263d Air Group commander, had two alternatives: attempt to move some of his troops out by barges, or break through the Marines' lines to join the Fonte defenders.[17] Within the next 12 hours he tried both.

The enemy commander could count on a force of 2,500 troops, composed of the main strength of the naval garrison force (54th Keibitai), remnants of the 38th Infantry (mostly men of the 2d Battalion commanded by Major Kiyoji Okujo), two companies of antiaircraft troops, and about 600 men from aviation squadrons. In addition, some naval laborers had been pressed into military service.[18]

[13] Capt P. D. Carleton, "The Guam Operation," Campaign for the Marianas, (Washington, 1946), II–23.

[14] Ltr LtCol C. B. Lawton to author, 19Dec51.

[15] 1st ProvMarBrig Jnl.

[16] 2/22 Jnl.

[17] Col Tsunefaro Suenaga, Commander of the 38th Inf, was the original commander of the Agat Defense Sector which included Orote Peninsula. Cdr Tamai succeeded to command of the Orote defenses after Col Suenaga was killed on the night of 21–22Jul44. Takeda Letter.

[18] IIIAC SAR, IntelRpt, Final Enemy O/B; IIIAC C–2 Periodic Rpt 7; Takeda Letter.

In the afternoon of 25 July, Commander Tamai decided to try his first plan by evacuating parts of the garrison force from Orote. At approximately 1700, enemy barges could be seen moving out into Apra Harbor from the vicinity of Sumay. Some individual Japanese even tried to swim across to the mainland. Neither of the attempts proved successful. A handful of enemy may have penetrated the hail of fire that air and artillery dropped on the harbor area, but the major formation was quickly scattered and destroyed.[19] Now with the rear exit banged shut, the enemy commander prepared his remaining forces for frontal assault against Marine lines.

JAPANESE BID FOR VICTORY

After dusk, the intermittent showers that had been falling all day became more frequent. A heavy downpour hampered organization of the brigade's defense for the night. On the other hand, the pitch blackness and the unpleasant weather aided the Japanese in making preparations for their supreme effort.

Marines in the front lines could hear screaming, yelling, laughter, and the breaking of bottles as the Japanese made final arrangements. At times so much clamor could be heard that reports reached the command post that the assault had started. Afterwards someone aptly said that the confusion "sounded like New Year's Eve in the Zoo."

While the enemy made ready and drank, Marine artillerymen laid down normal barrages along the swamp's edge and at all other points of possible penetration. Shortly before midnight the Japanese commanders felt that their men had reached the proper emotional state, and the assault began. *Sake*-crazed attackers swarmed from the cover of the mangroves in front of the 3d Battalion, 22d Marines. Led by flag-waving, sword-swinging officers, the enlisted men stumbled forward, carrying everything conceivable. Unsteady hands clutched pitchforks, sticks, ballbats, and pieces of broken bottles, together with the normal infantry weapons.

When the surging Japanese mass came within range, Marine forward observers and company commanders gave the order to commence firing. Brigade, 77th Division, and corps artillery, 37mm guns, 81mm and 60mm mortars, machine guns, rifles, and grenades saturated the entire area. At one time officers brought the fire of the Pack Howitzer Battalion, 22d Marines, to within 35 yards of 3/22's front lines in an attempt to stop the swarming horde.[20] One weapons company lieutenant reported: "Arms and legs flew like snowflakes. Japs ran amuck. They screamed in terror until they died."[21] But in a powerful attack it is inevitable that some men will seep through the blocking fire. Company L, 3/22, received the brunt of the subsiding attack and repulsed it before too much damage could be done. Those Japanese who survived fled to the momentary safety of the swamp. But observers shifted the artillery fire and between midnight and 0200 some 26,000 shells took a heavy toll of the remaining peninsular defenders.[22]

On the right flank of the 22d Marines a second counterattack hit. *The Island War* describes the action quite vividly:

> . . . At its height, flares revealed an out-of-this-world picture of Nipponese drunks reeling about in our forward positions, falling into foxholes, tossing aimless grenades here and there, yelling such English phrases as they had managed to pick up, and laughing crazily, to be exterminated in savage close-in fighting. Succeeding waves were caught in a deadly cross-fire. Not until dawn did this attack finally dwindle out, at which time more than four hundred bodies were counted in front of the position.[23]

In contrast to the frenzied close quarter action in the 3/22 zone, the platoon from Company A (1/4) that filled the gap between the two regiments participated in a shooting gallery affair with the Japanese. Enemy troops made no attempt at a concerted attack, and the platoon plus artillery, without the loss of a

[19] 1st ProvMarBrig WD, 1Jul–10Aug44, 9; 14th DefBn WD, July 1944, 5.

[20] Interview with Col E. C. Ferguson, 28Nov52, hereinafter cited as *Ferguson interview*.
[21] *The Island War*, 279.
[22] To repulse the counterattack, fires of III Corps Arty and 77th Div artillery battalions assigned to the brigade were added to those of the pack howitzer units. 1st ProvMarBrig Jnl.
[23] *The Island War*, 281.

single Marine, killed 256 Imperial soldiers. This fantastic figure was verified by officers from regiment the following morning.[24]

Some of the companies exhausted their supplies of ammunition and had to be replenished during the night. With the torrential rains making the roads a quagmire, transportation could not operate. Everything had to be manhandled through the clutching muck: casualties moving to the rear and supplies to the front. Many of the wounded could not be evacuated until morning in spite of the tremendous efforts of corpsmen and stretcher bearers.

Daylight revealed a strange and gruesome scene. Within the lines many foxholes containing Marines and Japanese still locked in a death struggle gave evidence of the violence of the night. Broken sticks, ballbats, and weapons lay in bits, smashed by the force of hand-to-hand combat. Weary Marines could be seen trudging down the slope helping wounded men to aid stations. It had been a severe struggle, but the lines were still intact, and the Japanese break-through attempt had been stopped. Now Commander Tamai had no choice; his "Sunday punch" had failed, and he could do nothing but defend until annihilated.

While the brigade repelled its counterattack, the 3d Marine Division was engaged in an equally serious effort. As a part of the over-all plan of the enemy commander to "solve the issue of the battle at a single stroke by an all out counterattack," [25] the Japanese launched a well-organized assault against the Asan beachhead.[26]

When General Takashina found his beach defenses smashed, he planned to regroup his forces in the Fonte-Chachao-Tenjo area. Here he expected to beat back the Marine attack by

[24] 1/4 WD, 30May–9Sept44, 4; interview with Capt W. A. Kerr, 22Jan52.

[25] *Japanese Defense of Guam.*

[26] To obtain an accurate picture of the Japanese counterattack on the 3d MarDiv front a variety of sources have been consulted. The consolidated account presented was obtained from journals, diaries, histories, and operation reports of the units involved, both American and Japanese. Letters from key officer participants were especially helpful. Citations have been kept to a necessary minimum in this section to avoid needless confusion.

MANGROVE SWAMP on Orote Peninsula, breeding point of the *banzai* attack against the 22d Marines on the night of 25–26 July.

a defense in position. But by 23 July he felt that holding tactics were not accomplishing his mission. Therefore, he formulated plans to make a countermove calculated to drive the invaders into the sea.[27]

In contrast to the disjointed, unorganized, *banzai* charges that Marines had encountered throughout the Pacific fighting, Takashina planned a coordinated counterattack by the defenders. He dispatched orders and overlays with complete instructions to all units, and moved his reserves into position. Troops which had been located in the Tumon, Agana, and Pago areas were assembled to participate in the Fonte counteroffensive. Finally commanders reported everything in readiness.

The scheme of maneuver called for the 18th Regiment (less the 1st Battalion), commanded by Colonel Hiko-Shiro Ohashi,[28] to attack on a two battalion front. (See Map 16, Map Section) On the right, 2/18 would push down the east draw of the Asan River and set up a defensive position on the high ground above Asan Point. The 3d Battalion, after moving down the Nidual River valley, would take the commanding ground southwest of Asan Point. An unidentified unit, probably a company of the 10th Independent Mixed Regiment, was to protect the left flank of the assault regiment.

On the right of the 18th Regiment, Takashina assigned the 48th Independent Mixed Brigade

[27] *Takeda.*

[28] Col Ohashi and both of his battalion commanders were killed during the counterattack. *Takeda Letter.*

the task of destroying the 3d Marines. From the Fonte Plateau, the unit would drive toward Red Beach 2, then swing northeast to hit ammunition and supply dumps at the base of Chonito Cliff.[29] In conjunction with this part of the attack, special small units had been equipped with demolition charges to destroy artillery pieces, vehicles, and installations. The entire operation would be supported by mortar and artillery fire.

American high-level intelligence had not reported the imminence of a large scale counteroffensive but some lower unit commanders had sensed it and indicated to their headquarters unusual enemy activity on 24 July. At daybreak a patrol from 3/21 observed a group of about 12 senior Japanese officers on a hill overlooking the Marines' beachhead. Throughout the day probing attacks had stepped up in frequency and intensity. To some officers, these signs pointed toward a major counterattack.[30] Nevertheless, so effectively did the enemy conceal his exact plans that to this day it is hard to say at just what hour the operation started on the night of 25–26 July. Perhaps the first real indication was a 12th Marines forward observer's report sent in at 2330 that the Japanese had very active patrols in the gap between the 9th and 21st Marines.

During the next hour reports started to filter in from units all along the line telling of sharp probing attacks. Still there was nothing to cause undue alarm; these were not new tactics for the unpredictable Japanese. But this time the enemy intended to do more than just find infiltration routes through the lines. He planned to exploit these weak spots.

The strongest of the feeler attemps hit the reconnaissance unit patrolling between the 9th and 21st Marines. About 50 enemy soldiers forced the Marines to abandon this mission, thus leaving the 800-yard gap between the two regiments unguarded.[31] About the same time the men of 2/21 withstood a bayonet charge in the

center of the regiment's zone. All 15 of the attacking soldiers were killed.

Although all of these short, sharp thrusts hit different points along the entire front, they were part of the over-all plan to keep the Marines off balance. Enemy flares, many of which fell within Japanese lines causing considerable speculation among amazed Americans, lit up the sky over the perimeter. It was later determined that the flares lighted certain areas to guide the scattered Nipponese to their assembly points. Heavy mortar and artillery concentrations served to cover these movements and to harass the howitzer crews of the 12th Marines.

Artillery fired from gunpits that were knee-deep in water in an attempt to silence enemy guns firing from the vicinity of Agana. Front line infantrymen peered through the wet underbrush trying to see what moved in front of them. The cold and dampness became more aggravating and Marines crouched lower in their foxholes. Mortar and artillery shells burst more frequently on the ridge line. Suddenly at about 0400, a volley of hand grenades landed on and behind the lines of the 1st Battalion, 21st Marines. Then the mass attack began.

Major Maruyama's men (2/18) advanced noisily, shouting, "Wake up American and die." The initial impetus of the assault passed completely over Company B in the center, previously reduced to about 50 men, and streamed through the gap down a draw toward the cliff. Despite the breakthrough, companies held the shoulders of the penetration and Lieutenant Colonel Williams ordered the units to refuse their flanks to the cliff. Company A on the left, commanded by Captain William G. Shoemaker,[32] rallied in the face of the withering fire and overwhelming numbers. Shoemaker pulled back his right platoon to deny his flank to the enemy and to permit regrouping for a local counterattack.[33] Company C (Captain Henry M. Helgren, Jr.) also successfully re-

[29] The detailed plan of the Japanese attack was taken from a map found on the body of Maj Chusa Maruyama, Commanding Officer, 2d Bn, 18th Inf.

[30] *Duplantis, 1952.*

[31] Ltr LtCol E. A. Clark to author, 16Jan52, hereinafter cited as *Clark.*

[32] Capt Shoemaker was killed on 3Aug44 during the exploitation phase on Guam.

[33] Ltr Lt Col R. R. Van Stockum to Historical Branch, 15Oct52.

fused its flank to protect the position and immediately began firing into the onrushing Japanese.

Tanks parked in the rear of the Marine positions took a great toll as the intruders surged through the widening gap. One report described the rush on the tanks as resembling a horde of ants. It went on to say of the Nipponese:

Savagely they swarmed upon the mechanized vehicles, oblivious of the vicious machine-gun fire, and frantically pounded, kicked, and beat against the turrets in an attempt to get the crew within. When this seemed futile they leaped to the ground and continued their wild rush down the draw to the rear areas. . . .[34]

Demolition charges were forgotten in the mad scramble to reach deeper into Marine-held territory.

Machine gunners of 1/21 had a field day. Never had they seen such lucrative targets, but grenades and bayonets soon silenced the Marines as enemy soldiers overran the gun positions. Many of the Japanese were killed as they moved through the lines and into the ravine. However, enough of them got down the cliff to attack the 1st Battalion CP and the mortar platoons of the 2d and 1st Battalions, killing most of the mortarmen in the latter.

About the same time, the 3d Battalion, 18th Regiment (Major Setsuo Yukioka), launched its part of the coordinated drive. The assault hit 3/21 and momentarily gained the advantage by capturing two machine-gun positions. The Marine lines recovered quickly, however, and a local counterattack retook the guns. The enemy attack failed to crack the line again, but the Imperial soldiers were not to be denied. They slid along the front until they hit the vulnerable spot on the right flank of the battalion. It will be remembered that an 800-yard gap existed here between the 21st and 9th Marines.

Led by lantern carrying scouts,[35] Yukioka's men started through the unguarded part of the line in a column. But a roadblock Lieutenant Colonel Duplantis had posted astride a trail skirting the right flank of the battalion opened up with BAR's, bazookas, rifles, and hand grenades. Duplantis committed his reserve to protect the rear of Company K, but the enemy strength was too great; the roadblock and the reserve unit fought a losing battle against overwhelming odds. Yukioka took full advantage of the gap and exploited his success. He set up a line on the high ground behind 3/21. From these positions his men could harass the front lines and at the same time besiege the CP. The effectiveness of the stranglehold can best be judged by the fact that Duplantis sent word to the division commander that he was burying his cipher device in case the enemy captured his CP.[36]

Over in the 3d Marines sector, fighting was even more confused. The 2d Battalion, 9th Marines, in its exposed position, received the brunt of the Japanese 48th Brigade's attack. Just when the main push came is hard to tell. Pressure against Lieutenant Colonel Cushman's units had not let up since they moved onto the slopes leading to the Fonte Plateau in late afternoon. Evacuation of the wounded had been almost impossible and the situation at dusk was none too secure. After an intense day of fighting, ammunition was practically exhausted, and the dribble of supplies carried up the cliff trail could hardly be expected to replace even a third of that already expended. A platoon of tanks loaded with ammunition was dispatched to the battalion, but darkness settled with no word from this convoy.

Enemy pressure increased as the night wore on, and fighting in the 2/9 area became more bitter. Cushman moved his reserve company up to reinforce the position held by the advance assault unit; the right company, driven back in the afternoon, had been reorganized and now guarded the gap between the regiment's right flank and the 21st Marines. Riflemen had only two clips of ammunition per rifle, and mortarmen reported approximately six rounds per tube available. But still nothing was heard from the supply vehicles. Finally, just as the Japanese launched another strong counterat-

---

[34] 1stLt K. Cohlmia, preliminary draft of 3d MarDiv History, 16.

[35] Small metal lanterns with narrow slits in the rearward side were used by the Japanese scouts to maintain direction. The morning after the attack Marines found several lanterns scattered along the enemy's route of attack. *Duplantis, 1952.*

[36] *3d MarDiv History,* 154.

tack, the ammunition-laden tanks came into the position. The vicious fighting in the sector definitely subsided by 0900, but the attack had cost 2/9 over 50 percent casualties. It had, however, resulted in 950 Japanese dead.[37] Seven determined counterattacks had been made by the enemy, but the equally determined men of the 2d Battalion, 9th Marines had lost no ground.

Shortly after the main Japanese attack started, it became evident that all available personnel would have to be used to stabilize the bending lines. The division had been hard hit while securing the beachhead, and organized reserve units were not available. Any addi-

tional manpower would have to come from other than infantry units. Division headquarters alerted the 19th Marines at 0420 and ordered them to assemble, ready for any emergency. The 2d Separate Engineer Battalion [38] was assigned later to back up the 3d Marines. Within the next hour calls went out to Division Headquarters, 3d Service, and 3d Motor Transport Battalions, and the 797 men who could be spared were organized into makeshift units. Badly depleted 1/3 also received the word to stand by for possible action.

---

[37] Ltr LtCol W. T. Glass to author, 25Jan52, hereinafter cited as *Glass*.

[38] The 2d SepEngBn was part of the division engineer landing group whose other components were the 19th Mar (less 1st and 2d Bns), Co B, 2d NavConstBn, and the Garrison Beach Party. 3d MarDiv OpPlan 2–44, 13May44.

STRETCHERS for wounded Marines lie scattered among the bodies of Japanese dead in the wake of the attack on the 3d Division hospital which was repulsed by corpsmen, doctors, and walking wounded.

Artillery units set up their own perimeter defenses to try to avoid the capture or destruction of pieces, as had happened at Saipan.[39] Advance intelligence had warned of the special Japanese demolition teams trained for such missions, and the 12th Marines intended to be ready. Short handed crews stepped up their rate of fire to meet infantry requirements. A steady stream of shells whined overhead as they barely cleared the ridge line. Forward observers "crept" their fire toward the front lines, allowing only the minimum margin of safety.[40] Shells landed so close to friendly troops that the executive officer of the 4th Battalion, 12th Marines later wrote:

Shortly after the attack began, I was awakened by an unusual rate of artillery firing. In the early dawn light it could be seen that the shells were hitting the tops of the ridges in the vicinity of the 21st Marines front lines. Bodies could be seen flying in the air as the shells exploded. . . . not knowing of the counterattack, I rushed to the operations tent believing that the artillery was falling short on our own troops.[41]

While the precautionary measures were being carried out in the beach areas, the 1st Battalion, 21st Marines was trying to repel the attack on its CP. Regiment rushed its attached engineer company (Company B, 19th Marines) and three platoons of the Weapons Company up to Lieutenant Colonel Williams' headquarters. With this added strength, the battalion counterattacked and restored its lines. Cooks, clerks, bakers, and communicators, who had been organized into a platoon commanded by 2d Lieutenant Joseph Y. Curtis (S–1), cleared the enemy from around the CP. Then the group assisted the mortar platoons in mopping up the

rear area. Even though communications had been lost, the direct support artillery battalion (2/12) delivered close-in-fires throughout the night to assist in stopping the Japanese assault.[42]

When Colonel Butler found his front line units weakening from the heavy pressure and many casualties suffered, he hurriedly ordered the establishment of a regimental reserve line. Lieutenant Colonel Ernest W. Fry, Jr., regimental executive officer, set up the defense on the high ground immediately overlooking the beach. It was a composite group that manned the position, consisting of units from Company E, 19th Marines (pioneers); Headquarters and Service Company, 21st Marines; elements from the 3d Motor Transport Battalion, and some men from 2d Battalion, 12th Marines. This gave the regiment a second line of defense in case the Japanese broke through in force.

This set-up, however, was not organized in time to stop the enemy troops that had surged through the gap between the 9th and 21st Marines. Many of these parties were the demolition squads that had the mission of destroying the artillery and blowing up dumps near the beach. Following the ravines and defiles leading down to the sea, it was inevitable that they would stumble into the Division Hospital area.

The first warning came about 0630 when corpsmen reported that a number of enemy soldiers could be seen on the high ground to the right of the hospital. Division headquarters immediately ordered Lieutenant Colonel George O. Van Orden (Division Infantry Training Officer) to take command of two companies of pioneers standing by for just such an eventuality and clear the enemy from the hard-pressed area.

At the hospital, doctors ordered patients to evacuate the tents and go to the beach. Onlookers saw a pathetic sight as half-clothed, bandaged men hobbled down the coast road helping the more seriously wounded to safety. Forty-one of the patients grabbed rifles, carbines, hand grenades, and whatever else they could find and joined the battle. The hospital doctors, corpsmen, and pajama-clad patients

[39] For a complete description of this action see *Saipan*, 224.

[40] Normally, in adjusting fire, a forward observer will get a round over (beyond the target from the observer) and then decrease his range to be sure he gets a short round (one which is between the target and the observer). The resulting "bracket" is then split until the correct range is obtained and fire can be expected to be effective. However, with the fire already so close to friendly troops that it was dangerous to try for a bracket, the range was decreased bit by bit until any further drop in range would result in rounds falling on Marines. This process is referred to as "creeping" and is not considered proper adjustment procedure. It is used only in emergencies.

[41] *Belzer*.

[42] Ltr Col M. C. Williams to CMC, 6Oct52.

MARINE RESERVES hastily assembled from 3d Division headquarters, engineer, and service units scramble up a hillside near the Nidual River as they seek out Japanese that penetrated front lines in the 25–26 July counterattack.

presented a rare sight as they formed a defensive line around the tents. It was a solid line, however, and one that held until the recently organized reinforcements arrived.

Only one patient was wounded during the fighting, but one medical officer and one corpsman later died of wounds. The casualty list also included one medical officer, one dental officer, one Navy warrant officer, 12 corpsmen, and 16 Marines from the medical companies wounded in action.[43] This does not include those casualties suffered by Lieutenant Colonel Van Orden's force.

[43] Cdr R. R. Callaway, (MC), "The Third Medical Battalion in Action: Bougainville and Guam," Historical Study, MCS SenCourse (1948–49), hereinafter cited as *Callaway Study*.

After cleaning out the assigned area, Colonel Van Orden proceeded up the Nidual River Valley in pursuit of the fleeing Japanese. The attack had pushed the enemy back to the hill at the head of the ravine by 1100, but a request to send a Marine patrol to the ridge to determine the hostile strength was denied. Other plans had already been made for the assault of this dominating terrain.

It was from this high ground that Major Yukioka's men paralyzed the operation of 3/21's CP and threatened the flank of both the 9th and 21st Marines. Machine guns raked the back of Company K and deadly mortar fire fell on the command post. As it grew light Lieutenant Colonel Duplantis called for artillery fire on top of the hill but division headquarters denied the request because of the confused situation. Instead, the 9th Marines received orders to capture the hill.

Colonel Craig assigned the mission to the regimental reserve, Company L (Lieutenant David H. Lewis), but directed Major Harold C. Boehm, executive officer of 1/9 who had been over the ground previously, to take command. Covered by artillery fire, Boehm and Lewis moved their men up the left branch of the Masso River to get into position behind the defenders. Concealed by the ridge line, the unit inched its way to within 250 yards of the enemy before being detected. With supporting machine-gun fire from Company B (1/9), the assault carried the hill killing 23 Japanese [44] and forcing the remainder into the firing line built up by 3/21. Those not killed fled into the draw to the north. Casualties to the Marines during the action were one killed and three wounded.[45] Boehm then organized the hill for defense and tied in the flanks of the 9th and 21st. The success of this company action is best indicated by the remarks of the operations officer of 3/21:

Had not the unit commanded by Major Boehm relieved the 3d Battalion's CP, many of the wounded (of which there were about 25) would have died. Relief of the CP made possible the evacuation of the wounded from front lines to the battalion first-aid station and then to the rear. One of the outstanding aspects of this action was Major Boehm's speed, tactical skill, and unerring direction of attack. Had this attack been misdirected, his men could have killed many of the remaining personnel in the CP, as well as the Japanese.[46]

While this action was taking place, the 12th Marines CP and several of its battalions were engaged in stopping the suicide squad attacks.[47]

---

[44] Although only 23 Japanese were killed in taking the hill Marines counted over 300 bodies in the area of 3/21 CP, around the right flank of Company K, and immediately in front of that unit. *Duplantis 1952.*

[45] 3/9 SAR, 2.

[46] Ltr LtCol P. M. Jones to CMC, 21Nov52.

[47] These were units that were especially organized and equipped to destroy artillery. They were to force their way through the front lines under cover of darkness, make a surprise attack, and demolish the guns with demolition charges. This method of attack called for men of exceptional courage, determination, and daring and to quote the Japanese order, "men having a sincere desire to die for the Emperor." 12th Mar SAR for 26July44, 1.

In order to have these parties in position to make their foray in conjunction with the all-out offensive, enemy commanders had ordered the groups to infiltrate behind Marine lines on the night of 24–25 July. With typical Japanese patience, the raiders lay hidden in caves all day. As soon as darkness came on the night of 25–26 July they started firing random shots into the headquarters of the 12th Marines and began to move in small groups down the Asan Valley. A hand grenade duel went on during the early hours of darkness, but some of the intruders sought the safer confines of a cave not 20 feet from the headquarter's fire direction center. A harrowing incident that took place in this hideout was related by the regiment's executive officer:

. . . A Marine was already in the cave and had gone to sleep. It was an excellent shelter from the nightly mortar and artillery fire. The Japanese crawled in on top of him and he could not get out. He couldn't use his carbine because they were sitting on it. He stayed there with them all night without them discovering him. They must have thought, jammed against him in the darkness, that he was one of them. Just before daybreak the Japanese left the cave and the Marine got out and scrambled up the bank as the daylight fighting got well underway. I don't remember this Marine's name, but as I recall he had to be evacuated that day as a mental patient. The strain of spending the night packed into the cave with the Japanese drove him insane, at least temporarily.[48]

The artillerymen's perimeter defense held, and only one of the enemy succeeded in getting through to the guns. He was killed in the 3d Battalion's area before he could do any damage. In the five-hour long fighting around the regimental headquarters, 17 explosive-laden Japanese died. Most of them carried packs containing about 20 pounds of TNT with ready detonators, while others carried magnetic mines. With the coming of daylight, patrols went out to clean up any troops that might cause trouble later in the day. Men of the 12th Marines killed approximately 50–60 more enemy soldiers and drove the remainder into other areas where they were liquidated one by one.

Most of the confusion ended by noon, and although commanders did not know it at the time,

---

[48] Ltr Col J. S. Letcher to CMC, 14Mar47.

AFTERMATH of the Japanese counterattack finds bodies of the attackers strewn on a hillside typical of the terrain over which much of the battle was fought.

the backbone of Japanese resistance on Guam had been broken. From the standpoint of the enemy, the initial attack had been well planned, coordinated, and executed.[49] Excellent observation from the Mt. Tenjo-Mt. Alutom-Mt. Chachao massif enabled him to determine almost to a man the number of troops in the Marines' beachhead and their exact positions.[50] Reconnaissance in force had located the weak spots in the line, and units were massed to ex-

[49] It is of interest to note that the Japanese in carrying out their attack were able to follow some of the principles of warfare (mass, objective, surprise, security, cooperation, offensive, movement, economy of force, and simplicity) to the letter; others they violated with utter disregard or were unable to execute with proficiency.

[50] Upon capture of this massif three huge telescopes of 20 power were found. Looking through these one could almost make out the features of individual Marines below. Practically every part of the beachhead could be seen through these glasses from this high ground. *Craig 1952.*

ploit the advantage. But from this point on, the Japanese plan began to break down.

After the enemy broke through they could not maintain contact, and as a result had no cohesive force to withstand the Marines' counterattacks. Officers leading the assault were among the first killed. Without their leaders the men in the ranks, unable to think for themselves, forgot the over-all plan. Elements within each component soon lost touch with the others, and individuals began slinking off into the ravines and caves.

Another factor contributing to the failure of the attack was the American interdiction of all assembly areas by air, naval gunfire, and artillery. This stopped reinforcements from moving into the Fonte area to bolster the enemy forces and follow up the original assault.

But most credit for the defeat of the Japanese in this engagement must go to the individual Marine and his training. Men from every type of unit in the division found themselves engaged in close combat with the enemy. And the record stands for itself. They did more than a creditable job. In this regard the comments of the executive officer of 1/21 concerning Company B, 19th Marines are of interest:

> . . . The engineer company (Company B, I believe), or a major portion thereof, was placed into line and attached to 1/21. I was particularly impressed with the number of automatic weapons they were able to produce (from their organic vehicles). They advanced as a leading company in at least one of our attacks and performed infantry duties with credit. This is another advantage of basic training being given to all Marines.[51]

When the battle had subsided, the Japanese found themselves in desperate straits. General Takashina had thrown seven of his best battalions against the Marines and had lost approximately 3,500 (3,200 in front of the lines and 300 in the rear areas).[52] This defeat so disorganized the remaining units that the Japanese never again could regroup for any sizable counterattack on Guam.

This conclusion is confirmed by the testimony of the 29th Division's operations officer, Lieutenant Colonel Takeda:

> It was estimated that it was no longer possible to expel the American forces from the island after the results of the general counterattack of the night of 25 July were collected in the morning to about noon of the 26th. After this it was decided that the sole purpose of combat would be to inflict losses on the American forces in the interior of the island. The chief reasons for the foregoing estimate were:
>
> 1. The loss of commanders in the counterattack of 25 July, when up to 95% of the officers (commissioned officers) of the sector defense forces died.
>
> 2. The personnel of each counterattacking unit were greatly decreased, and companies were reduced to several men.
>
> 3. The large casualties caused a great drop in the morale of the survivors.
>
> 4. Over 90% of the weapons were destroyed and combat ability greatly decreased.
>
> 5. The rear echelons of the American forces on Agat front landed in successive waves and advanced. There was little strength remaining on that front and the strength for counterattacks became nonexistent.
>
> 6. The Orote Peninsula defense force perished entirely.

> 7. There was no expectation of support from Japanese naval and air forces outside the island.
>
> Considering the forgoing points all together, it became clear that it was impossible to counterattack and expel the enemy alone.[53]

The Marines could look at their performance with a good deal of satisfaction. Less than 7,000 front line riflemen had been covering over 9,000 yards of terrain and still had beaten back the best the enemy had to offer. Casualties had been heavy[54] but in the words of General Turnage, "It was a grand victory for us."[55] In the same memorandum, however, the general warned of a possible renewed attempt by an even greater force on the night of 26–27 July.

This ominous warning was followed with a defense order issued at 1340 setting up an emergency division reserve, composed of service and support troops, under command of Lieutenant Colonel Van Orden. Each unit of the task organization was assigned an alert area that would be occupied prior to darkness each day until further notice. In official terminology, the employment of the reserve would be:

> . . . on Division order to prevent a penetration of the beach area and, in case of such penetration, to immediately drive the enemy out. In case of penetration by night, the enemy spearheads will be held at all points and a strong counterattack launched as soon after daylight as practicable.[56]

Other safeguards that had been taken earlier in the day (1145) included the ordering of one battalion of the 307th (corps reserve) to assemble in the vicinity of Piti Navy Yard. And to help tighten the perimeter, the 9th Marines had shortened their lines by pulling back about 1,500 yards to better defensive positions. About the same time division directed all combat teams to start preparing strong defensive positions for the night. This included instructions to use barbed wire and to get the most

---

[51] *Van Stockum.*

[52] 3d MarDiv SAR, OpNarrative, 6.

[53] *Takeda Letter.*

[54] Casualty figures for the 3d MarDiv (Reinf) for the period 25–27Jul44 were reported as 166 KIA, 645 WIA, and 34 MIA. The majority of these casualties were incurred during the counterattack period. 3d MarDiv D–3 Periodic Rpts 5–7.

[55] Ltr CG, 3d MarDiv to distribution list, 26Jul44, in D–1 Jnl.

[56] 3d MarDiv DefOrder 1, 26Jul44, in D–1 Jnl.

effective coverage from mortars, naval gunfire, and artillery.

The division was a cautious, alert, and expectant unit when corps moved ashore at 1300 and set up its CP near Agat.[57] Even though the desperate enemy sortie of the previous night had seemed an all out effort, General Geiger also felt the Japanese had enough force remaining for another large-scale attack. No one except the Japanese themselves knew the destructive blow that had been dealt the defenders.

BATTLE FOR OROTE: MARINE BARRACKS, GUAM RECAPTURED

The spirited Japanese night assault against the brigade did not delay the Orote Peninsula attack of the 4th Marines on the morning of 26 July. (See Map 17, Map Section) Following an excellent and well-coordinated preparation by aviation, naval gunfire, and artillery, the 4th jumped off at 0700. The plan of attack called for a column of battalions with the 1st spearheading the advance. With the 3d mopping up behind, units made good progress against light opposition until they encountered difficult terrain on the left.

As the 22d Marines waited for the softening-up preparation prior to its 0700 attack hour, shells began to fall on units of that regiment. At first the men thought that friendly artillery or naval gunfire caused the trouble, but further checking indicated the enemy was again using one of his old tricks, timing his own artillery to coincide with American barrages. In any case, the fire had a demoralizing effect on the troops, and disorganized the 22d to such an extent that it crossed the line of departure an hour late.[58]

This delay coupled with the initial rapid movement of the 4th Marines resulted in the right flank of that unit becoming exposed. Consequently, Lieutenant Colonel Shapley sent a message shortly before noon requesting permission to take over part of the 22d's zone of action and continue the advance to the O–4 line (vicinity of old Marine rifle range). This

would give Shapley room to employ all battalions, protect his right, and at the same time provide some relief to the depleted and fatigued assault units of the 22d. At 1145, General Shepherd ordered the regimental boundary changed to the Agat-Sumay Road, making the 22d responsible only for the area east of that road.[59]

Meanwhile, the 22d had reorganized and left the line of departure at 0800. Immediately to the front of the assault elements was the swamp that had been the breeding spot of the Japanese counterattack the night before. Despite the blocking high-arched roots in the mangrove swamps, patrols waded through mud and water waist deep to make certain that no sizable enemy unit still lurked there. Snipers slowed the advance, but by 1245 Marines had successfully cleared the area and contacted the 4th Regiment at RJ 15.

Here the assault had to be channelized because of the mangrove growth on the right of the road and a marsh on the left. The enemy had mined the 200-yard corridor with aerial bombs and was covering the area with automatic weapons from cleverly concealed pillboxes west of the road junction. Tanks that had been following directly behind the infantry were called forward to set up a base of fire for the riflemen who would move in to knock out the strong point.

When the assault platoon got half-way across the gap between the tanks and the pillboxes that had halted the advance, the Japanese opened fire from many brush-hidden mounds and stopped the Marines in their tracks. Tank commanders stepped-up their rate of fire, and observing with field glasses from open hatches adjusted within one and two foot margins to penetrate the bunker openings. This silenced the Japanese gunners long enough for the infantry to crawl back to the protection of the tanks which had been firing only three or four feet over the heads of the troops.

Mortar fire continued to fall on the attackers, and the 22d Marines Tank Company commander contacted his liaison team at the artillery fire direction center and asked for high-angle

---

[57] IIIAC C–3 Jnl.

[58] 1st ProvMarBrig WD, 1Jul–10Aug44, 10.

[59] 1st ProvMarBrig Jnl.

fire.[60] This would enable the tank observers to bring fire on the mortars emplaced behind the well-camouflaged mounds. This fire was promptly delivered and adjusted on to the target by means of smoke shell bursts. The enemy mortar shells ceased falling, and two large fires which started to burn indicated an ammunition and fuel dump in the same area had been hit.[61]

By this time it was too dark to try to continue the advance. The brigade dug in just beyond RJ 15, with its right flank anchored on the swamp; artillery blocked the gap from there to the beach.[62] On the left, Marines prepared night positions generally along the O–3 line.

Satisfactory progress had been made by the evening of 26 July, not only by front line units but also by other elements of the brigade. All ships had been completely unloaded,[63] and ammunition problems greatly reduced. Engineers had moved equipment into position to be ready for a hurried reconstruction of Orote airfield as soon as it was secured.

The outlook for a quick capture appeared good, even though the brigade as a whole had suffered 1,266 casualties since landing, most of them concentrated in the two infantry regiments.[64] The enemy had not been encountered in any strength during the day, and the only heavily fortified positions met were those at RJ 15. But the full extent of this strong point remained unknown. The Japanese had been observed organizing defenses near the airfield, and artillery and mortar fire still came from the cliffs behind Neye Island. Air and naval gunfire had not been able to knock out these positions even with constant pounding.

During the night the Japanese guns were comparatively quiet, but friendly artillery, mortars, and naval gunfire kept the air full of harassing fires. This limited the enemy ground action to minor infiltration attempts. The jump-off on 27 July, originally scheduled for 0700, was delayed 15 minutes because brigade headquarters feared the original time might have been intercepted on a SCR 300 channel.[65]

The heavy pre-attack preparation had made little impression on the enemy, and the Marines moved only 100 yards before being stopped by intense automatic-weapons fire. The rolling terrain, covered with heavy undergrowth, interspersed with swamps, restricted the avenue of advance to the Sumay Road and the narrow strip of land in front of the 4th Marines. Tanks could not assist the infantry until the mine fields were cleared from around RJ 15. Fortunately, the mines were poorly camouflaged, and a bomb disposal officer from the 22d, covered by a smoke screen, disarmed many of them.[66] Tanks, guided by infantrymen, then threaded their way between the aerial bombs and got into supporting position.

The 4th Marines jumped off on time with the 3d Battalion on the right, next to the road. A ridge 300 yards to the front, from which the Japanese laid down their withering fire, was the first objective. Beyond this a coconut grove extended 500 yards on gently sloping ground to meet a higher brush-covered ridge. Behind this, hidden from view, lay the important Orote airfield.

Major Hoyler's 3/4 assault companies found it impossible to make any progress against the well-camouflaged and mutually-supporting positions along the base of the first ridge. But Marine Shermans, firing at point-blank range, soon silenced the heavy and light machine guns in the dugouts. With the automatic weapons knocked out, Hoyler's men moved in and occupied the ridge.[67]

In the afternoon, the advance through the coconut grove proved to be a painstaking job. The fighting was extremely bitter, and tanks could not get forward to help because of the congestion on the road. Assault elements fought ahead yard by yard and finally, at 1530, broke out of the grove only to be brought up

[60] Fire delivered in such a manner that it falls similar to mortar fire is called high-angle fire. Its use is appropriate when firing into or out of deep defilade, sharply eroded terrain, or over high terrain features near friendly troops.

[61] TkCo, 22d Mar SAR, 5.

[62] Ltr Maj S. A. Todd to author, 21Jan52.

[63] 1st ProvMarBrig WD, 1Jul–10Aug44, 10.

[64] Casualties as of 1800, 26 July were: KIA 247, WIA 960, and MIA 59. IIIAC C–2 Jnl.

[65] 1st ProvMarBrig Jnl.

[66] 22d Mar Unit Rpts.

[67] TkCo, 4th Mar SAR, 14.

MEN OF THE 1ST PROVISIONAL MARINE BRIGADE advance through a coconut grove 500 yards from the old Marine Barracks.

short by fire from the next ridge. Mopping up and trying to soften the strong enemy defenses on the hill just short of the old Marine Corps rifle range consumed the remaining hours of daylight of 27 July. During these operations the regimental executive officer, Lieutenant Colonel Samuel D. Puller, was killed by a sniper.[68]

On the right of the brigade zone, the 22d Marines had been unable to move until 3/4 cleared the road to a point beyond the swamp. With the left boundary set at the Agat-Sumay Road and the mangrove swamp on the right, the regiment's front was limited to 50 yards.

Colonel Schneider's battalions could do nothing but hold up until they had room to maneuver. When 3/4 moved ahead, Schneider pulled his 3d Battalion up on the right of the 2d, which had been in the lead.

The two units advanced slowly against opposition that increased as the day wore on. By midafternoon the attack stalled when it encountered numerous pillboxes, dugouts, mines, and intense mortar and automatic-weapons fire from positions on the rising ground near the site of the old Marine Barracks.

The Japanese had been resisting more fanatically as they were driven back and compressed in the remaining half of the peninsula. Although the remaining men of the 38th Regiment

[68] 1/4 WD, 30May–9Sept44, 5.

and the composite naval units still had organization, there was some evidence that they felt their defeat inevitable. One incident that bore this out was the attack on a tank by a lone Imperial officer armed only with a sword.[69] Another action that had questionable value found 30–40 of the enemy marching in column down the road toward the brigade's front lines. Led by an officer carrying a large battle flag they made an excellent target for a tank of the 4th Marines. Shell bursts quickly scattered the column, killing most of the marchers.[70]

But men of the 22d Marines witnessed a sight almost unique in Pacific fighting during the afternoon of 27 July. In an attempt to reach the high ground before digging in for the night, the regiment called for a heavy preparation on that area about 1700. All aircraft available bombed and strafed the hills in front of the 22d, after which artillery and naval guns fired a devastating barrage. As the men waited for the lifting of fires the Japanese suddenly broke in a mad, headlong retreat abandoning their well-organized defensive line.[71]

Major John F. Schoettel, who had relieved Lieutenant Colonel Hart in command of 2/22 that afternoon, sent his men in hot pursuit. The 3d Battalion followed, and by 1945 the regiment had surged ahead of the 4th Marines on the left, seized the dominating terrain in its zone, and started making preparations for the night. This incident proved to be the turning point of the battle for Orote. From these positions above Sumay, the Marines flanked the enemy line extending along the rifle range and the airfield. The day's advance also had broken the bottleneck around RJ 15 and opened the way for supplies and ammunition to be moved forward more rapidly.

On the right, the brigade lines were within 300 yards of the former Marine Barracks, but a 500-yard gap existed between the two regiments because of the rapid advance of the 22d. The 4th had prepared its night lines along the unimproved road about 300 yards short of the rifle range. Fighting during the day had been severe, with both regiments suffering heavy casualties. Supplies in front line units were low with some tanks completely out of ammunition.[72] On the brighter side, enemy pressure had lessened and the worst of the swamp areas had been successfully passed.

General Shepherd's operation order for 28 July called for a preparation designed to blast the enemy from his defenses in front of the airfield. Shepherd requested a 45-minute air strike and a 30-minute naval gunfire barrage to precede the 30-minute artillery pounding that would be given the Japanese positions prior to the 0830 attack-hour. As an indication of the volume of artillery fire desired, six Army 105mm and three 155mm howitzer batteries would augment the six pack howitzer batteries of the brigade. To give still more weight, two corps artillery 155mm howitzer and two 14th Defense Battalion 90mm gun batteries were added.[73]

After an uenventful night along the entire front, the air, naval gunfire, and artillery preparations went ahead on schedule. At 0830 the brigade resumed the attack to seize the airfield and the remainder of the peninsula. The operation order for the 28th had given a new boundary and assigned the former Marine Barracks and Sumay to Colonel Schneider's 22d Marines and the rifle range and airfield to Lieutenant Colonel Shapley's 4th.

The enemy in front of the 22d continued to fight a delaying action, dropping back only when artillery and the infantry's superior fire power drove them from their holes. Although Japanese artillery and mortar fire decreased during the morning, automatic-weapons fire did not slacken. With tanks leading the way, Schneider's regiment reached the O–4 line by 1005.[74] This increased the already existing gap between the 22d and 4th, and necessitated echeloning units to the left rear to gain contact.

Plagued by terrain covered with heavy vegetation, as well as a dug-in enemy who had cut firelanes through the dense underbrush, the 4th Marines made slower progress. Extremely bitter resistance developed in the center and on the

[69] 1st ProvMarBrig Unit Rpts.
[70] *Bergren.*
[71] 2/22 Jnl.

[72] TkCo, 4th Mar SAR, 14.
[73] 1st ProvMarBrig OpOrder 27, 30Jul44; IIIAC Arty WD, July 1944, 3; *Ferguson Interview.*
[74] 1st ProvMarBrig Jnl.

TANK-INFANTRY TEAM from the 4th Marines advances slowly through the dense scrub growth that characterized most of the terrain in the regiment's zone of action on Orote Peninsula.

right of the regiment's zone, with two strong points causing most of the trouble. Tanks were called in as quickly as possible, but the thick foliage made control and observation practically impossible.

Initially, two platoons of the tank company were assigned to the 3d Battalion and the other to the 1st when 2/4 reported it could not use armor because of the terrain. With the help of the tanks, 3/4 on the right broke through the coconut log pillboxes and reorganized prior to advancing to the O–4 line. Intense automatic-weapons fire kept the 2d Battalion from making any headway, and when flanking fire from the left started to cut Company I to ribbons, Major Messer called for tank assistance. Regiment

ordered a platoon of Shermans from the 3d Battalion to report to Messer. The 2d Tank Platoon withdrew and at 1430 was guided into position to help Company E. Unfortunately, it had been led into the midst of the strong point and could not fire because the 1st Battalion, on the left, had also advanced and there was danger of hitting units of that battalion.

During the early afternoon, while this situation was being rectified, General Shepherd went forward on a reconnaissance of his front lines. Quickly sizing up the gravity of the situation he sent a request to General Bruce for a platoon of Army tank destroyers to augment the fire from the brigade's tanks and a platoon of Army light tanks that had just arrived on the scene.

Shepherd then issued oral orders to Lieutenant Colonel Shapley to organize a tank-infantry attack, employing all available tanks in a mass effort to break through the strong line of Japanese-held bunkers. At 1530 Shapley launched the assault all along the regimental front. The massed armor cracked the rifle range defense line and infantry units followed closely behind to exploit the breakthrough. This had been one of the most formidable enemy positions encountered by the brigade, and it was here that the Japanese command had ordered its soldiers to hold until killed. Marines counted approximately 250 pillboxes and emplacements in this general area after the attack. Their reduction permitted the advance to sweep forward to within 150 yards of the airfield, where units set up for the night.[75]

After making certain that his left flank was secure, Colonel Schneider had ordered his 22d Marines to resume the attack at about 1015. By 1208, Companies E and G had driven to the rubble and skeleton buildings of the former Marine Barracks. Only a cigar box containing pre-war PX papers and receipts, a bronze plaque, and a star-covered pillow, which a Japanese had made from the blue field of an American flag, gave evidence of previous Marine occupancy.[76]

Halting only for a moment, the 22d pressed on in an effort to capture Sumay before darkness fell. The left flank of the regiment held up about 150 yards in front of the fallen buildings, but the units on the right continued on to the cliffs overlooking the village.

Tanks and demolition teams quickly sealed any caves that slowed down forward movement. Marines encountered little resistance as they entered the village, but the debris and extensive mine fields made the streets impassable to tanks. It is believed that the town was the most heavily-mined area on Guam. One hundred and seventy-two aerial bomb mines, two torpedo mines, and many ordinary land mines were disarmed in Sumay alone.[77]

One tank fell victim to these fields, and the

LIEUTENANT GENERAL HOLLAND SMITH (right) stands with the leaders of the successful conquest of Orote Peninsula (left to right: Lieutenant Colonel Shapley, General Shepherd, Colonel Schneider) behind the plaque taken from the wreckage of the Marine Barracks on Guam.

remaining vehicles hurriedly withdrew while infantry moved through the wreckage of buildings to make certain that the enemy was not bypassed in force. Units completed the job by 1750 and then established defensive positions 100 yards east of the town.[78]

The brigade spent a quiet night, and in the morning (29 July) the attack jumped off at 0800. Desiring to conclude the Orote campaign that day, General Shepherd had ordered a tremendous supporting arms preparation. The heaviest air strike since W–Day backed up the six battalions of artillery (which included units from the 77th Division and 12th Marines) and eight ships that laid down a curtain of fire prior to the assault.[79]

Results speak for themselves, as both the 4th and 22d advanced half the length of the airstrip against only meager resistance by 1000. Army and Marine tanks led the way, supported by six M–10 tank destroyers from the 77th Division that had reported to the brigade during the

[75] TkCo, 4th Mar SAR, 15.
[76] 2/22 Jnl.
[77] 22d Mar Unit Rpts.

[78] 1st ProvMarBrig Unit Rpts.
[79] 1st ProvMarBrig WD, 1July–10Aug44, 12; CTG 53.2 OpRpt, OpNarrative, 21–23; 1st ProvMarBrig **Jnl.**

AMERICAN COLORS are again raised over the remains of Marine Barracks, Guam. Men of the 22d Marines salute as "To the Colors" is sounded on a captured Japanese bugle.

morning. Shortly after 1400, Marines held Orote airfield and had established a defensive line about 150 yards beyond the end of the landing strip.

Earlier in the day the brigade commander had ordered that, upon reaching this line, the 4th Marines would take over the entire front, relieving the 22d for mopping-up details. This relief was effected by 1500, and an hour later Lieutenant Colonel Shapley sent a strong tank-infantry patrol to the tip of the peninsula. The tank-riding infantry found only two Japanese soldiers during the entire expedition. When this patrol came back with its information, General Shepherd reported Orote Peninsula secured.[80]

After relief of the 22d at the O–6 line, the 3d Battalion with the Pioneer Company attached returned to Sumay to flush out any enemy troops that might have returned during the night. Little hostile activity met the Marines as they proceeded through the town along the coastal road. But as the men from 3/22 pushed on to investigate the cliffs paralleling the road west of Sumay, Japanese resistance increased. From positions that had been constructed and armed to interdict Apra Harbor, the enemy commanded the entire area. Installations dug high in the rocks were inaccessible from the heights above, and finally LCI(G)'s were called to pound the cave defenders with 40mm and 20mm guns. But not until late the next after-

---

[80] 1st ProvMarBrig Jnl.

noon did the firing from these cave positions subside.[81]

As mopping-up patrols continued their aggressive action, isolated enemy soldiers destroyed themselves by using hand grenades or cutting their throats. Others tried to escape by swimming to Fort Santa Cruz,[82] but these attempts proved futile when a platoon of LVT(A)'s was dispatched to the scene to discourage such rash procedure.[83]

Another cliff area that had caused trouble throughout the Orote fighting received a check during the day. A LVT-borne squad from the 9th Defense Battalion investigated Neye Island and the cliffs behind it, but found no enemy. Evidence indicated that the island had been used primarily as an observation post; nothing pointed to the mortar and artillery positions previously reported. The difficulty of landing and the danger of mines precluded a thorough investigation of the cliffs. From the amphibian tractor in the water observers noted many caves but could see no guns in their vicinity.[84]

Meanwhile, a group of high ranking Navy and Marine officers, including Admiral Spruance, Lieutenant General Holland Smith, Major General Geiger, Major General Larsen (soon to become Guam Island Commander), and Brigadier General Shepherd gathered on the ground of the former Marine Barracks. Lieutenant Colonel Shapley, Colonel Schneider, and all other officers and men who could be spared were also there.

Sporadic small-arms fire was still going on west of the airstrip on Orote Peninsula, and to the north, the 3d Division's artillery could be heard in the distance. At the command from General Geiger, a Marine sounded "To the Colors" on a Japanese bugle, and at 1530 the United States flag once more flew over Orote Peninsula.

It was a solemn ceremony. Marines from 2/22, who had helped capture the site, furnished the honor guard, and the men in the vicinity paused momentarily to pay tribute. General Shepherd expressed the thoughts of every one there:

On this hallowed ground, you officers and men of the First Marine Brigade have avenged the loss of our comrades who were overcome by a numerically superior enemy three days after Pearl Harbor. Under our flag this island again stands ready to fulfill its destiny as an American fortress in the Pacific.[85]

The next day, 30 July, mopping up continued with the 4th Marines responsible for the entire peninsula except Sumay. Lieutenant Colonel Shapley ordered extensive patrolling to the end of Orote. Maximum use was made of the war dog platoon, but the patrols encountered only one unarmed Japanese soldier.

On order, the 22d left one battalion behind, and the rest of the regiment moved into corps reserve in a bivouac area about 2,000 yards southeast of Agat, just north of Harmon Road. The remaining unit, 3/22, continued the job of cleaning up Sumay and the caves west of it.[86] One platoon, sent to Fort Santa Cruz to make certain that the enemy escape attempts had failed, took two prisoners and found six dead.[87]

It did not take long for the Marines to get Orote airfield into operational condition. Only six hours after the first engineer units moved on to the strip, a Navy TBF was called in for a test run. With Lieutenant (jg) Edward F. Terrar, Jr. as the pilot, the plane came in, touched its wheels to check the ground, and took off again to circle the field for the actual landing. At 1650 it touched down, and Orote airfield was ready for use.[88] Soon after, observation planes

[81] CTG 53.2 OpRpt, OpNarrative, 23.

[82] On 21 June 1898 the first American flag was raised over Guam at Fort Santa Cruz, signifying the bloodless capture of the island. At the time of the American landing in 1944, the fort was a low-lying mass of ruins on the coral reefs near the center of Apra Harbor, and 1,200 yards from Sumay. Its derelict condition and periodic inundation by the sea rendered it ineffectual for use as a Japanese strong point.

[83] 1st ArmdAmphGru Action Rpt, 2. The tanks poured 600 rounds of 37mm and 10,000 rounds of .30-caliber machine-gun fire into the ruins of the fort.

[84] IIIAC C–2 Jnl.

[85] Lt M. Kaufman, "Attack on Guam," MC Gazette, April 1945, 63.

[86] 1st ProvMarBrig OpOrder 27, 30Jul44.

[87] 1st ProvMarBrig Unit Rpts.

[88] The landing of this plane disappointed several Marine officers who had laid plans to insure that the first plane to land on Orote would be flown by a Marine. VMO–1, which was embarked on a CVE, had been alerted but the Navy plane landed before the VMO–1 pilot arrived over the field. Ltr Col F. P. Henderson to CMC, 21Nov52.

FIRST PLANE (piloted by Lieutenant (jg) E. F. Terrar, Jr.) to land on Orote airfield after its capture is welcomed by the engineers who prepared the strip for the landing.

(OY's) from VMO–1 began flying missions from this strip.

Earlier in the day, the corps operation order for 31 July had been received. It directed the brigade to take over the southern half of the final beachhead line from Inalas to Magpo Point. Extensive patrols were to be conducted to determine the presence or absence of the enemy in the southern portion of Guam. Those units of the 77th being relieved (the 306th was to remain in position and continue its patrols), would regroup with the remainder of the Army division for an attack to the east.[89]

The task of rooting out the well-organized and cleverly entrenched enemy on Orote Peninsula had been accomplished in four days of severe fighting The aggressive action of the 1st Provisional Marine Brigade in securing the strategically important Orote Airfield and Apra Harbor earned the unit the praise of General Geiger and the subsequent award of the Navy Unit Commendation. To destroy the approximately 2,500 enemy troops, the brigade reported that it had suffered 115 KIA, 721 WIA, and 38 MIA.[90]

FONTE PLATEAU: SECURING THE FBL

While the brigade opened the attack on Orote on 26 July, the 3d Division continued preparations for another strong enemy assault expected

that night. Commanders made close inspections of front line installations to make certain that all units were tied in. During such a check a sniper killed Lieutenant Colonel de Zayas, commanding officer of 2/3.[91]

The expected large-scale Japanese assault did not materialize, and only minor infiltration attempts were made during the night of 26–27 July. Naval guns and artillery kept the air full of shells most of the night to discourage any attack ideas that the enemy might have. This, plus the heavy preparation fired in the morning, softened up positions for the 0900 jump-off.

It had become increasingly evident that the principal Japanese battle position now lay along the Fonte-Chachao-Tenjo ridge line, with its right flank on the northern nose of Fonte. Operations for 27 July were designed to bring the greatest possible pressure to bear against this line. The 9th Marines, on the right, was to hold its position and give maximum fire support to the 21st until that regiment reached the D–3 line. The 3d Marines, on the left, would attack in conjunction with the 21st.[92]

Colonel Butler's 21st started forward with the 3d, 1st, and 2d Battalions abreast, from right to left. With a platoon of tanks attached, 2/21 had advanced approximately 200 yards when enemy machine guns in the vicinity of the radio towers slowed down the attack. The tanks tried to move around a swamp, blocking the route of progress, to get into position to take the weapons under fire, but bogged down. The tankmen continued to throw shells into the area, however, and knocked out the guns causing the trouble, allowing the 2d to move up just short of the power line by noon. Here a halt was called until units on the right and left could come abreast.

The 1st Battalion had been unable to advance because of heavy resistance from Japanese in caves on the reverse slope of a small hill to the left front, and from a quarry. Air and artillery put concentrations into the area but to no avail; tanks expended 90 percent of their ammunition, but still the unit could not move.[93]

[89] IIIAC OpOrder 7–44, 30Jul44.
[90] 1st ProvMarBrig Jnl.

[91] 3d Mar SAR, 3.
[92] 3d MarDiv D–3 Jnl.
[93] 3d TkBn SAR, 8.

On the right, Lieutenant Colonel Duplantis' 3d Battalion met only slight resistance and lunged forward to the D–2 line by 1000. Companies had to be echeloned on the left to keep in touch with the stalled 1st and on the right to maintain contact with the 9th Marines. One company of 3/9 was attached to 3/21 at 1630. The Army's 3/307, which had been committed by General Geiger in the wake of the 25–26 July counterattack, received orders to relieve the remainder of 3/9. When this had been completed 3/9 (–) moved into an assembly area behind the 21st as division reserve.[94]

On the left flank of the division the 3d Marines, with 2/9 still attached, ordered that battalion and 2/3 to make the main effort to reduce Fonte Plateau in the center of the regiment's zone of action. The 3d Battalion was to remain in position north of Adelup Point and patrol as far forward as possible. The 1st Battalion remained in division reserve at the foot of Fonte, but division headquarters released Company C to the regiment with instructions not to commit it without prior authority.[95]

Lieutenant Colonel Cushman (2/9) issued his attack order for the day at 0800, although at the time Company G was already in a fire fight. As though this were not enough trouble, at 0930 friendly artillery and aerial bombs fell on the same unit as it prepared to cross the line of departure. This disrupted the attack and necessitated a one-hour delay to effect reorganization.[96] Then Companies E and G, supported by two platoons of tanks, edged forward and recaptured the ground from which they had withdrawn the day before. Cushman moved Company F from battalion reserve at 1100 to fill a gap that had developed between the two assault units. (See Map 18, Map Section)

Just as the attack was resumed, about 150 Japanese made a wild *banzai* charge against Company G. Even though that unit had been hard hit during the morning, it stopped the rush without allowing any penetration. The battalion then launched its drive toward the

CAPTAIN LOUIS H. WILSON, JR., Commanding Officer, Company F, 2d Battalion, 9th Marines, awarded the Medal of Honor for action on 25–26 July when, although wounded three times, he successfully led his men in capturing their assigned objectives and repulsing repeated enemy counterattacks during a fierce ten-hour hand-to-hand struggle.

power line, and by midafternoon all units declared their sectors secure.

Meanwhile, the 2d Battalion, 3d Marines, now commanded by Major William A. Culpepper, jumped off on time. With Companies F and G in assault, the attack progressed against moderate resistance. Several pockets of the enemy were by-passed, but the attached engineer unit (C/19) quickly cleared the areas. The day's objective, the power line, was reached early in the afternoon, and units reorganized for the expected continuation to the D–3 line. But regimental headquarters decided to hold up the attack when 2/9 encountered serious opposition from a depression on top of Fonte Plateau. Orders went out to all units to dig in for the night.

The division's line had not advanced too far during the day, but the situation was brighter

[94] 9th Mar SAR, 2.
[95] 3d MarDiv D–3 Jnl.
[96] 2/9 SAR, 4.

FONTE PLATEAU, scene of bitter fighting by the 2d Battalion, 9th Marines, is highlighted by the sun's rays in this photograph taken by a plane from the USS *Sangamon*. (Navy Photograph.)

than it had been. There was contact all along the line, and good progress had been made toward capturing the troublesome Fonte area; units now held the last intermediate phase line before the top of the ridge.[97] The day's fighting had carried troops through the strongly defended Japanese 29th Division's command post defenses.[98]

Pockets of the enemy still remained behind the Marine lines, but they were being contained and systematically reduced. Sporadic enemy artillery and mortar fire that fell on the beaches proved more effective and caused a slow-down in unloading. Further delay resulted from the

tactical demand for shore party and service troops. Nevertheless, TQM's reported the remaining division assault shipping (LST's) 80 percent unloaded.[99]

During the night 27–28 July, the Marines repulsed several small-scale enemy counterattacks with little loss to themselves, and at 0830 the big push to capture the FBL got under way. The 3d Marines, with the same units (2/3 and 2/9) bearing the brunt of the advance, moved out on schedule. The 2d Battalion, 3d went slowly up the hill, meeting only light opposition. Halting shortly before noon to make contact with 2/9, which was momentarily held up, Major Culpepper's men renewed their attack at 1300. An hour later Company G

[97] This is the general line that was to be reached at 1800 on W-Day by the 3d Marines. *Aplington.*
[98] 3d MarDiv D–2 Periodic Rpt 74.

[99] 3d MarDiv D–3 Jnl.

reached the D–3 line overlooking the Fonte River.[100]

Meanwhile Companies E and F of 2/9 on the right of the depression, advanced against moderate resistance and reached their objective (D–3 line) before noon. On the other hand, Company G, which had the job of cleaning out the pit and the area immediately around it, made slow progress. By noon only one officer remained in the company, the others having become casualties, and the fourth commander since W-Day had taken over. This officer, Captain Francis L. Fagan, arrived just in time to find his unit's thin right flank being pushed back by an enemy counterattack. With the help of one platoon of the weapons company, Fagan reestablished the line, and by 1500 the Japanese force had been annihilated.

While his battalion reorganized to renew the advance, Lieutenant Colonel Cushman reconnoitered the depression on top of Fonte. This pit was generally circular in shape, its very steep sides honeycombed with caves, which made it difficult for the Marines to check the area without coming under fire from all angles. Cushman planned to surround the area, but that would take time and he had been ordered to capture the objective as soon as possible. He requested a delay until the next morning (29 July) which was granted. Consequently, at 1800 the night positions of the battalion stretched along the D–3 line, but were bent back in the center around the pit where Company G still held just forward of the power line. For all practical purposes, however, 2/9 now controlled the area in its zone to the FBL.[101]

During the remaining hours of daylight Cushman's units made up special demolition loads, refueled flame throwers, and brought forward extra rocket launchers. A careful reconnaissance disclosed a site where a tank could fire into the pit, firing positions for machine guns and rocket launchers that could cover all sides of the depression, and a path for the descent of troops. This completed Cushman's plans for reducing the Fonte bowl, and as troops dug in for the night orders went out for the attack at 0830 the next morning.[102]

The operation order for the capture of the FBL had been designed not only to take the Fonte area but to secure the beachhead line along the entire division front. To assure a coordinated attack on the strategic Chachao-Alutom-Tenjo ridge line, division had enlarged the zone of action of the 9th Marines on the morning of 28 July. This placed the entire zone under one commander, Colonel Craig.

With 2/9 still operating with the 3d Marines, it was necessary to attach two battalions to Craig's regiment for the ensuing assault. The Army's 3/307 relieved the 3d Battalion, 9th, on the right flank of the regiment's zone; 3/9 then moved to the other flank and relieved 3/21 on position. This gave Colonel Craig three battalions on the line, 3/307, 1/9, and 3/9 from right to left. The released 3/21 (attached to the 9th until D–3 line reached) went into regimental reserve with the mission of following 3/9 in the attack and protecting the left flank.[103]

Following an hour-long air strike and a 15-minute artillery and naval gunfire preparation, the assault started at 0830. By 0945, 3/9 had advanced in its zone to come abreast of the rest of the regiment. Colonel Craig then ordered a general advance all along the line to begin at 1045.

As the 9th advanced on Mt. Chachao and Mt. Alutom, men from the 77th Infantry Division could be seen on Mt. Tenjo. Craig immediately contacted the Army commander and arranged for a boundary between the units. Later when the corps overlay designating the dividing line arrived, it was found the two corresponded. The new division boundary ran along an unimproved trail 400–500 yards south of the Aguada River and then along the high ground southeast of Mt. Alutom.[104] (See Map 19)

The 9th Marines renewed its attack with orders to seize the high ground on the new boundary and prepare to continue on to the FBL. By 1500, 3/307 had gained its objective on the

[100] 2/3 Jnl.

[101] Ltr Col R. E. Cushman, Jr. to CMC, 8Oct52.

[102] LtCol R. E. Cushman, "The Fight at Fonte," *MC Gazette*, April 1947, 16.

[103] 9th Mar SAR, 2–3.

[104] IIIAC C–3 Jnl; *Craig 1952.*

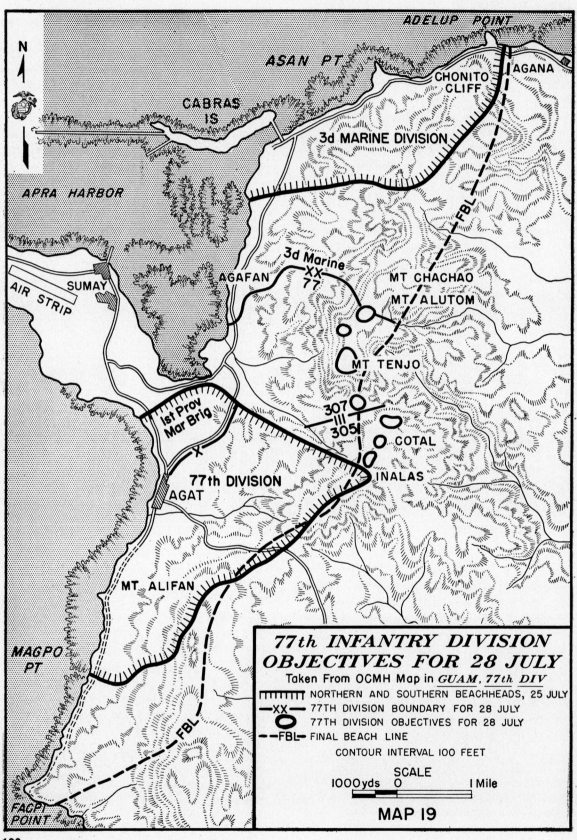

N

ADELUP POINT

ASAN PT.

CABRAS
IS

3d MARINE DIVISION

CHONITO
CLIFF

AGANA

APRA HARBOR

AGAFAN

3d Marine
XX
77

MT CHACHAO
MT ALUTOM

AIR STRIP

SUMAY

MT TENJO

1st Prov
Mar Brig

307
III
305

COTAL

77th DIVISION

AGAT

INALAS

MT ALIFAN

MAGPO
PT

FBL

FACPI
POINT

77th INFANTRY DIVISION OBJECTIVES FOR 28 JULY

Taken From OCMH Map in *GUAM, 77th DIV*

|¯¯¯¯¯¯¯¯| NORTHERN AND SOUTHERN BEACHHEADS, 25 JULY

—XX— 77TH DIVISION BOUNDARY FOR 28 JULY

◯ 77TH DIVISION OBJECTIVES FOR 28 JULY

—FBL— FINAL BEACH LINE

CONTOUR INTERVAL 100 FEET

SCALE

1000 yds   O   1 Mile

MAP 19

TANKS of the 3d Tank Battalion lumber up the twisting trail from the beach to assist the 21st Marines in its drive toward the FBL.

right and was only 200 yards short on the left; 3/9 was ready to attack Mt. Chachao and Mt. Alutom, while 1/9 made preparations to contact Army patrols from Mt. Tenjo.

On Mt. Chachao, the Japanese had constructed a concrete emplacement in the center of the summit, with a series of foxholes and machine-gun positions nested in the surrounding cliffs to protect it. Circular gun pits at either end of the crest guarded the trail running across the ridge and leading down the slope. Manned by a company of troops, the Mt. Chachao fortification was formidable.

Major Donald B. Hubbard's 3d Battalion, 9th went up the ridges to the road, quickly overcame the enemy outposts, and formed for the assault to reach the top of the objective. Artil-lery neutralized the defenses while tanks moved forward through the assault units and around the peak to prevent escape of the enemy. The infrantry then formed in a column of companies and, protected by the steepness of the cliff faces, drove the length of the ridge line and made ready to rush the top. A shower of grenades hurled into the positions preceded a final charge that carried the Marines to the crest and the FBL.[105]

In conjunction with this assault, Lieutenant Colonel Carey A. Randall's 1/9 moved up on the right and made contact with men from the 77th Division near Mt. Tenjo.[106] On the left,

[105] *Craig.*
[106] 9th Mar SAR, 3.

3/21 had completed its mission of guarding the 9th's flank and had returned to its parent organization's control.

The 21st Marines (less 3d Battalion), in the center of the concerted drive to capture the FBL, had met less resistance than the other regiments of the division. The only heavy opposition was encountered in the vicinity of the radio towers. Two tanks from Company B worked in close and cleared the enemy from that area and the nearby caves, allowing the infantry to move in. The pocket had been reduced by 1630 and the regiment rushed forward to the FBL.[107]

For the first time since W-Day, the 3d Division could look at the situation on the evening of 28 July with satisfaction. The FBL had been reached along the entire front with the exception of that area in front of Company G, 2/9 on Fonte Ridge. This gave complete command of the center of the island, and of equal importance permitted observation to the north. Enemy opposition had diminished during the day to the point where it was now evident that the Japanese could not launch a counterattack without time to reorganize their scattered remnants. Phase I of the recapture of Guam could now be considered closed.[108]

During the night of 28–29 July the Japanese made an attempt to free some of the isolated groups that still hid inside the Marines' perimeter. One such try was made on the right flank of 3/21 where that unit tied in with the 9th. Two enemy forces communicated with each other by colored flares, but signals got mixed and the coordinated effort turned into just another small unit counterattack that was broken up without much trouble.[109]

The preparations that 2/9 made the night before paid off on the morning of 29 July. From two sides of the depression a heavy crisscross of bazooka, machine-gun, and tank fire pinpointed every cave. Assault groups rapidly worked their way down into the pit and systematically cleaned out the caves and emplacements. Marines did not suffer a single casualty while they killed an estimated 35–50 Japanese.[110]

Company G then went forward to the FBL to complete the fight for Fonte. From a later study of the terrain from both sides it was evident the Fonte hill mass was the strategic high ground along the entire D–3 line and the FBL. It had been organized and defended by about a battalion of Japanese. As the enemy losses mounted, General Takashina had rushed approximately another battalion and a half into the area.

The value placed on this terrain by the Japanese can best be judged by the 11 separate counterattacks launched to retain it and the 800 Imperial dead, including many officers, left on the battlefield.

The enemy defenses were not unusual, consisting of individual and automatic weapons positions on the high ground, protected by mortars and artillery. But the caves and other shelters cut into the reverse slopes protected the defenders from naval gunfire and artillery, making the entire position difficult to reduce. The only solution found to be effective by the Americans was the use of naval gunfire on the reverse slopes,[111] artillery on top of the hill, 81mm mortars on the forward side, and close overhead machine-gun fire in support. In this manner the Marines could creep up the bare slopes to gain the top where they had to engage in fierce hand-to-hand battle to retain the hill and push on to the military crest.

Even with the intelligent use of all available supporting weapons, two rifle companies of the assault battalion (2/9) had 75 percent casualties while the other company suffered 50 percent. The battalion as a whole had 40 percent killed or wounded.[112]

The division spent the remainder of 29 July in consolidation and reorganization of the FBL. Mopping up in the rear and patrolling to the front disclosed few enemy concentrations of any size. But many supply dumps and several air-

---

[107] 21st Mar SAR, 6.
[108] 3d MarDiv SAR, OpNarrative, 6.
[109] *Jones.*

[110] Cushman, *op. cit.*
[111] The ships were maneuvered along the coast to enable them to fire on Japanese defensive positions on the reverse slopes of the plateau. 2/9 SAR, 5.
[112] *Ibid.*

plane parts storage areas were uncovered, one of which held six new undamaged motors.[113]

While this activity progressed, 1/3 received orders to relieve the battered 2d Battalion, 9th Marines. This maneuver was completed by 1800, and 2/9 entrucked to move into an area near the Asan River fork where the unit became division reserve.

Meanwhile, a shift of command had taken place. A division order reassigned Colonel W. Carvel Hall as D–4 and Colonel James A. Stuart (D–3) as commanding officer of the 3d Marines. Lieutenant Colonel Ellsworth N. Murray (D–4) replaced the D–2, Lieutenant Colonel Howard J. Turton who became D–3. Other changes included giving Colonel Robert G. Hunt (Division Inspector) the additional duty of Liaison Officer, IIIAC, and the assigning of Lieutenant Colonel Ralph M. King (in-

fantry operations officer on division staff) to the 9th Marines where he became regimental executive officer. On the same order Major Irving R. Kriendler was listed as taking over as D–1 on 22 July after Lieutenant Colonel White was killed.[114]

Earlier in the afternoon, Admiral Spruance, General H. M. Smith, General Geiger, General Turnage, and General Noble made a hurried inspection tour of the front lines,[115] after which the visiting dignitaries went to Orote Peninsula to witness the flag raising over the old Marine Barracks. (See page 95)

RECONNAISSANCE PATROLS TO THE SOUTH

When the 77th Infantry Division took over the southern beachhead line from the brigade

[113] 3d MarDiv D–2 Periodic Rpt 75.

[114] 3d MarDiv D–1 Jnl.
[115] 3d MarDiv D–3 Jnl.

MAANOT RIDGE is the scene of bivouac of the 2d Battalion, 305th Infantry, first Army unit to see action on Guam. Patrols from this unit and others searched the southern half of the island for signs of Japanese resistance. (Army Photograph.)

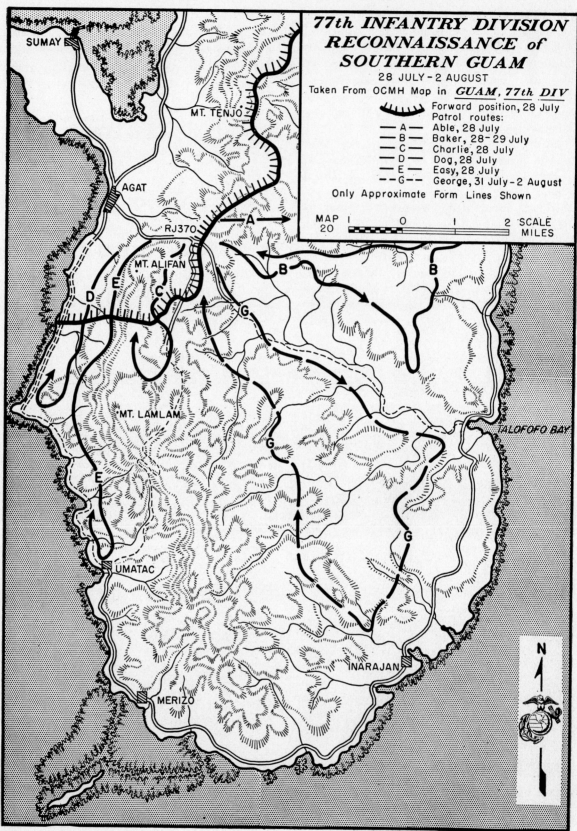

77th INFANTRY DIVISION RECONNAISSANCE of SOUTHERN GUAM

28 JULY - 2 AUGUST

Taken From OCMH Map in *GUAM, 77th DIV*

Forward position, 28 July
Patrol routes:
— A — Able, 28 July
— B — Baker, 28-29 July
— C — Charlie, 28 July
— D — Dog, 28 July
— E — Easy, 28 July
— G — George, 31 July - 2 August

Only Approximate Form Lines Shown

MAP 20   1   0   1   2   SCALE MILES

SUMAY
MT. TENJO
AGAT
RJ370
MT. ALIFAN
MT. LAMLAM
UMATAC
MERIZO
INARAJAN
TALOFOFO BAY

N

on 24 July, it immediately made plans to send patrols to the south and east. Originally this was a precautionary measure to ensure the safety of the perimeter, but General Geiger requested the action be expanded in an attempt to determine the enemy's defensive intentions. The two infantry regiments (305th and 306th) manning the main defenses carried out the early patrols which were limited to 500–1,000 yards to the front.[116]

On 27 July, however, the 77th Reconnaissance Troop, which had been guarding the Maanot Reservoir, received orders from General Bruce to prepare for extensive operations. Intelligence as to what moves the Japanese would make after they had been driven from their beach defenses was lacking, and corps headquarters did not know for certain whether the enemy would elect to defend the northern or southern part of Guam. The corps did not have enough strength to make simultaneous attacks on both ends of the island. Nor could it block off one half and have sufficient strength left to assault one end at a time. From the information expected to be obtained by the patrols, General Geiger could better make a decision concerning the future employment of troops.[117]

About noon on 27 July overlays came in to the 77th Division's Headquarters, detailing the plans and showing the routes to be taken by the reconnaissance patrols. (See Map 20) Five units of five men each, with native guides, would leave at 1300 and penetrate up to seven miles to the south and east. Patrols A and B would proceed from RJ 370 to the east coast, while C, D, and E would move directly south along the ridge line below Mt. Alifan toward Umatac and return.

Only two of the patrols, B and E, covered the entire assigned area; the others had to return because of illness and impassable terrain. Another unit (Patrol G) was dispatched on 30 July to move southeast to Talofofo Bay, then to Port Inarajan, and back across the center of the southeastern part of the island. All patrols had returned with negative reports on enemy contacts by 31 July. The native Guamanians encountered reported that the Japanese had moved to the north and that only small groups of 10–15 of the enemy remained in the south.[118]

The aggressive patrolling of the 305th Infantry between 24–27 July indicated the area around Mt. Tenjo was lightly defended by the Japanese. Consequently, on 27 July General Bruce requested he be permitted to seize Mt. Tenjo. Permission granted, he ordered Company A, 305th to reconnoiter the mountain and to occupy its crest if the enemy offered only light resistance. By 0830 on 28 July, Company A had reached the top of Mt. Tenjo without meeting opposition. At 1500 that afternoon, 2/307 took over the defense of the hill mass, and it was these troops that tied in with the 3d Marine Division, thus securing the III Corps FBL.[119] The ground work had now been laid for Phase II, the attack to the east and northeast.

---

[116] 77th InfDiv G–3 Jnl.

[117] Ltr Col W. F. Coleman to CMC, 1947, hereinafter cited as *Coleman*.

[118] 77th InfDiv OpRpt, 3; LtCol F. C. Bridgewater, "Reconnaissance on Guam," *The Cavalry Jnl*, May–June 1945, 46–48.

[119] 77th InfDiv G–3 Jnl.

CHAPTER V Other Parts of the Team

The effective support given IIIAC units throughout the Guam campaign drew unqualified praise from the ranking survivor of the Japanese garrison, Lieutenant Colonel Hideyuki Takeda. After witnessing the overwhelming power of the air and naval units of the Southern Attack Force he concluded that it was no longer possible to defend an island properly with isolated ground troops. This tribute by the operations officer of the main defensive force on Guam adds emphasis to American reports that all supporting arms available to corps functioned with precision and produced excellent results.

NAVAL GUNFIRE SUPPORT

The continuous 13-day bombardment of Guam prior to W-Day by the battleships, cruisers, and destroyers under Admiral Conolly has been cited as the most systematically conducted "shoot" in the Pacific up to that time. The proximity of the Saipan task groups with additional gunfire support vessels made a greater supply of ammunition available to TF 53. An indication of the volume of fire delivered during this period is shown by the following table of ammunition expenditure:

836	rounds of	16-inch
5,422	rounds of	14-inch
3,862	rounds of	8-inch
2,430	rounds of	6-inch
16,214	rounds of	5-inch [1]

---

[1] TF 56 NGF Rpt, 71.

As to the effect of the continuous pounding, in the opinion of the naval gunfire officer for IIIAC, Major William M. Gilliam:

The extended period for bombardment plus a system for keeping target damage reports accounted for practically every known Japanese gun that could seriously endanger our landings. When the morning of the landing arrived, it was known that the assault troops would meet little resistance.[2]

At the next higher command level, Admiral Conolly's staff believed "that not one fixed gun was left in commission on the west coast that was of greater size than a machine gun." [3] The above estimates of the damage already done to the enemy installations did not lessen the W-Day scheduled fires which let loose with a barrage that lasted until 90 minutes after H-Hour. Originally scheduled fires had been set to last until H-plus 30 minutes but after studying the results of naval gunfire at Saipan Admiral Conolly decided to lengthen that part of the gunfire plan. This covered the period between the landing and the establishment of fire control agencies ashore.[4] During the day, 21 July, 342 rounds of 16-inch, 1,152 rounds of 14-inch, 1,332 rounds of 8-inch; 2,430 rounds of 6-inch, 13,130 rounds of 5-inch, and 9,000 rounds of 4.5-inch rockets were hurled into the landing areas.[5]

---

[2] IIIAC SAR, NGF Rpt, 3.
[3] CTF 53, OpRpt, NGF Comments, 11b.
[4] Gilliam.
[5] TF 56 NGF Rpt, 72.

From the Japanese viewpoint naval gunfire had been effective but not as completely destructive as the above reports indicate. One Marine officer who landed five minutes after H-Hour later wrote:

I was particularly impressed to see Japanese soldiers still alive right on the landing beaches after almost 24 hours of incessant bombardment by naval gunfire . . .[6]

Of even more significance is the enemy analysis of damage done:

Fortifications

1. Construction consisting of ordinary simple buildings reinforced on an emergency basis which received direct hits were completely destroyed.
2. Field positions hit by shells were completely destroyed. Over 50% of all installations built in the seashore area of the landing beaches were demolished. (Since there was much use of sand, they offered little resistance.)
3. Half permanent positions in which the hard agent *cascajo* [7] was used and which were reinforced with concrete about 50cm thick remained in good condition except in cases of direct hits. Positions receiving direct hits were more than half destroyed.
4. Permanent construction (concrete over one meter thick) positions which received direct hits without exception remained perfectly sound.

Defense Installations

1. All naval gun emplacements in the open were completely demolished before the landings. About half of the guns emplaced in caves with limited fields of fire remained operational, but soon after opening fire at the time of the landings the cave entrances were demolished and the guns could fire little.
2. Antiaircraft artillery sustained damage from naval gunfire only once.
3. Communications installations were not damaged, since they were constructed in dead spaces where they could not receive direct hits.
4. Harbor installations received almost no damage.
5. Only once did water pipes receive a direct hit.
6. Power installations were not damaged because generating was done in caves.
7. Most boats in military use were sunk, but by strafing rather than by naval gunfire.

Cases Where Naval Gunfire Had No Effect

1. Antiaircraft gun positions were operational until the very last.

[6] *Kunz.*
[7] A type of coral used as gravel in concrete construction.

LCI GUNBOAT fires rocket barrage against Japanese positions behind Agana holding up the advance of the 3d Marine Division. (Navy Photograph.)

2. There was no effect against construction in valleys or in the jungle. Also there was very little effect against the interior of the island over four kilometers from the shore line.
3. Incendiary shells started fires in grassy areas and exposed our positions but had almost no demolition or antipersonnel effect.[8]

Whatever the exact extent of the damage caused by naval gunfire, its success is best measured by the fact that most enemy guns were silenced during the critical period that Marines were first establishing themselves ashore. In addition, naval gunfire contributed considerably to the demoralization of the Japanese. A staff officer for the 29th Division reports:

After several days there were scattered outbreaks of serious loss of spirit. After another week of bombardment, as in the period before the landings, there were some whose spirit deteriorated so that they could not perform their duties in a positive manner. This was especially true of the units on the landing fronts. However, in contrast to such personnel whose courage fell, there was a minority who were just as though insane with the remarkable power of their spiritual strength.[9]

[8] *Takeda Letter.*
[9] *Ibid.*

Probably the best over-all opinion that the enemy had of naval gunfire was expressed by one of the prisoners of war captured on Guam:

We had been thinking that the Japanese might win through a night counterattack, but when the star shells came over one after the other we would only use our men as human bullets and there were many useless casualties and no chance of success . . . I was horrified by the number of deaths on our side due to the naval gunfire which continued every day.[10]

There is one thing on which both the Americans and Japanese did agree: that night illumination, using star shells, was an important factor in Phase I operations. The procedure of assigning each front line battalion a ship for illumination and other fires furnished that unit with the means of sighting and stopping any counterattack that might develop. In addition, it provided light for organizing positions when it was impossible to accomplish the task prior to darkness. Star shells proved so beneficial to infantry commanders that almost all recommended that a more adequate supply be made available in the future.[11]

Shore fire control parties not only conducted illumination firing but also effectively employed naval gunfire on call, preparation, and harassing missions. The split landing resulted in there being no single control agency either ashore or afloat. As a consequence, different agencies directed fire support activities and there was some loss of control, coordination, and flexibility. Call fire was good but limited by the lack of training in the Shore Fire Control Section of the 3d JASCO (Joint Assault Signal Company).[12] Nevertheless, within the limitations indicated naval gunfire rendered very effective support whenever ground troops requested fire.[13]

---

[10] *CominCh P-007*, Chap 3, 13–14.

[11] *Ibid.*, Chap 3, 11

[12] The 3d JASCO was not scheduled to complete training at AmphibTraComd, PacFlt until too late to be employed on Guam. Such a need was felt for the JASCO, however, that it was made available in a state of limited training and attached to the 3d MarDiv for the operation. TF 56 NGF Rpt, 67.

[13] *Ibid.*, 138.

AIR SUPPORT

Until noon nothing unusual occurred, but a formation of about 30 planes strafed and bombed the airfield and other places throughout the afternoon. I realized that finally the enemy striking force was closing in.

This entry on 30 April 1944 in the diary of Lieutenant Kanemitsu Kurokawa was the first of many indicating the unwelcome visits of Admiral Mitscher's carrier planes over Guam. A month later so frustrated had the lieutenant become by the unceasing air bombardment that he wrote he now understood, in view of the lack of friendly planes overhead, the meaning of constant requests in the Japanese press for increased aircraft production to send even one extra plane to the front lines.[14]

Higher ranking Japanese officers, however, concerned themselves more with how the air strikes delayed defense preparations. According to the 29th's operations officer:

[Before the landing] The fact that Japanese air forces were as nothing against American air power (in quantity) certainly had its effect on morale. But this effect was not great because casualties were avoided through use of every inch of the terrain. However, a very heavy blow was the fact that transportation and work on positions could not be conducted in the daytime because ground movements were severely restricted. Daylight movements [after the landing] could not be carried out in cases such as advancing reserves for changing operational maneuvers, causing situations disadvantageous for the direction of combat to arise everywhere. Because of this we could not employ effective strength quickly, and [attempts to] recover the situation and counterattacks made at opportune times ended in complete failure.[15]

Confirmation of the telling effect on both personnel and emplacements of continual air strikes is pointed out by the following extracts from Japanese diaries and prisoner of war interrogations:

. . . The enemy, circling overhead, bombed our airfield the whole day long. When evening came our carriers bombers returned, [airgroups from carriers returning to Guam to refuel and rearm during the Battle of the Philippine Sea] but the airfield had just been destroyed by the enemy and they could not land. Having neither fuel nor ammunition the 15 or 16 planes were unable to land and had to crash on [Orote Airfield]. It was certainly a shame. I was unable to

---

[14] CinCPac-CinCPOA Item 11,943—Diary of Lt Kanemitsu Kurokawa, IJA.

[15] *Takeda Letter.*

watch dry-eyed. "The tragedy of war" was never so real. . . . Towards evening enemy planes appeared and halted our construction. . . . As usual, the enemy planes attacked furiously, so we could not venture out. . . . Our position demolished today by bombs.

On the other hand, the Joint Expeditionary Force Commander considered the close air support given front line troops on Guam "not very good."[16] In the early stages of the landing there appeared to be a reluctance on the part of Commander Support Aircraft (CSA) to turn over aircraft to the control of battalion air liaison parties. In the later days of Phase I, when it was demonstrated that by so doing no time was lost in carrying out the mission, pilots conducted closer and more accurate strikes.[17] Even with this increased precision, the 3d Marine Division's operations officer wrote that "pilot error, resulting in strafing or bombing of our own troops, did not improve the troops' confidence in close air support."[18]

The same unit reported that it had been necessary to cancel some missions because of the lapse of time between requests and the execution of strikes. This lag varied from nine minutes to five hours and 30 minutes, with the average for 31 missions being one hour and a half. Similar complaints came from the brigade, which added that delays were also caused by radio nets being overcrowded. Use of the same frequency by both the brigade and the division, separated by a hill mass which prevented them from hearing each other, made it extremely difficult to coordinate requests.[19]

To General Geiger, the answer lay in employing Marine aviation to a greater extent. He cited the fact that "the use of Marine Bombing Squadrons for close (100 to 500 yds) air support of ground troops has been clearly demonstrated on several occasions,"[20] as his main argument. This opinion was supported by the repeated requests of his troop commanders for Marine aviation to furnish the close support. General

TORPEDO BOMBERS move in formation toward the Agat Beach to support the landing of the 1st Provisional Marine Brigade. (Navy Photograph.)

Holland Smith made the same recommendation after the operation and set down specific details of his plan. He suggested that "sufficient air groups be designated and trained as direct support groups and be assigned to CVE-type carriers." For this specialized task, General Smith concluded that Marines should be used:

The troop experience of senior Marine pilots combined with the indoctrination of new pilots in infantry tactics should insure greater cooperation and coordination between air and ground units.[21]

ARTILLERY IN THE FIGHT

The Guam operation was memorable as the first campaign in which the Marines placed a sizable corps artillery unit of their own in the field.[22] Of equal importance is the fact that during this operation the forerunner of the present FSCC (Fire Support Coordination Center) was used extensively. The corps NGF officer and air officer worked together in the same tent, using a common situation map. In turn, a direct telephone line connected them to the corps artillery fire direction center. In this way the three major supporting arms achieved close cooperation and coordination.[23]

[16] Ltr Adm R. K. Turner to Maj C. W. Hoffman, 13 Mar52.
[17] Ltr Col J. R. Spooner to author, 12Aug52.
[18] 3d MarDiv SAR, Air Support Comments, 1.
[19] 1st ProvMarBrig OpRpt, 14.
[20] IIIAC SAR, Air Rpt, 5.

[21] TF 56 Air Rpt, 6.
[22] VAC artillery battalions participated in the Saipan operation, but were attached to the 10th and 14th Mar. Corps artillery support was supplied by battalions of the Army's XXIV Corps Arty.
[23] *Henderson.*

GUN CREW swabs the bore of No. 4 Gun, Battery C, 7th 155mm Gun Battalion after firing in support of the 3d Division beachhead.

Within the artillery set-up itself, General Geiger assigned operational control over all artillery on the island to the Commanding General, IIIAC Artillery. This tied all units together, enabling fires to be massed quickly and reinforcing missions assigned with dispatch. In addition, priorities on ammunition, transportation, and position areas were easily controlled. However, as a result of the piecemeal unloading and landing of the 155mm units of corps, the artillery commander felt the maximum efficiency was not obtained from the big guns and howitzers during the first two days on Guam.[24] Of this situation General del Valle later wrote:

The unloading of Corps Arty was completely out of control of the Commanding General, Corps Arty and at variance with the planned scheme of unloading and entry into action. . . . The loading and unloading must be under control of the Corps Arty Commander and in accordance with the projected employment. . . . As long as this control is vested in other officers, not especially concerned with, nor interested in, the operation of Corps Arty, satisfactory results will not be achieved.[25]

On the other hand, even though loaded in many ships of the convoy,[26] the 12th Marines and the brigade's artillery did not meet with such difficulties. The DUKW's and LVT's, loaded with the howitzers and sufficient men and ammunition to start firing, moved ashore soon after H-Hour. Although both the division and the brigade had some of their amphibious

---

[24] IIIAC Arty SAR, Enclosure B.

[25] *Ibid.,* 18.

[26] LtCol A. L. Bowser's 3d Bn, 12th Mar landed from nine LST's, two AP's, and one AK. *Bowser.*

trucks stranded on the reefs during the landing, commanders were unanimous in their praise of the vehicle. As soon as the "A-frame" unloaded the howitzers, the vehicles returned to the ships to get more shells to bring into the battery positions.

In addition to solving the problem of maintaining an adequate supply of ammunition around the firing pieces during the early phases of the amphibious assault, the DUKW also supplied the solution to another difficulty. Previous thinking on equipping the artillery regiment with 105mm howitzers had been tempered by the lack of a suitable vehicle to get such weapons into the fight early. However, as a result of the DUKW's satisfactory performance at Guam, Colonel John B. Wilson, commanding officer of the 12th Marines, recommended that the remaining 75mm pack howitzer units be given 105mm weapons. This would not only give the regiment more power and flexibility, but would do away with the necessity for handling both 105mm and 75mm shells.[27]

Communications between forward observers and the fire direction centers proved to be adequate, with the SCR 300 once more giving reliable radio service. As usual, most of the traffic was carried over telephone lines, and the use of the forward switching central[28] proved to be the answer to keeping artillery fire missions coming through from front line observers.

Inasmuch as no Japanese planes penetrated the air cover over Saipan to get to Guam,[29] the anti-aircraft batteries of the 9th and 14th Defense Battalions and the Army's 7th AAA (AW) Battalion were not tested. Nevertheless, commanders employed all weapons in support of ground troops. On the left flank of the corps the 3d Marine Division made full use of the fire power of the 20mms and 40mms in reducing the Fonte position. Shells from guns emplaced on the shore near Agat and on Cabras

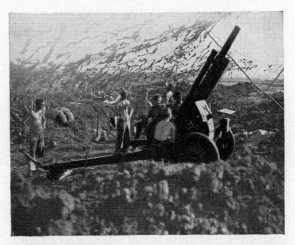

CAMOUFLAGE NETTING covers the gun pit of a 105mm howitzer as a 12th Marines crew prepares to place high-angle fire on Japanese positions.

Island pounded both faces of Orote Peninsula, while searchlights of the 14th enabled night surveillance of possible water routes of withdrawal.

The over-all effectiveness of artillery during the assault phase is found in General Shepherd's remarks at the conclusion of the campaign:

It is the opinion of the Commanding General that artillery was the most effective weapon employed during the operation. Close support was given to the infantry in both attack and defense and harassing fires at night were particularly effective. The troops have great confidence in the power of our own artillery. . . . The groupment of battalions and massing of fires in vital zones of action greatly assisted the advance of the assault troops against strong enemy resistance from well-prepared emplacements. The 105-mm Howitzers were particularly effective. Reports from prisoners of war indicate that artillery fire has a great demoralizing effect on their troops.[30]

ENGINEER OPERATIONS

As was usual throughout the Pacific theater campaigns, engineers on Guam carried out with precision their endless and dangerous duties during the assault phase. The unspectacular nature of this work did not lessen its value to the corps mission. The absolute necessity of

---

[27] 12th Mar SAR, 5.

[28] This system established a switching central in the vicinity of the infantry regimental CP from which wire was laid forward to observers and trunk lines run back to the fire direction center. Forward observers and liaison wire teams were able to maintain the shorter line much more easily, which resulted in better wire communications to the firing elements.

[29] Ltr Col E. O. Price to CMC, 26Aug52.

[30] 1st ProvMarBrig OpRpt, 18. As an indication of the effect of artillery on the Japanese, a POW from an infantry company of 2/38 stated that his unit was nearly wiped out by artillery after the landing. IIIAC POW Interrogation 24.

SEABEES on bulldozers prepare the bed of a new road linking the Agat Bay area with the IIIAC front lines.

maintaining supply routes, disarming mines, clearing road blocks, and establishing water points can leave little doubt of the engineer's important role in any tactical scheme of maneuver.

If any one job assigned to the engineer units can be considered more important than another during Phase I, it was maintaining an adequate network of roads. The existing improved roads disintegrated in one day under the traffic of a single division. When of necessity both the 3d and 77th Divisions used the same highway, the situation became critical at times. To add to the difficulties, several factors hindered construction of new supply roads. First, the restriction of cargo space limited the amount of engineering equipment lifted to the target area. Second, the addition of the Army division without adding heavy construction equipment increased the demands on existing graders beyond their capacity. Finally, engineers found it difficult to place new coral surfacing during the many rainy days. The mixing of relatively small amounts of mud prevented the coral from binding together, resulting in an increased depth of muck on the road.[31]

Even the versatility of the bulldozer could not supply the answer to road maintenance and drainage. As a result the corps engineer recommended that in the future:

. . . a minimum of one engineer battalion with heavy grading equipment (a Naval Construction Battalion, a Marine Separate Engineer Battalion, or an Army Aviation Engineer Battalion) be included in the assault echelon of each Marine or Army division, or fraction thereof, in the assault forces.[32]

The bulldozers, however, proved so valuable that corps artillery was requested to turn over most of its organic dozers[33] until gun emplacements had to be dug. This enabled the engi-

[31] IIIAC SAR, SerGruRpt, 5B.

[32] *Ibid.*, 6B.

[33] These dozers were prime mover tractors equipped with angle dozer blades and could be used for the dual purpose of moving artillery pieces and digging gun pits.

POLE AND SATCHEL CHARGES are carried by a 19th Marines patrol moving forward to investigate a cave reported by 21st Marines scouts in the vicinity of the Japanese division command post.

neers to complete work on the brigade beaches expeditiously, and as soon as the 155mm units landed, their equipment was returned.[34]

During the initial phase all units of the 19th Marines (engineers, pioneers, and attached Seabees) except the Headquarters and Service Company were assigned to combat teams. Brigade carried out a similar plan and both units employed personnel in the same fashion. The Seabee units worked the beach areas, being charged with the responsibility of maintaining the main supply road. Marine engineers supported the infantry regiments to which attached, and in addition occupied defensive positions at night to back up weak spots in the thinly-held front lines.

In the 3d Division's zone, the 19th Marines formed the backbone of the Division Shore Party. Lieutenant Colonel Robert E. Fojt, the engineer's commanding officer, also served as Division Shore Party commander while his battalion commanders headed the regimental shore parties in addition to their regular duties. Each infantry regiment had as part of its task organization a pioneer company and a Seabee company; these two units furnished the ele-

ments around which the three regimental shore parties were organized and operated.[35]

In the 77th Division, the 302d Engineer (Combat) Battalion regained control of its companies upon the landing of division headquarters. The 302d then assigned missions according to the needs of the infantry regiments in assault. Three other combat engineer battalions (132d, 233d, and 242d) were attached to the division solely for shore party activities.[36]

To say that the engineers and pioneers were wholly responsible for the smooth flow of supplies during the first phase of the Guam campaign would be somewhat exaggerated. It cannot be questioned, however, that their work greatly facilitated this tremendous task.

SHORE PARTY ACTIVITIES

The other part of the combat-service team came in for its share of acclaim, too. General Geiger commented that "both the division and brigade not only kept assault troops constantly

[35] *Williams.*
[36] 77th InfDiv OpRpt, DivEngRpt, 1.

DYNAMITE STICKS tossed by Marine engineers explode as they seal another cave in the continuous task of silencing bypassed enemy positions.

[34] *Henderson.*

supplied but unloaded the entire assault echelon of shipping over assault beaches prior to W-plus 7." [37]

The accomplishment of this task was in the main the result of the ingenuity of the shore party personnel from assault and garrison units. Since the 25 cranes, mounted on pontoon barges offshore, assigned for transferring supplies at the reef's edge were not sufficient, other means of doing the job had to be devised. Piers were improvised by tying ship's life rafts and rubber boats together, anchoring them and laying dunnage on top. Landing craft then approached the piers, dropped their ramps, and had their cargo manhandled onto rafts which troops floated ashore. By this and other such impro-

visations an average of 6,650 tons per day passed over the corps beaches during the first eight days. [38]

In order to expedite unloading activity in the brigade zone, General Geiger had included a replacement unit with the assault force. This organization, the 1st Provisional Replacement Company (11 officers, 383 enlisted men), was the forerunner of the replacement battalions that accompanied other combat units in later Pacific operations. The men operated as part of the shore party in the vital first stages of the compaign and then were fed into front line companies as replacements for casualties. [39]

Another reason why unloading progressed so

---

[37] IIIAC SAR, SerGruRpt, 1C.

[38] TF 56 TQM Rpt, 26.
[39] IIIAC SAR, Personnel Rpt, 1; *Scheyer*.

MEN OF THE SHORE PARTY roll gasoline drums through the water over the reef toward a temporary dump on the beach.

WAR DOGS and their handlers accompany advancing troops of the 3d Division as they move forward from the northern beachhead.

rapidly was that Admiral Conolly permitted some of his ships to continue discharging cargo throughout the first night.[40] Thereafter, when commanders assured Conolly that sufficient materials were ashore for any emergency, unloading activities ceased between midnight and 0530. This did not affect the shore party personnel on the beach, however. Work continued on an around-the-clock basis except when the tactical situation required the men to occupy defensive positions.

Initially, because of the restricted beachhead and the many rice paddies, it was difficult to find suitable dump areas. Moreover, the number of available vehicles of all types did not meet requirements. The high casualties of LVT's during the assault landing reduced the original inadequate allotment. And with only 64 of the assigned 100 DUKW's in operation at the end of the assault phase, a similar situation existed with these vehicles.[41] When the 77th Infantry Division moved ashore without amphibious vehicles, an additional burden had to be carried by those already on the scene. Of this particular situation, the operations officer of the 4th Amphibian Tractor Battalion recalls:

... I can remember long lines of GI's from the reef to the beach trying to bring in even a bare minimum of supplies for their troops. Our CO noticed this

---

[40] CTF 53 OpRpt, OpLog, 35A.

[41] IIIAC SAR, SerGruRpt, 6.

condition and immediately contacted their Shore Party Commander who literally wept over the offer of part of our LVT's to help him out. (As our supply problem was well licked we could divert LVT's to aid the Army with no loss of efficiency to our main effort.) This diverting of LVT's for Army use was a godsend to their supply problem for soon sufficient quantities were moving ashore to bring their dumps up to safe levels.[42]

This type of cooperation by all hands helped to overcome the transportation situation and surmount all other supply problems that arose during the landing. As a result, one author wrote, "As in other phases of the operation, unloading of supplies was conducted in general more expeditiously on Guam than on Saipan." He adequately summed up the over-all logistics activities by concluding that, "with . . . few exceptions, the supply system on Guam worked smoothly and efficiently." [43]

WAR DOGS, MILITARY POLICE, AND COMMUNICATORS

There were conflicting opinions as to the usefulness of the war dogs during the initial phases of the campaign. The 4th Marines, the only unit in the brigade zone having a platoon of dogs attached, found little use for the animals. When brigade initiated patrolling a squad or a fire team had one dog and his handler attached; used in this manner the canines proved of some help. They were not infallible, however, and in several instances enemy troops went undetected and surprised the patrols.[44]

In the northern sector the 3d Division had a provisional war dog company of two platoons. It found the dogs a welcome addition to protective forces and particularly effective when used for night security. During the early stages of the fighting the dogs were nervous and inclined to bark if the enemy came too close, but handlers quickly overcame this habit by teaching the animals to alert silently. Even before this fault was corrected, their mere presence on the front lines had a good effect on troop morale. Men felt secure and could spend more restful nights when not actually on watch.

---

[42] Ltr Maj R. J. Parker to author, 6Feb52.

[43] J. A. Isley and P. A. Crowl, *The U. S. Marines And Amphibious War*, (Princeton, 1951), 387–389.

[44] 1st ProvMarBrig OpRpt, 13.

WIREMEN close behind assault troops lay a line to a forward command post.

Because of the excellent communications, only one messenger dog was used, and it carried word to an isolated outpost. But troops found a new use for the animals when Marines encountered enemy caves near the beach. A Doberman was sent into a cave and if it met no resistance a scout followed to investigate more thoroughly. Even though the animals had not been trained for this duty the most vicious ones proved reliable.[45]

Another task assigned to the four-footed fighters was working with the military police companies to patrol areas, protect supply dumps, guard trails, and insure protection of other installations. This released regular MP personnel, permitting them to carry out other duties.

Initially the most important work of the MP's was to maintain traffic discipline in the beach areas and guard supplies on shore. Later their efforts were turned toward keeping vehicles moving on the crowded main road. As

---

[45] 2d and 3d War Dog Plats SAR, 1–4.

usual, MP's guarded all prisoner of war stockades and also maintained a protective watch over civilian camps.

In addition to all other services during Phase I, the MP's rendered invaluable aid to communications personnel by constantly warning vehicle drivers of vital telephone wires that had not yet been overheaded. Generally, communications functioned well after W-Day, but at times there was some delay in wire repairs because of the shortage of wiremen.[46]

The only other complaint was that the long voyage had caused idle storage batteries to lose their charges. At first this created some concern, but the situation was quickly rectified and thereafter radio communications proved reliable. The use of Navajo talkers[47] kept radio transmission interception at a minimum, but the Japanese attempts at jamming were more successful. However, this interference proved more of a harassment to operators than a stumbling block to the accomplishment of their mission.

---

[46] IIIAC SAR, SigCommRpt, 1.

[47] These were Indians of the Navajo tribe especially recruited and trained by the Marine Corps to operate voice radio nets. They used their own language, completely incomprehensible to the Japanese, to transmit vital messages.

USS SOLACE bringing the first ship borne whole blood bank into a combat area, as it arrived off Guam on 24 July to begin evacuation of casualties. (Navy Photograph.)

The system of having division wire teams work with infantry regiments paid high dividends. Formerly these teams would advance along hastily laid ground wires of the battalions. These lines then became circuits between regiment and division and presented a maintenance problem that lowered efficiency of wire communications. On Guam division teams moved with the regiments and kept two overhead lines close behind the front in the direction of anticipated CP displacements. In this manner wire communications were usable more quickly and once established more easily maintained. Corps wiremen advanced with division CP's in the same fashion to keep overhead lines constantly ready for use.[48] As a result of having both radio and wire transmission available most of the time, commanders had few complaints about communication breakdowns during Phase I activities.

MEDICAL EVACUATION

"Too much praise cannot be heaped upon these units for the marvelous performance in the evacuation of casualties."[49] This was the opinion of the 3d Medical Battalion commander

BANDSMEN in their combat role of stretcher bearers carry a wounded Marine down out of the hills.

---

[48] Ltr Col A Sutter to CMC, 25Sept52.

[49] Callaway Study.

CABLE LIFT built by the 19th Marines used to evacuate casualties from the top of the steep cliff in the 21st Marines zone of action.

when he commented on the activities of the shore party medical sections at Guam. So effective were these units that less than an hour after the first troops landed, casualties had been received aboard the APA's.[50]

As in other Pacific campaigns, naval corpsmen and army aidmen with the assault infantry units forged the first link in the chain of evacuation. After treatment by these front line medical personnel, the wounded moved to the rear as rapidly as possible. Ambulance jeeps carried much of the load, but when the terrain proved impassable for vehicles, manpower was employed. Marine bandsmen who put aside their instruments to perform their combat mission as stretcher bearers bore the brunt of this assignment.

On reaching the beach, casualties were loaded

into LVT's and DUKW's and then dispatched by beach medical parties to APA's and LST's which had been equipped and staffed to handle them. Although the LVT proved adequate, the DUKW gave smoother handling to the more seriously wounded. In spite of the fact that neither the LST nor the APA is designed for handling many casualties, 2,552 were on board these ships on W-plus 8 when they left the area.[51]

In addition to these ship evacuees, two hospital ships carried 1,132 wounded to rear areas during Phase I operations.[52] The USS *Solace* arrived on W-plus 3 and brought the first known blood bank to be waterborne to a fighting front.[53] She departed two days later with

---

[50] IIIAC SAR, MedRpt, 3.

[51] TF 56 MedRpt, 2A.

[52] *Ibid.*

[53] At Eniwetok, Capt John T. Bennet, (MC), USN, the *Solace's* Medical Officer, decided to attempt to

approximately 428 litter and 153 ambulatory cases. The USS *Bountiful* steamed into the area on W-plus 7 (28 July) and received orders to anchor off the southern beaches. The next day she moved to the vicinity of the 3d Marine Division's beaches to complete loading the 551 patients she would carry to the Marshalls.[54]

The stark whiteness of the hospital ships lying off shore, with their distinctive red cross, was a great comfort to the man in the front lines. To him they were a symbol of cleanliness and reassurance that casualties would receive the best medical treatment in the world. Coupled with this was his faith in the corpsmen and aidmen whom he had seen day after day saving many a life at the risk of their own. Much credit must be given to the medical services for the high morale of the men on Guam and the aggressiveness they showed in securing the FBL.

take whole blood into the combat area on board the ship. Success of the experiment depended on the ability of the living blood to survive the disturbance created by the engines and the pitching and rolling of the ship. On 21 July volunteers were requested from the Marine garrison and over 300 men from the 10th AAA Bn (Reinf) came forward. Of this number, 100 were chosen and the following morning, 22 July, the ship set sail for Guam with a 100-pint blood bank. The experiment was a success and at Guam there was ample whole blood for required transfusions. 10th AAA Bn (Reinf) WD, July 1944, 3.

[54] CTF 53 OpRpt, MedComments, 21.

CHAPTER **VI**

Into the Jungle

Looking back on Phase I operations, the men of the III Amphibious Corps could view their accomplishments with satisfaction. They had executed a difficult landing across a wide, dangerous reef in the face of a well-organized Japanese force concentrated, as expected, in the Asan, Orote, and Agat areas. The costly, bitter, often hand-to-hand struggle that ensued dealt a death blow to any hopes that General Takashina had of driving the Americans off Guam.[1] There now remained little for the surviving half of the original Imperial garrison to do but fight a futile delaying action to the north.

Marines and soldiers now held the entire southern half of the island. Apra Harbor was once more in American possession and already in the process of being developed into a forward fleet anchorage. The airfield on Orote Peninsula had been made operational for light planes, and would shortly be ready for planes from MAG–21 to fly close support strikes over the front lines.

To date the operation had been one of fighting an uphill struggle over some of the most rugged and densely wooded terrain in the Pacific. It had been a campaign of maneuver with units being shifted from one front to the other. Each tactical situation was met with the number of battalions required for the job, regardless of the unit's parent organizations. The flexibility of General Geiger's plans had paid off well.

The turning point of the campaign, securing the FBL, saw the Guamanians beginning to flock to the protection of the Americans. Corps estimated that military agencies had 1,331 civilians under their care by 31 July. The number had swelled to 5,530 by 2 August and two days later it had leaped to 12,100.[2] Unfortunately, the combat units were ill prepared to handle this tremendous civilian problem. However, after the treatment the Japanese had given the Guamanians, they appreciated any help offered. Before long civil affairs sections took over and brought the situation under control.

General Turnage sent a message to his troops on 30 July commending them for their fine work during the past fighting, but at the same time he pointed out the possibility of heavy resistance in and north of Agana.[3] From positions on the commanding ground of Fonte-Chachao-Alutom-Tenjo, men of the 3d Marine Division and the Army's 77th Division could

---

[1] Units of IIIAC reported 989 KIA, 4,836 WIA, and 302 MIA from H-Hour to 2400, 30Jul44. During the same period counted enemy dead totaled 6,205; there were 50 POW's and several thousand enemy were estimated to be sealed in caves. Also, an undetermined number still lay unburied in areas recently captured. IIIAC C–1 and C–2 Jnls; 3d Mar Div WD, July 1944, 12.

[2] IIIAC C–1 Jnl.
[3] 3d MarDiv D–1 Jnl.

get a bird's-eye view of the terrain they would soon be fighting over. (See Map 21, Map Section)

Across the Fonte Ravine, immediately to their front, lay the rubble of the capital, Agana. Behind it stretched a marsh area covered with cogon grass and weeds 15–20 feet high. From these lowlands a broad limestone plateau rose from an elevation of 100 feet in the center to 600 feet near the end of the island.

Dense jungle consisting of a maze of tree-like plants and undergrowth covered this sloping terrain. Fields and roads left idle had become overgrown with weeds, trailing vines, and underbrush that had grown to a height of six to eight feet. Troop movements away from the established roads or trails would be next to impossible. Jutting above the landscape were the bare slopes of Mt. Santa Rosa and the thickly covered crests of Mt. Barrigada and northernmost Mt. Machanao. It was quite evident that the terrain would continue to hinder military activities during the second phase of the operation.[4]

ATTACK PREPARATIONS

The period 29–30 July was spent in resting, reorganizing, and preparing for the coming attack. The 3d Marine Division and the Army's 77th sent patrols far to their front in an effort to determine the strength of the enemy and get a first-hand look at the terrain. Individual Marines and soldiers improved their positions and gave weapons a much needed going over. For the first time since W-Day, Marines stopped to wash, shave, and get into fresh clothes.

During this rest on Fonte Plateau the men witnessed one of the most unusual sights of the Pacific War. There can be little question that the unstable situation of the Japanese called for some master stroke to restore organization and morale. It is questionable, however, if the full dress parade in Agana, staged in full view of the Marines, was the answer. Decked in full combat regalia, the unpredictable Nipponese marching with militant precision made an impressive sight. But the brilliantly polished bayonets and Samurai swords did not bewilder the alert fighting men on the ridge to the point

GUAMANIANS, guided by an MP, move down a road outside of Agana to the temporary refugee camp where they will be fed and housed.

of inactivity. Forward observers quickly called for an artillery concentration, but it fell too late to hit the formation that dispersed as rapidly as it had appeared.[5]

On the more serious side, during these two days (29–30 July) unloading had progressed so satisfactorily that the Division Shore Party was deactivated at 1600 on 30 July.[6] All men from division and the garrison forces assigned to unloading operations returned to their parent organizations. The 19th Marines now assumed control of shore party activities. This release of riflemen to the 3d Marines enabled the regiment to rebuild its badly depleted assault units.

In an effort to obtain a last minute check on terrain and enemy, the 3d Division's Reconnaissance Company sent two patrols well forward of front lines on 30 July. The only enemy activity observed was some movement on the airstrip east of Agana. After being over the ground, the patrols reported it would be impossible to build supply roads behind the 9th and 21st Marines.[7] As a result, the coast highway would have to carry the entire supply load in addition to necessary troop traffic.

[5] *3d MarDiv History,* 157.
[6] 3d MarDiv Jnl.
[7] 3d MarDiv SAR, IntelRpt, Patrol Rpts 1 and 2.

[4] *WD Survey,* 3–12.
250254°—53——9

With heavy foliage concealing enemy movements, the exact location of their next stand was unknown. Intelligence reports indicated Japanese concentrations in the Sinajana-Yona area and suggested the advance probably would encounter defensive positions near the Agana-Pago Bay Road. Of the 8,500 troops now estimated to be available to Japanese commanders to defend northern Guam, only 6,000 were believed to be combat troops, the remainder being labor personnel.[8]

This figure later proved to be very accurate; the actual location of enemy defenses was somewhat different. After machine-gun fire killed General Takashina on 28 July (about 1400) as he tried to leave his Fonte CP, General Obata, the 31st Army commander, took direct control of the remaining forces.[9] Still following Takashina's plan of fighting a war of maneuver, Obata ordered a general withdrawal to the Mt. Santa Rosa area for the final defensive stand on Guam. To protect this area by fighting a delay action, he established two strong positions about six miles forward of his main defenses. By daybreak of 31 July the right sector unit was deployed in the vicinity of Finegayan, the other in the left sector near Mt. Barrigada.[10]

During the move of the 29th Division to its new defensive area around Mt. Santa Rosa, men of the unit celebrated the anniversary of its organization: "In an environment how different from last year," wrote one of the Imperial officers. "I was deeply moved. There was only a little *sake* to drink each other's health. The American . . . shelling is awful and a wounded man, Corporal Nakaji, committed suicide." [11]

With General Geiger not certain of just where the corps would encounter the main enemy defenses, his operation order of 30 July outlined a plan to meet with any contingency.

The over-all scheme of maneuver called for cutting the island in half on the general line Agana-Famja-Pago Bay (O-1 line), and then swinging to the northeast for the continuation of the attack. To seize O-1, the 3d Marine Division would swing to the left, capture Agana, also that portion of the Agana-Pago Bay Road in zone, and maintain contact with the Army division on the right. From its present positions along the Tenjo-Alifan Range the 77th would have to move nearly ten miles to take its part of the O-1 line.

The boundary between the divisions extended from Mt. Alutom, along the Sigua River to Lonfit at the O-1 line; from there to Road Crossing 120 on the Agana-Pago Bay Road, and then to Chochogo Village at the O-2. This divided the island approximately in half, putting Agana and the important Tiyan Airfield in the 3d Division's zone of action and Mt. Barrigada and Mt. Santa Rosa in the 77th Division's. (See Map 21, Map Section) Corps set the jump-off time at 0630, 31 July.[12]

To make the 77th available for the operation to the north, corps ordered the 1st Marine Brigade to take over the southern part of the FBL. General Shepherd's units were to protect the force from any Japanese that might be in the south and to make further reconnaissance to determine the presence or absence of the enemy in that area.

Aware of corps' future plans for his 77th Division, General Bruce had started to get his units into position on 29 July in anticipation of the move. The 3d Battalion, 305th went into corps reserve in an assembly area 1,200–1,400 yards northeast of RJ 5 and just south of the old Agat Road. Upon completion of its mission with the 3d Marine Division, 3/307 returned to control of its parent organization but remained in the same defensive positions. By nightfall all of the 307th had reverted to division control, and the 302d Engineer Combat Battalion had started construction of a supply road through the gap between Mt. Tenjo and Mt. Alifan.[13] (See Map 22)

The next day warning orders went out to all units. The 77th's plan called for the 307th to

[8] IIIAC C-2 Periodic Rpt 12.

[9] MajGen Toyashi Shigematsu, commander of the Tumon-Agana-Asan defense sector, next in line to assume division command, was killed during the Fonte action (probably on 26 July). With all of the higher unit commanders killed, General Obata felt he should assume command. *Takeda Letter.*

[10] *Japanese Defense of Guam; Takeda.*

[11] F. Pratt, *The Marine's War*, (New York, 1948), 286.

[12] IIIAC OpOrder 7-44. 30Jul44.

[13] 77th InfDiv OpRpt, 4.

advance eastward and turn north across the Pago River; the 305th would follow, protecting the division's south flank, cross the river, and extend to the east coast. The 306th, reinforced, would pass to the control of the Marine brigade on 31 July. This Army unit would then shift its strength to the left of its sector, and when relieved move east behind the 305th. To round out the plan, the 902d Field Artillery Battalion was assigned as direct support of the 307th; all other artillery would be general support.[14] (See Map 23, Map Section)

On the left flank of the corps, the 3d Marine Division's operation plan called for the advance with three regiments abreast: 9th, 21st, and 3d, from right to left. The mission called for seizing the important cross-island Agana-Pago Bay Road and being prepared to continue the attack on order. Initially all air, naval gunfire, and artillery support would be on call. Division reserve would be made up of the depleted 2/9 and the tank battalion which now had all of its tanks back under operational control.[15]

AGANA AND ITS AIRFIELD

While infantry units made their preparations for the attack to the north, artillery and naval gunfire did their share by two days of intense and well-placed interdiction and harassing fires. All road junctions, known and possible assem-

[14] 77th InfDiv OpOrder 4, 30Jul44.
[15] 3d MarDiv OpOrder 8, 30Jul44.

LIEUTENANT GENERAL TAKESHI TAKASHINA, Japanese commander on Guam killed on 28 July while directing the evacuation of the Fonte defensive position.

bly areas, observation points, and other selected targets were kept under constant fire. As a last minute effort to limit Japanese movements,

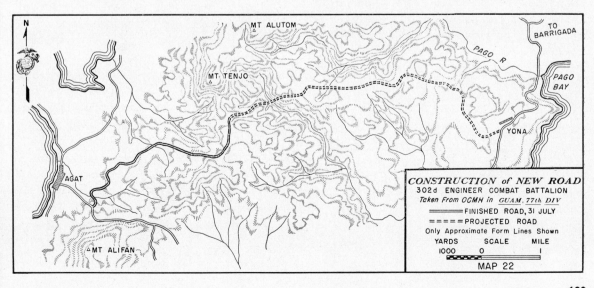

MAP 22

CONSTRUCTION of NEW ROAD
302d ENGINEER COMBAT BATTALION
Taken From OCMH in GUAM, 77th DIV
======= FINISHED ROAD, 31 JULY
===== PROJECTED ROAD
Only Approximate Form Lines Shown
YARDS   SCALE   MILE
1000   0   1

naval guns fired over 1,600 rounds and artillery nearly 500 rounds during the night before the 31 July advance.[16]

The III Corps launched its attack to seize the northern portion of Guam at 0630, as scheduled. On the left the 3d Marines moved out with three battalions abreast. The 3d Battalion, along the coast highway, headed generally north; 2/3, in the center, having been on a line with part of the unit facing north and the remainder east, started northeast. To complicate further the regiment's maneuver, the 1st Battalion was in position along the east lip of Fonte Ravine and tied in with the 21st Marines, which would move to the north. This advance would cause the 21st to cross in front of 1/3, which would soon be pinched out and go into regimental reserve.[17] (See Map 24, Map Section)

Little opposition met the forward movement of Colonel Stuart's forces. Although the thickly mined roads into Agana caused some casualties, Marines were in the Plaza of the former capital by 1045. The enemy did not defend the razed town, and the only Japanese encountered were wounded hiding in huts in the 2d Battalion's sector.

By noon the remainder of Agana had been occupied and assault units of the 3d Marines had seized their portion of the O-1 line. They immediately reorganized and occupied positions along the Agana-Pago Bay Road and awaited orders to continue the advance.[18]

The 21st Marines left its line of departure on 31 July with two battalions in assault, the 2d on the left, which quickly pinched out 1/3 and then extended to contact 2/3 and 3/21. The latter unit, coming down from the slopes of Mt. Macajna, passed through an area where the Japanese had large supplies of food and equipment stored and pushed on against little or no opposition. Following orders to bypass any small enemy groups, the assault elements moved through the heavy underbrush as rapidly as possible. Contact was difficult but was maintained with the 3d Marines throughout the morning; none was made with the 9th.

Even though the rugged terrain had slowed the advance somewhat, the 21st Marines reported its front line elements on O-1 at 1340.[19] Only the 3d Battalion encountered organized resistance. In attempting to establish the right limiting point near Famja, this unit found it necessary to reduce a small opposing force centered around a concrete pillbox. As soon as the regiment reached the day's objective, 1/21, which had been in reserve, was put into the line on the left to cover the assigned frontage adequately.

When Lieutenant Colonel Duplantis (3/21) brought his command post forward, a curious incident occurred which illustrated the confusion of the Japanese. Someone in the battalion command group sighted one of the by-passed enemy groups, estimated to be about 15–20, led by an officer, moving toward the new CP area. The Marines held their fire, and when the small unit got to within 150 yards of the waiting men, an interpreter called to the Nipponese to surrender. Apparently thinking they had finally reached friendly lines, they started forward, then stopped to hold a hurried conference. The chattering was interrupted by the interpreter urging them forward, but by this time the aggregation had decided they were in unfriendly territory. They broke and ran in all directions; the Marines opened fire, killing and wounding about half of the intruders. Those still alive escaped into the protecting foliage.[20]

With 2/9 still division reserve, Colonel Craig ordered his remaining two battalions to make the attack to the north. Forward elements had moved 2,500 yards ahead of the line of departure 40 minutes after the regiment began its advance. For the remainder of the morning, terrain and not the enemy turned out to be the time-consuming factor. The only real fight took place near Ordot where a detachment of Japanese had been left behind in defense of dumps containing hundreds of tons of equipment and supplies.

Overwhelming this opposition, the attack continued to make progress until two Japanese tanks halted the drive at 1415. The 3d Tank

[16] 3d MarDiv D-3 Jnl; 12th Mar OpSummaries.
[17] 3d Mar Jnl.
[18] 3d Mar SAR, 4.

[19] 3d MarDiv D-3 Jnl.
[20] Clark.

Battalion, now under division control, could not send armor to help because of mines and congestion on the cross-island road. However, a bazooka man attached to one of the assault squads of 1/9 took the matter in his own hands and knocked out both tanks. The regiment met no further resistance, and at 1510 Colonel Craig had his units on the O–1 line.[21] Contact during the day had been an intermittent affair because of the rough terrain, and as the units arrived at the day's objective there was physical contact with the 77th Division but none with the 21st Marines.

The 9th sent patrols out beyond its limiting point in an effort to contact the 21st, but had no success until about 1800 when patrols met approximately 300 yards to the left of the 9th's boundary. A readjustment of lines then took place. Colonel Craig filled the gap with Company C (1/9), and the troops began to dig in for the night. By this time a platoon of Company B tanks, which had been dispatched to the 9th earlier, arrived to strengthen the defense and guard against any possible enemy tank attack on the flank.[22]

General Turnage and his ADC, General Noble, had been well forward all day to keep abreast of the situation. When the left and center of the division had reached the O–1 line, a message was sent to corps requesting permission to continue the advance. At 1400 General Geiger authorized this move but ordered that particular attention be paid to contact between units.[23]

About 1500 the 3d Marines sent its 3d Battalion along the coast road north of Agana, and the 1st passed through the 2d to enter the swamp beyond the city. The passage of the swampland with its streams and 15-foot reeds was not completed until dusk. Emerging on the north side, 1/3 set up all-around security and established roadblocks on the trail forward of the position. That night, 31 July–1 August, both assault units of the 3d Marines set up perimeter defenses north of Agana a mile and a half apart with the rest of the division echeloned to the right rear.

RUINS OF AGANA surround the first troops of the 3d Division to reach the island's capital.

When division ordered the renewal of the attack on the afternoon of 31 July, it also alerted the Reconnaissance Company to send two motorized patrols forward at about 1700: one to check the road to Tumon Bay, the other to go to the vicinity of the airfield. The unit heading up the coast road stopped short of its objective when it encountered a roadblock; the other, after making the only enemy contact, completed its mission. Three Japanese were fired on in a house near the airfield with undetermined results.[24]

The first day's advance to the north had been almost unopposed, and the division's front lines surged forward more than 5,000 yards. The former capital of Guam had been occupied, and 4,000 yards of the important cross-island road had been opened for traffic. With the rapid advance came the necessity to move supply distribution points closer to the front. Trucks began to roll over the already crowded coast highway to establish an advanced division dump in the Agana Central Plaza area. Artillery units

---

[21] 3d MarDiv D–3 Jn1; *Craig 1952.*
[22] 3d TkBn SAR, 10.
[23] 3d MarDiv D–3 Jnl.

[24] 3d MarDiv SAR, IntelRpt, Patrol Rpt 3.

COLUMN OF MARINES moving up the Agana-Piti Road on the first day of the attack to capture the northern end of Guam.

started to displace forward so that continuous direct support would be available to the assault units.

This added traffic, plus the fact that the 77th Division would have to move supplies over the same road, presented a problem to the engineers. In an effort to alleviate the situation, the 25th Naval Construction Battalion and the 19th Marines put all available men to work improving existing roads and trails.[25]

There had been little need for artillery and naval gunfire during daylight of 31 July, but that night both took up where they had left off in the morning. Artillery fired 753 rounds and

NGF 1,028 on harassing and interdiction missions from 1900 to 0530.[26]

Not a unit reported any enemy activity during the night. Nor did the 3d Division meet any opposition when it renewed the attack at 0700, 1 August. The advance started with three regiments abreast, having the mission of seizing Tiyan airfield and continuing to the northeast. On the left, 1/3 and 3/3 regained contact and moved forward to the D–2a line, where they held up until the situation on their right developed.

The planned maneuver called for the 3d and 9th Marines to pinch out the 21st at the D–2a

---

[25] 19th Mar SAR, 2.

[26] 3d MarDiv D–3 Periodic Rpt 13.

line across the narrow waist of the island.[27] As the two regiments advanced, they would close toward the center of the division zone of action, gradually converging in front of Colonel Butler's unit. In the 21st's zone, the 1st Battalion remained on line as the 2d and 3d advanced abreast; near the Agana Pumping Station the 2d halted until covered by the forward movement of the 3d, and then pulled out of the line. At 0910 the 3d Battalion was ordered to pivot on its right flank and occupy the boundary between the 3d and 9th Marines, establishing contact with each.

The 9th, plagued by the dense vegetation, had moved up more slowly, with a resultant widening gap between the 3d and 9th Marines. It was this gap that 3/21 would cover until the 9th moved abreast of the 3d Marines on the D–2a line; 3/21 would then be attached to the 3d Regiment. The Marines completed this maneuver by 1300 against negligible opposition and the 21st (less 3d Battalion) replaced 2/9 as division reserve;[28] 2/9 then reverted to regimental control.

General Turnage ordered resumption of the attack at 1500 and alerted the Reconnaissance Company for an afternoon mission. The two assault regiments pushed steadily ahead toward the airfield against slight enemy resistance and at 1745 began preparing positions for the night.[29] The 3d Marines stopped 300 yards beyond D–2 with 1/3 strung out across the southwest end of the runway without cover or concealment; the remainder of the division tied in along a line just short of the Tiyan landing strip.[30]

The problem of getting supplies forward was becoming more serious. The main coast road over which all traffic had to move had been heavily mined. The Japanese had placed aerial bombs and single-horned mines at road junctions and intersections in and around Agana. The 3d Marines suffered at least three serious accidents involving the loss of life and equipment by 1000, 1 August. Among those killed were Major John A. Ptak and Lieutenant Arthur C. Vivian, Jr., respectively the executive officer and the intelligence officer of 1/3.[31] Later in the day the 19th Marines attached additional bomb-disposal sections to the regiment in order to cope with the increasing menace.

Mines also hindered the motorized patrol led by Lieutenant Donald S. Floyd which scouted the beach road. When it had to turn back because of the mines, the tank-led unit went to the airfield area to reconnoiter for a route to the north. The nine tanks and one half-track checked the entire western side, finding little in the way of usable roads. However, one uncharted trail, later developed into a passable route, was found half-way up the airstrip. Floyd continued on and covered three-quarters of the length of Tiyan field before being forced back by enemy fire.[32]

With the apparent lack of Japanese strength to the immediate front of the corps, General Geiger ordered the advance to continue with all possible speed. He wanted to contact the enemy before strong defensive positions could be prepared in the Mt. Santa Rosa-Mt. Barrigada area. In an effort to harass the enemy while they went about their work, III Corps Artillery shifted the positions and normal zones of several units to enable them to take the Japanese under fire. At the same time Admiral Conolly sent eight ships around to the east side of the island to give Mt. Santa Rosa a working over.[33]

The remainder of the fleet continued its mis-

[27] 3d MarDiv OpOrder 9, 31Aug44.

[28] 21st Mar SAR, 7.

[29] On this day (1 Aug) at 1855 Marines of the VAC (elements of 2d and 4th Marine Divisions) secured the island of Tinian after a bitter nine-day battle. For a complete story of the Tinian operation see Maj C. W. Hoffman, *The Seizure of Tinian*, MC Historical Monograph, (Washington, 1951), hereinafter cited as *Tinian*.

[30] 3d MarDiv D–3 Jnl.

[31] *Aplington*.

[32] 3d MarDiv SAR, IntelRpt, Patrol Rpt 4.

[33] At 0800 on 2 August the NGF support was reorganized to cover the advance up both coasts. TU 53.5.2 (RAdm W. L. Ainsworth) with the battleship *Colorado*, cruisers *Honolulu* and *New Orleans*, and five destroyers took position off the east coast to support the 77th InfDiv. TU 53.5.3 (RAdm C. T. Joy) with the battleship *Pennsylvania*, cruisers *Wichita*, *Cleveland*, and *Minneapolis*, five destroyers, and four LCI(G)'s supported the 3d MarDiv on the west coast. CTF 53 OpRpt, OpLog, 61A.

AGANA AIRFIELD less than two months after its capture is the scene of bustling activity as planes of MAG–21 line both sides of the runway. (Air Force Photograph.)

sion of interdiction and harassing, with most of the fire delivered at night. Artillery also kept up the constant pounding of road junctions and known or suspected enemy assembly areas. Everything possible was being done to press the attack as rapidly as practicable.

The 3d Division jumped off at 0630, 2 August, with two regiments abreast to secure the airfield and continue to the D–3 line. The attack progressed slowly but steadily. The terrain remained the biggest obstacle, with heavy underbrush making the advance difficult and tedious. The 9th Marines took the airfield by 0910. Instead of the stubborn fighting that had been expected, the Japanese offered only minor resistance.

On arriving at the D–3b line, Colonel Craig's regiment received instructions to hold up until it could gain contact on both the right (77th

Division) and left (3d Marines).[34] Colonel Stuart's 3d Marines had run into almost impenetrable jungle that slowed its advance to a snail-like pace. Not until 1400 could that unit move up adjacent to the 9th Marines.

The 3d Division spent the remainder of the afternoon trying to make an advance that was hampered by unsuccessful attempts to keep contact. The 3d Marines pushed ahead 1,800 yards on the left, but Colonel Stuart and his executive officer (Colonel James Snedeker) had to tie in battalions by the light of the moon. The 3d and 9th Marines had contact but the 77th Division had been retarded by the jungle growth; General Turnage attached 2/21 to the 9th to fill the gap between the Marines and the Army.[35] Meanwhile, the 3d Battalion, 21st had

[34] 9th Mar R–2 Jnl.
[35] 3d MarDiv D–3 Jnl.

128

cleared the Saupon Point-Ypao Point area of small enemy groups, and at 1630 reverted to control of its own regiment.

Earlier in the day one enterprising Japanese tank crew had taken advantage of the Marines' extended lines and had driven through a gap near the airstrip, then sped down the road. As the vehicle raced toward the CP of 1/3, the assistant battalion surgeon looked up and remarked, "Look at the Japanese tank we must have captured." About that time one of the crew opened the turret and brandished a pistol, firing wildly at anything in sight. A few hundred yards farther and the tank ran into a ditch, whereupon the crewmen jumped to the ground and fled into the jungle. Just prior to darkness two tanks from Company B, 3d Tank Battalion destroyed the enemy vehicle.[36]

With the Tiyan airfield secured, the Marines now controlled the area that would be developed into one of the finest fighter strips in the Pacific. On Orote, work on that airstrip had been on a 24-hour basis, and the runways would soon be ready for MAG–21. The entire peninsula had been cleared of all but isolated Japanese, and the garrison force had taken over its defense, as well as that of Cabras Island, at 0800, 2 August.[37]

In contrast to the deepest penetration of 5,000 yards during the first eight days on Guam, the 3d Division as a whole had surged ahead 8,000–9,000 yards with the 9th Marines taking over 12,000 yards in just three days (31 July– 2 August) since starting the drive to the north. Casualty figures for this phase of the operation showed 44 KIA, 52 VIA, and none MIA for the division.[38] The fact that of the 96 casualties listed, nearly 50 percent were killed in action reflects the character of the fighting during those few days. Enemy resistance had been light and contact with the main force of the retreating Japanese could not be made. But the rear guard units were so posted that the advancing Marines came upon them unexpectedly. At close quarters the point-blank fire could not miss and resulted in the disproportionate death toll.

The dense junge growth and rugged terrain provided cover and concealment that added to the effectiveness of this delaying action.

During this period, the rapid advance began to tax the inadequate transportation of the division. The reduced number of organic vehicles brought ashore increased the burden of keeping supplies forward. There had been combat losses and operational defects, and with the necessity of keeping the already old trucks on the road most of the time, preventive maintenance had to be neglected.[39]

With the cut in the efficiency of the transportation, and the lack of an adequate road net to carry the heavy supply load, corps began a search for an alternate solution to the situation. General Geiger on 2 August requested that a harbor reconnaissance be made of Pago Bay and the Agana Bay channel to determine the feasibility of their use as unloading points.[40] This would bring the supply origination closer to the using arms and shorten the haul to dumps, particularly in the case of the 77th Division, which had been unable to get a road cut through the mountainous country behind its units.

The 302d Engineer Battalion had made a gallant effort to construct a passable road, but by nightfall of 31 July the jungle had won, and the project had to be abandoned.[41] From that point on, supply would be by hand-carry until the Agana-Pago Bay Road could be opened.

"WATER AT LAST"—BARRIGADA VILLAGE

With the Reconnaissance Troop protecting the south flank, General Bruce's 77th Infantry Division started toward the east coast of Guam at 0700, 31 July. Elements of the 307th, with 3/305 attached, led the way in a column of battalions. Lack of enemy resistance permitted battalions to move with companies in column; even so, the march proved most difficult. The troops initially scaled steep slopes, slid down into narrow gorges, and followed along the foothills southwest of the central mountain range of Guam.

---

[36] *Aplington.*
[37] IIIAC SAR, OpRpt, 6.
[38] 3d MarDiv WD, July 1944, 13; August 1944, 2–3.

[39] 3d MT Bn SAR, 1–7.
[40] IIIAC C–3 Jnl.
[41] 77th InfDiv OpRpt, 4.

SOLDIERS OF THE 77th DIVISION reach the end of the road bulldozed by the 302d Engineer Combat Battalion. Forward elements strike out cross country in the advance on 31 July. (Army Photograph.)

For a time, vehicles followed, but soon the terrain became so rough that even jeeps could not traverse it. As one infantryman later wrote:

The distance across the island is not far, as the crow flies, but unluckily we can't fly. The nearest I came to flying was while descending the slippery side of a mountain in a sitting position. . . . After advancing a few yards you find that the [bolt] handle of the machine gun on your shoulder, your pack and shovel, canteens, knife, and machete all stick out at right angles and are as tenacious in their grip on the surrounding underbrush as a dozen grappling hooks. . . . The flies and mosquitos have discovered your route of march and have called up all the reinforcements including the underfed and undernourished who regard us as nothing but walking blood banks. We continue to push on. . . .[42]

The rapid movement of the infantry despite the rough terrain prompted General Bruce to decide to push on to the Pago River before stopping for the night. A liaison plane dropped orders to the 307th to this effect at about 1200.[43] The assault elements continued moving and kept small units forward to report any enemy activity while the main force followed in column.

One of these patrols from Company L, 3/307 had the distinction of liberating the first large group of Guamanians. Late in the afternoon of 31 July scouts met several natives who told of a concentration camp near Asinan which was guarded by only a few Japanese civilians. When the unit reached the compound, 2,000 Guamanians were found and immediately freed. Soldiers willingly gave their rations and cigarettes to the undernourished men and women who were almost overcome with joy at once again seeing Americans. Men of the 77th Division soon forgot the long, tiresome cross-island march as the full realization of the expression, "liberation of enslaved peoples," came to the troops.[44]

Earlier in the day (1150) 3/305 had reverted to control of its parent regiment which had been ordered to move to the Pago River with two battalions. The remaining unit (2/305) after connecting with the northern flank of the brigade had orders to guard the MSR (main supply route) as far as possible to the east. Company I (3/305) made the only enemy contact on 31 July. As the unit moved up the road leading into Yona late in the afternoon, several Japanese opened fire on the advance elements. Platoons deployed and the soldiers quickly overran the former Japanese supply center; five enemy were killed.[45]

The 307th had occupied the high ground on the southwest bank of the Pago River by 1700, but a wide gap existed between it and 3/305, which had set up a perimeter defense after its skirmish at Yona. Colonel Tanzola echeloned the remainder of the 305th to the right rear to protect the south flank of the corps. Colonel Smith's 306th still remained in position on the FBL.[46]

At daybreak, 1 August, 2/306 went into corps

[42] *Guam, 77th Div,* 65.

[43] 307th Inf S–2, S–3 Jnl.
[44] *Guam, 77th Div,* 68–69.
[45] IIIAC C–2 Periodic Rpt 11.
[46] 77th InfDiv G–3 Jnl.

reserve, and the remainder of the regiment started the march to the vicinity of Pago Bay to join the division. About an hour later, 0700, with the 307th on the left and the 305th next to the coast, the 77th attacked to gain the O–2 line. The 305th had secured the bridge across the Pago River by 0800, but the 307th made slower progress as the men hacked their way through jungle near the river.

The 307th captured the all-important Agana-Pago Bay Road shortly after noon, thus making it available for the movement of equipment and supplies. The 77th immediately requested permission to use the coast road in the 3d Marine Division's zone to enable it to get supplies forward. It was an unusual thing indeed for two divisions to utilize the same supply route but as General Bruce so aptly put it, "The books would say it can't be done, but on Guam it was done—it had to be." [47]

Little or no opposition met the advancing Army troops as they pushed on toward the O–2 line and Barrigada. The route of march led the soldiers cross country over rough terrain covered with heavy undergrowth that made the going slow and tiresome. Individuals began running low on food and canteens were almost dry. Lacking pure water, the troops started drinking coconut milk or creek water made usable with halazone tablets. Captured Japanese canned salmon and gum drops added variety to K-rations, the only food that had been carried on the long trek across the island.

Fortunately some relief would arrive when the O–2 line was secured. Sufficient roads could be cleared to permit some traffic to bring forward the urgently needed food, reserve ammunition, and water. However, as the advance moved farther to the north, the sources of water became scarcer. The northern half of the island had few streams and the sub-surface coral quickly absorbed even the heaviest rainfall. This necessitated the speedy capture of Barrigada with its deep well that could provide 30,000 gallons of pure water daily.[48] But the

INFANTRYMEN of Company B, 305th Infantry send out flankers as they move from the FBL toward Barrigada. (Army Photograph.)

task was expected to be a difficult one since intelligence estimates indicated the enemy had established defenses in this area to block the American advance to the Japanese battle position which aerial observers reported under construction at Mt. Santa Rosa.

On the evening of 1 August, the 305th dug in for the night near Manguilao, a mile and a half northeast of RJ 171 where the 306th had halted at 1900. The 307th, under its new commander, Lieutenant Colonel Thomas B. Manuel,[49] extended its left northward to make contact with the Marines on the O–2 line.

The newly captured Agana-Pago Bay Road was soon a scene of bumper-to-bumper traffic as direct support field artillery battalions moved forward and supply trucks began to roll to newly established dumps. The absence of enemy aircraft and the improper employment of Japanese artillery permitted the use of lights

[47] MajGen A. D. Bruce, "Administration, Supply, and Evacuation of the 77th Infantry Division on Guam," *Military Review*, December 1944, 8.

[48] *Ibid.*, 4.

[49] Col. Stephen S. Hamilton, the former CO, was evacuated because of illness at 1600 on 1 August. 307th Inf OpRpt, 2–3.

FORWARD OBSERVERS check the progress of assault units of the 307th Infantry as they reach jungle growth near the Pago River. (Army Photograph.)

as supply trains continued to grind throughout the night.[50]

Late in the afternoon of 1 August commanders decided that after the 307th Infantry had captured the Price Road within its zone of action the next morning, the regiment would be permitted to halt temporarily. This would allow trucks to bring much needed rations forward to resupply units before they launched a concerted effort to seize Barrigada. At 0700 on 2 August, the 77th jumped off to accomplish this mission.

A half-hour earlier 14 light tanks from Company D, 706th Tank Battalion had moved out on a reconnaissance of the Barrigada area. When the column reached a point 800 yards beyond the road junction at San Antonio it drew moderate fire. After spraying the underbrush with machine guns, the force withdrew and returned to regimental headquarters with the report of having seen only eight enemy soldiers. The same unit was ordered out at 0800 to complete its mission of scouting as far as the O–3 line.[51]

Retracing its previous route along the Agana Road, the patrol passed through Barrigada, turned at RJ 306, and proceeded up the Finegayan Road toward Mt. Barrigada. An empty pillbox at the junction and an unmanned roadblock were the only enemy positions seen. When the tanks were almost abreast of the hill mass, Japanese soldiers opened fire from behind three enemy trucks stalled in the road. The leading tanks killed an estimated 35 defenders and then turned their guns on the trucks to demolish them.

Returning to the road junction at Barrigada, the tankmen started up the road toward the O–3 line. The way became rougher and narrower, and the dense jungle closed in around the tanks as they plowed forward. About 1,000 yards from the junction the platoon leader's tank got hung up on a stump and blocked the rest of the column. The Japanese had been waiting for this and the jungle immediately came alive with enemy soldiers. They swarmed over the lead tanks, and 20mm cannon and heavy machine guns commenced firing on the vehicles that followed. The Army tank crews recovered from their surprise immediately and drove the attackers back into the protective cover of the heavy foliage. Some of the Japanese were shot from their exposed positions on the tanks and others picked off as they scrambled into the jungle. After the tank on the stump had worked itself loose, the reconnaissance commander received permission to return to the regimental lines. The patrol accomplished this without further incident by 1100.[52]

The 14 tanks arrived back at their assembly area shortly after the 307th had jumped off from Price Road. The regiment had secured the road by 0830, and immediately issued the rations and supplies that had been rushed forward. Two hours later the general advance to capture Barrigada got under way.

The 305th, with its 1st and 3d Battalions in assault, met little resistance initially. The 3d, which encountered less troublesome terrain and jungle, pushed almost a mile ahead of its flanking units. As the battalion approached Barrigada enemy opposition from outposts increased,

---

[50] 77th InfDiv OpRpt, 4.
[51] 77th InfDiv G–3 Jnl.

[52] 706th TkBn OpRpt, 5.

and at 1020 a Company I patrol was hit by withering fire from concealed machine-gun positions near the Barrigada Well, 100 yards northwest of RJ 306. The company deployed and initiated an attack supported by battalion mortars, but the effort gained only 100 yards. Japanese troops, well dug in and excellently camouflaged, held their fire until Army units endangered their positions. These tactics stopped any attempt at a flanking movement, and allowed the enemy to take full advantage of the terrain around Barrigada.

A platoon of light tanks from the 706th Tank Battalion, requested earlier, arrived about noon and plans got under way for a coordinated battalion attack at 1230 to be supported by tanks and artillery. Radio difficulties with the supporting artillery and word of the expected arrival of a platoon of medium tanks caused the jump-off time to be delayed until 1330.

Lieutenant Colonel Chalgren took advantage of the extra time to make a more detailed reconnaisance and to contact the commanders of the flanking battalions to assure coordination of all units. Chalgren's men jumped off on time but even with the strong artillery and tank support the battalion gained less than 200 yards.[53] It now become apparent that the Japanese planned to put up a determined resistance in this area.

On the left, the 307th's plan for 2 August called for its 1st Battalion (Lieutenant Colonel Joseph B. Coolidge) to maintain contact with the 3d Marine Division flanking units, reach the Finegayan Road north of the town, and seize the western slopes of Mt. Barrigada. Major John W. Lovell's 3d Battalion was to keep abreast of the 305th, push directly through Barrigada, and take the mountain's southern slopes. Directional control would be by compass on an azimuth of 45 degrees.[54]

The regiment moved out anticipating little or no opposition, but within the hour small arms and machine-gun fire hit both assault battalions. Immediately after leaving the line of departure Company A met scattered resistance which forced it to veer to the right. The change in

ARMY SHERMANS of the 706th Tank Battalion grind through the rubble of Agana before taking the cross island road to join the 77th Division prior to the Barrigada action. (Army Photograph.)

direction brought the company out on the Agana Road so that its advance was now in the zone of action of the 3d Battalion. The latter unit had been moving steadily ahead on the prescribed axis of attack. The inevitable happened as the units approached Barrigada; Company A collided with L, which in turn forced K into the 305th's sector.

As a result of crowding three companies into an area not wide enough for two, the possibilities for a balanced attack no longer existed. The resultant 1,000-yard gap on the left of Company A reduced the chances of any flanking pressure on the enemy entrenched around the village. Furthermore, only one platoon of Company A could be used effectively, and K had almost no front at all.[55]

Major Gerald G. Cooney, executive officer of the 1st Battalion, quickly took command in his zone and ordered Company B into the gap in an effort to adjust the front lines.[56] As men of that unit tried to get into position, a Japanese tank shot out of a burning grass shack and headed down the Agana Road toward the thinly-held lines. Crashing blindly into build-

---

[53] *Chalgren.*

[54] 307th Inf OpRpt, 3.

[55] *Guam, 77th Div*, 85–86.

[56] The battalion commander, LtCol Coolidge, had gone with Co C along the division boundary and was now out of contact with the remainder of his battalion. Later in the day Col Coolidge was wounded and evacuated. Maj Cooney took over full command at about 1600. 307th Inf OpRpt, 3.

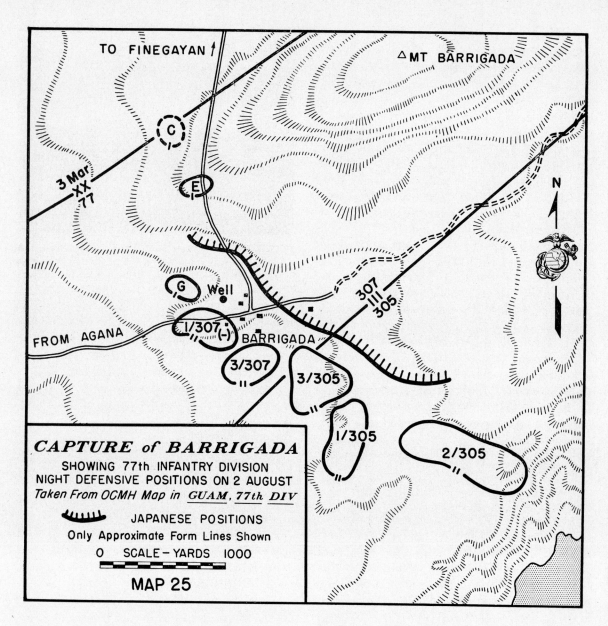

TO FINEGAYAN ↑ △MT BARRIGADA

3 Mar
XX
77

N

307
III
305

Well

G

FROM AGANA

1/307 (-)

BARRIGADA

3/307

3/305

1/305

2/305

CAPTURE of BARRIGADA
SHOWING 77th INFANTRY DIVISION
NIGHT DEFENSIVE POSITIONS ON 2 AUGUST
Taken From OCMH Map in GUAM, 77th DIV

JAPANESE POSITIONS
Only Approximate Form Lines Shown
0   SCALE – YARDS   1000

MAP 25

ings, including a temple in the village, the enemy tankmen whose vision slit was covered by the temple roof, whirled and churned their vehicle in every direction. The thatch-roofed tank overran Army machine-gun positions and continued down the road, wildly firing at everything in its path.[57] Curiously enough, no available records show how, or when, this tank was destroyed, but at any rate it did not return to the Barrigada action.

Repeated attempts by the 307th failed to

dislodge the enemy. Finally, Company G (2/307) launched a tank-supported attack at 1500 which penetrated the Japanese line but did not lessen the gap on the left. Lieutenant Colonel Charles F. Learner committed Company E at 1630, and with light tanks leading the way the unit successfully filled the breach and gained contact with the 1st Battalion. Darkness halted any further advance, and the regiment dug in just beyond the road junction at Barrigada.[58] (See Map 25)

[57] *Guam, 77th Div*, 88.

[58] Ltr LtCol C. F. Learner to author, 26Nov52.

Meanwhile, on the right, the 305th had moved up and consolidated its lines with the 307th, destroying an enemy tank in the process. Both regiments prepared all-around defensive positions on the night of 2–3 August to ensure against enemy infiltration attempts.

It had been a day of frustration for men of the 77th Division. The intense fire from Japanese weapons could be felt as the attacking troops tried to move forward, but locating the concealed soldiers was another matter. Positions were so well camouflaged that the size of the force opposing the Americans could not be intelligently estimated. In any case, the enemy had sufficient strength to kill 29 and wound 98 Army officers and men during the day.[59]

Before the advance got under way on 3 August, General Bruce ordered a regrouping of battalions. Regimental boundaries stayed the same, but in the 307th's zone the 2d Battalion replaced the 1st, and the 3d shifted back to cover its normal frontage. The 1st Battalion, 305th relieved the 3d on the left, and the 2d remained in the assault on the right. This realigned the regiments so that the division covered its assigned sector, and it also assured a coordinated attack against the enemy positions around Barrigada.[60]

The assault started at 0630, and much to the surprise of everyone, encountered only a few snipers as units went forward. By 0930 the regiments had advanced through the Barrigada clearing, and the all-important well had been secured. Five hours later a water point had been rushed into service and thirsty troops could once more be assured of a good supply.[61]

In conjunction with the attack plans for 3 August, artillery had been ordered to fire an hour-long preparation on Mt. Barrigada, starting at 0630. The 304th and 306th Field Artillery Battalions were assigned the mission, completing it on schedule. Again at 1330 Mt. Barrigada received a going over when all of the division's artillery opened up with a five-minute barrage prior to the 307th's main effort against the hill. After the regiment started

TERRAIN photograph taken from Mt. Santa Rosa shows the zone of action of the 77th Division in the advance to the north. (Army Photograph.)

to move, the barrage would be lifted 100 yards every two minutes until the infantry reached the summit.[62]

With tanks spearheading the drive, the 307th beat a path through the jungle, meeting only scattered opposition on the lower slopes of the hill mass. As the troops neared the top, enemy resistance diminished to only occasional sniper shots. The 3d Battalion reached the summit at 1500, but its advance had been more rapid than the 2d's on the left. The 2d Battalion's attack on Mt. Barrigada tended to pull it to the right, and when the zone became too wide to cover, contact was lost with the 3d Marine Division. (See Map 26, Map Section)

About 1,000 yards to the right of the 307th, isolated pockets of Japanese slowed the 305th's attack. Also the trails that had provided the avenues of advance had dwindled to nothing, further hindering progress. In an attempt to maintain control within the regiment, Colonel Tanzola reduced the front and ordered patrols to cover the remainder of the zone to the coast.[63]

Although the day's advance had been limited to only about one mile by the dense jungle, the

[59] 77th InfDiv G–1 Jnl.
[60] 77th InfDiv G–3 Jnl.
[61] 77th InfDiv OpRpt, 5.

[62] 77th InfDivArty Action Rpt, 9.
[63] 305th Inf Action Rpt, 3.

expected heavy Japanese opposition had not materialized. This in part was due to the air, naval gunfire, and artillery harassment, but of more significance is the fact that the Japanese did not consider Mt. Barrigada a good defensive position. An enemy terrain appreciation study of the island contains these remarks concerning the area:

> Mt. Barrigada is densely wooded. A single road over the summit is barely passable for foot troops. The level summit has no field of vision, and for a future military position a firing area must be cleared. [The Japanese did not see fit to do this.] [64]

Further attempts late in the afternoon of 3 August failed to close the existing gaps in the line. As the division dug in for the night across the summit of Mt. Barrigada, there was no contact between regiments and none with the Marines.[65] Again the men of the division had seen few of the enemy but plenty of the thick jungle that would plague them for the remainder of the Guam campaign. During the day they had also seen the first Army fighters and bombers over the island. Sixteen P–47's and three B–25's of the Seventh Air Force, based at Saipan, flew deep support missions in the afternoon. One of the P–47 pilots, Lieutenant Howard H. Barret, USA, had the dubious honor of being the first Air Force pilot to land on Guam when he made a forced landing on Orote Airfield.[66]

Following a five-minute artillery preparation at 0655 on 4 August, the 77th Division pushed forward to capture the day's objective. General Bruce ordered that contact should be made with the Marines as soon as possible and that the O–3 line be secured. There the advance would be temporarily halted for consolidation and reorganization.

To accomplish the first mission, a reinforced platoon of 2/307, with two tanks attached, started toward the division's left flank. The tanks reduced two enemy roadblocks and proceeded on down the road. As they neared a third barrier they opened fire for a quick destruction of the obstacle in their path.

Unfortunately, men of Company G, 2/9 of the 3d Marine Division occupied this position. The hail of bullets and 75mm shells quickly drove the Marines to cover. Before the fire fight was halted by Captain Fagan, company commander of the 9th Marines unit, who stood up and waved his helmet at the onrushing tanks, seven Marines had been wounded. Later investigation revealed that the Army patrol had been told that friendly troops would identify themselves by firing red smoke grenades. The Marines had not been informed, and when the soldiers started to throw colored grenades after the action had gone on for some time, it meant nothing to them. Fortunately, Captain Fagan stopped the skirmish before further casualties and loss of equipment took place.[67]

Earlier in the morning the 307th's commander had ordered his 1st Battalion to pass through the 2d (Major Thomas R. Mackin)[68] and secure the road near the O–3 line; the latter unit would then pass to regimental reserve. The 1st completed the passage of lines at 0915, but did not move abreast of the 3d Battalion (Major Joseph W. Hanna)[69] until 1245. Bruce ordered the general advance to start about the

---

[64] JICPOA Item 9174–Guam; Military Terrain and Beach Conditions. Translation of Japanese map dated February 1944.

[65] 77th InfDiv G–3 Periodic Rpt 11. It should be pointed out that some officers feel it is not necessary to maintain a solid line across the entire front in this type of terrain against scattered opposition. The advocates of this method of jungle fighting advance in columns, make contact only on certain favorable terrain features, and establish perimeter defenses to provide all-around security. Still another group of officers push through the jungle on existing roads and trails but maintain contact by the use of connecting files and patrols throughout the advance. Strong points, roadblocks, and patrols keep visual contact between perimeter defenses at night. No attempt is made in this monograph to evaluate the different methods of jungle warfare but only to present the facts as they existed during the campaign.

[66] 318th FtrGru, VII FtrComd, Seventh AF, Organization History, August 1944; 48th BomGru(M), VII BomComd, Seventh AF, Organization History, August 1944.

[67] *Guam, 77th Div*, 104–105; *Glass.*

[68] Assumed command on 3 August replacing LtCol Learner who was wounded and evacuated. *Guam, 77th Div*, 102.

[69] Assumed command on 3 August replacing LtCol Lovell who was hospitalized because of illness. Lovell resumed command of 3/307 on 6 August. Ltr LtCol J. W. Lovell to author, 15Dec52.

same time division headquarters received the following message from General Geiger:

Corps commander is sorry but he feels he will have to hold up advance of 3d MarDiv until 77th Div lines are a little better organized and gap between divisions is closed. Orders to Turnage are being issued accordingly.[70]

Major Hanna's battalion (3/307) had taken its objective without meeting any enemy resistance, and shortly thereafter the 1st moved up on line. But the contact that had been gained in the morning had once more been lost because of heavy underbrush. Patrols from both the Army and the Marines failed to meet, and preparations had to be made to try again at daylight.

On the right flank of the division the 305th's progress had been slow because of the narrow and indistinct paths. Tanks broke trail for the two assault battalions, 1st and 2d, but the heavy foliage still retarded the advance. Nevertheless, by nightfall the regiment had been able to reduce an ambush, overcome other scattered resistance, and move 500–1,000 yards beyond the O–3 line.[71]

The movement from the O–2 to O–3 line was ended by the night of 4 August. The 77th Division had captured the town of Barrigada with its important water supply and had secured the mountain north of the town. It had been an advance opposed not only by a well-concealed enemy but also by difficult terrain which made contact within the division difficult and practically nonexistent with the Marine division throughout the drive to the north. Although during the five days of fighting 46 were killed, 228 wounded, and 18 reported MIA, the 77th Division was in good condition to continue the push northward.[72]

FIGHT FOR FINEGAYAN

The officers and men of the 3d Marine Division had been hearing the word "contact" as often as those of the 77th Division since the start of Phase II operations. The difficulty of maintaining contact is indicative of the effect that the close-knit vegetation had on the advance of both divisions. Fortunately, the Japanese had not been encountered in any organized strength the first three days the Marines were in the jungle. But this was not to be the case during the next three.

All artillery battalions of the 12th Marines had displaced forward by 2 August in order to be in position to provide continuous support to regiments of the division. Corps artillery had also moved, so that its longer range guns could now be used more effectively. By nightfall, units had brought forward a good supply of ammunition in anticipation of the increased need for artillery support in the Finegayan area. During the night 2–3 August, the 12th Marines delivered 777 rounds of harassing and interdictory fires on roads and trails within the division's zone of action.[73]

The division renewed its advance at 0700, 3 August, with two regiments in assault. The 3d Marines, on the left, moved ahead against little opposition, but the 9th did not meet with such good fortune. (See Map 27, Map Section) As its 1st Battalion approached RJ 177 just west of Finegayan village at 0910, an estimated platoon of Japanese opened fire on Company B. The enemy was dug in on either side of the road across an open area that gave excellent fields of fire to the defenders. This well-organized position, according to the commanding officer of 1/9, Lieutenant Colonel Randall, constituted one of the strongest his battalion hit during the Guam campaign.[74] Nevertheless, a platoon of infantry supported by two tanks and the fire of company weapons, overran the stronghold, disclosing it to have been held by a force of about company instead of platoon size. After the half-hour action Randall's men counted 105 enemy dead.[75]

At RJ 177 about 500 yards farther up the Finegayan-Mt. Santa Rosa Road, Company B ran into more enemy soldiers. This force consisted of riflemen with machine guns dug into positions taking full advantage of the ravines and ditches in the area. Heavy brush and palm

[70] 77th InfDiv G–3 Jnl.
[71] 305th Inf Action Rpt, 3.
[72] 77th InfDiv G–1 Jnl.

[73] 12th Mar OpSummaries.
[74] Interview with Col. C. A. Randall, 27Mar52.
[75] 9th Mar R–2 Jnl.

PRIVATE FIRST CLASS FRANK P. WITEK, 1st Battalion, 9th Marines, posthumously awarded the Medal of Honor for action on 3 August during the advance on Finegayan when he covered the temporary withdrawal of his platoon, exposed himself to safeguard a wounded comrade, and then led an attack, personally accounting for 16 Japanese and a machine-gun position before he was struck down by an enemy rifleman.

groves provided concealment that made individual Japanese hard to discover. The light opposition at the road junction, however, made it apparent that the Imperial troops planned to fight only a delaying action in this vicinity.

After RJ 177 was secured at 1300, Companies A and C passed through B and received orders to prepare to spend the night in the vicinity of Finegayan. Company B pulled back and set up in the open area it had cleared earlier in the day.[76] As the advance elements of 1/9 dug in for the night of 3–4 August, a column of jeeps, half-tracks, tanks, and trucks came speeding up the road and continued on past the road junction toward Yigo. But 400 yards farther the column pulled up short when 75mm guns, automatic weapons, small arms, and one tank fired on the leading vehicle of the convoy.

This reconnaissance unit had been in a state of uncertainty all day. As early as 0750 the 21st Marines had been alerted to furnish one company for a motorized reconnaissance patrol to Ritidian Point. Throughout the remainder of the morning other units were dispatched to RJ 125. When the complete patrol assembled, its makeup consisted of:

> One section of Reconnaissance Company (2 half-tracks and 4 radio jeeps).
> Company A and staff tanks of 3d Tank Battalion.
> One squad of mine detection and demolition men from 19th Marines.
> Company I, 3/21 mounted in 6 trucks.

Over-all commander of the Armored Reconnaissance Group was Lieutenant Colonel Hartnoll J. Withers (Commanding Officer, 3d Tank Battalion), with the reinforced infantry unit being under command of Major Edward A. Clark (Executive Officer, 3/21).[77]

Unfortunately, the haste with which some units had to organize their part of the patrol resulted in trucks reporting to haul troops without sufficient gas to make the entire trip. Nor were drivers properly equipped or oriented for their mission which caused confusion as to the route to be followed. The drivers had been engaged in hauling rations to a forward dump, and the first six trucks unloaded had been pressed into service on short notice. Lack of time prevented correction of all the inadequacies, and at 1245 commanders received the word to proceed on the mission.[78] At 1455 Lieutenant Colonel Withers sent the following message to division headquarters:

> Patrol is held up at front lines where firefight is going on. Recommend patrol remain together behind front lines tonight and clear at 0730 tomorrow. Insufficient time remains today to accomplish mission . . . .[79]

A half-hour later headquarters directed Withers to proceed on the assigned mission at once, but to return by 1800. That part of the route not covered would be checked the next morning, 4 August.

[76] 1/9 SAR, 1.

[77] 3d TkBn SAR, 11.
[78] *Clark.*
[79] 3d MarDiv D–3 Jnl.

When Marines had cleared the way the column continued along the road. But the limited vision from the lead half-track caused it to miss the left fork at RJ 177, its assigned route, and continue in an easterly direction. It was this patrol which sped through the lines of 1/9 and was stopped at 1610 by heavy enemy fire. Only the point had advanced beyond the road junction, but before these elements could break contact one half-track had been destroyed, one 6 x 6 truck damaged and abandoned,[80] and one tank slightly damaged.

Two hours later remaining units had returned to the front lines, and a check of casualties showed one KIA and 14 WIA in addition to the vehicles destroyed or abandoned. Japanese equipment put out of action included two 75mm guns, one tank, and several machine guns. An undetermined number of enemy soldiers were killed.[81]

With the exception of the action around RJ 177, the 3d Division had advanced against only moderate resistance throughout the day. The left flank had moved about 3,000 yards ahead of the right, which had been stopped at noon because of lack of contact with the 77th Division. As a consequence, on the night of 3 August the Marine front lines extended eastward from Naton Beach to the coastal highway. From there they ran along the road through Dededo and Finegayan, joining the division boundary at a road junction 1,000 yards west of Mt. Barrigada.[82] (See Map 28, Map Section)

The early hours of darkness were quiet, but at 2100 the 3d Marines started receiving mortar fire. An hour later the same unit reported killing an eight-man Japanese patrol led by an officer; all had been wearing white arm bands, and as they neared the front lines the last member of the group fired a red rocket. This evidently signaled two enemy medium tanks to go into action. They cruised down the road into the lines held by the 9th Marines, passed

through RJ 177, and continued on their way, impervious to the fire of several 37mm guns. After crushing the trail of one of the 37's, the tanks turned west into the rear of the 3d Marines, fired a 57mm projectile at a Marine tank, and then withdrew. Fortunately, the 57mm round failed to explode, though it did penetrate the armor on the right sponson.[83]

During this tank action an enemy force of undetermined size made an attack, supported by 90mm mortars, in the area of the boundary between the 3d and 9th Marines. Division headquarters warned the 21st Marines and the 3d Tank Battalion about 2330 to be prepared to repel the counterattack. Twenty minutes later, after artillery had broken up the Japanese effort, the alerted units were secured.[84] The remainder of the night passed without incident.

Earlier in the day the 4th Marines of the 1st Brigade had moved into an area northeast of Agana near Toto. This was in compliance with a corps order issued the previous day, 2 August, placing that regiment in force reserve. The first indication that General Geiger intended to use General Shepherd's brigade in the north had come the day before (1 August), in the form of a warning order, issued at 1900.[85] This decision had been made after one day's extensive patrolling by units of the brigade, which reported seeing few Japanese soldiers or installations.

These patrols, consisting of platoons or larger units from both regiments, had started their search mission at daylight on 1 August. The largest, Company A (1/22) Reinforced, departed from Magpo Point and was to proceed along the south coast via Facpi to Umatac, Port Merizo, Port Ajayan, Agfayan Bay, Inarajan, Talofofo Bay, and Togcha Bay to Ylig Bay and then return overland, reentering the brigade's lines at Maanot Pass. It had the mission of determining enemy strength and movements, destroying or capturing all Jap-

[80] The damaged truck was subsequently recovered and the only damage evident was a large hole in the left front door. Ltr LtCol T. R. Stokes to CMC, 25Nov52.

[81] 3d MarDiv D–3 Jnl; 3d TkBn SAR, 11.

[82] 3d MarDiv D–3 Jnl.

[83] A sponson is the hollow enlargement on the side of the hull of a tank, used for storing ammunition, or as a space for radio equipment or guns.

[84] 3d MarDiv D–3 Jnl.

[85] 1st ProvMarBrig WD, 1Jul–10Aug44, 16.

anese encountered, and assisting friendly natives to enter the Marine lines. Corps authorized the sending of two DUKW's with the patrol to carry seven days' ration and two units of fire, and to be available for evacuation of casualties if needed.[86] LCM's were to meet the DUKW's at Umatac with additional supplies consisting mostly of fuel.

The patrol arrived at Umatac at 1400 that afternoon (1 August) without encountering resistance other than two stragglers. It also arrived minus rations. About one mile south of Bangi Point one of the DUKW's became mired in the sand, obliging the crews to redistribute the supplies and reload the remaining vehicle. This then put to sea but did not arrive at Umatac until after dark.

Meanwhile, the reconnaissance flight that had been assigned to locate the unit each day learned of the patrol's plight. The brigade observer in the plane, Captain William R. Norton, returned to Orote Airfield and loaded 90 pounds of rations and dropped them to Company A at 1800. The supplies scheduled to arrive at Umatac by LCM had failed to do so when the sea became too rough for small boat operations, but brigade headquarters directed the patrol to continue its mission. Supply would be by OY airdrop.[87]

To search the southern portion of the island more thoroughly, brigade ordered the 22d Marines, which had completed the relief of the 306th Infantry by 1000, 1 August, to send one company with three days supplies to Umatac. After establishing a base camp there, it would comb the western half of the brigade zone. The 4th Marines was to set up a base at Point Agfayan and check the eastern half of the zone south of the Maanot-Talofofo Road. The northern part of the eastern zone would be patrolled by a unit from the 4th, operating from a position near Togcha Point.[88] (See Map 2, Map Section)

At 1030 the following morning (2 August), in accordance with verbal instructions from corps directing the brigade to be prepared to move to the vicinity of Toto in corps reserve,

General Shepherd issued his operation order. The 4th Marines, less the two companies (A and F) on distant patrol, received orders to assemble in the vicinity of Maanot Pass and be prepared to move to the north at 0800 the next morning. The 22d Marines, less the 1st Battalion, would continue on its present mission of patrolling and be ready to move on 5 August.[89]

Shortly after noon, however, corps directed that the 4th get under way at 0630, 3 August, and pass to force reserve at that time. Late in the afternoon when reports started coming in from the day's patrols few enemy contacts were noted. Marines had sighted only one organized group and that consisted of 12 soldiers who had holed up in a cave in the heights south of Mt. Lamlam. All were destroyed, but not until one Marine had been killed and two others wounded.

At daylight on 3 August, the 4th Marines began the move to Toto. Upon departure of that regiment from the south, the 22d received the responsibility of evacuating the wounded of the two 4th Marine companies remaining in the area. Other units assigned the searching mission continued their patrol activities. To assist in the mopping up of the Japanese stragglers, Guamanians in the Talofofo area were armed, at their own request.[90]

At 1415 General Shepherd received dispatch orders from corps directing the movement of the brigade (less 1/22, 9th Defense Battalion, and 7th AAA (AW) Battalion) to join the 4th Marines at Toto. The order would be effective at 0700, 4 August, at which time the detached units would become a task force under command of Lieutenant Colonel Archie E. O'Neil, Commanding Officer, 9th Defense Battalion. The mission of this newly-activated unit would be to protect the force south flank from a point in the vicinity of Inalas along the FBL to the west coast opposite Anae Island. (See Map 15) In addition it would defend the Agat-Dadi Beach area and patrol the island south of the general line Pago Bay-Agat Bay.[91]

At 0700, 4 August, Headquarters, 1st Marine

[86] 1st ProvMarBrig OpOrder 30, 31Jul44.
[87] 1st ProvMarBrig Jnl.
[88] 1st ProvMarBrig WD, 1Jul–10Aug44, 16.

[89] 1st ProvMarBrig OpOrder 33, 2Aug44.
[90] 1st ProvMarBrig WD, 1Jul–10Aug44, 18.
[91] 1st ProvMarBrig Jnl.

Brigade and the 22d Marines, less the 1st Battalion, commenced the move to get into position to support the corps in its seizure of the remainder of Guam. At the same time the 3d Division jumped off to straighten its lines so that the 21st Marines could move into position as planned. The operation order called for that regiment (less 3d Battalion) to go into the center of the division's zone between the 3d and 9th Marines as soon as those two assault units secured the O-3 line. The division's widening sector north of RJ 358 made this maneuver necessary.[92]

As the 9th's right flank went forward, the breach between the Marines and the Army kept widening. At 0800, when the gap continued to widen, the right flank was halted 1,000 yards short of the O-3 line. Division headquarters directed 2/9 and 3/21 to fill the gap and protect the right flank of the division. In carrying out this directive, 2/9 established a roadblock on the Finegayan-Barrigada Road. It was this position that the tank-led patrol of the 77th Division fired on at about 1045.[93]

The 1st Battalion, 9th tried to push on to the O-3 line, but moderate resistance slowed the advance. When it became apparent that the day's objective could not be reached without exposing the division's right flank even more, a change of plans occurred. At 1450 the 21st Marines was directed to take over its zone of action immediately, and in compliance with General Geiger's instructions the division would hold up until contact could be gained with the 77th Division.

While this maneuver took place, another incident occurred that showed the need for closer liaison between adjacent units. As 2/9 and 3/21 prepared their positions on the boundary between the 3d and 77th Divisions, friendly planes hit the Marines. Two B-25's flying support missions for Army units opened up on the CP area of 3/21 and also strafed troops moving along the road toward the front lines.[94]

Elements of the 21st had completed the relief of Companies B and C, 1/9 by 1730. The remaining units of the 1st Battalion, 9th, held the area around the Japanese-manned roadblock that had stopped the armored reconnaissance patrol on 3 August. From this position the enemy had successfully delayed the advance throughout the day by the use of antitank (AT) weapons, 75 mm guns, machine guns, and riflemen concealed in the 10-20 foot high brush. (See Map 27, Map Section)

When intelligence reports indicated the possibility of a counterattack from this position during the night of 4-5 August, Lieutenant Colonel Randall sent reinforcements to his advance company. Before dark two platoons of infantry and a machine-gun platoon had gone forward and were dug in for the night.[95] Contact had not been made with the 77th Division, but the Marines did have a solid line extending from Naton Beach along the O-3 line north of Dededo. From there it bent back to a point 1,000 yards short of O-3 along the division boundary.

During the afternoon of 4 August the 22d Marines started to move into its assembly area, and by nightfall the entire regiment and brigade headquarters group were set up in force reserve. General Shepherd's CP officially opened in the vicinity of San Antonio at 1200, and at 1400 the 4th Marines reverted to brigade control.[96]

In the south, patrols of the 4th Marines had returned from Togcha Bay and Port Inarajan, reporting no enemy contact. Other units, under Lieutenant Colonel O'Neil's new task force, also failed to find any organized resistance, further strengthening the intelligence that the Japanese would only defend in the north. As the units of the 4th completed their mission in the south, they immediately joined their parent organization at Toto.

The 3d Division renewed its attack at 0630, 5 August, with orders for the 9th and 21st Marines to seize the O-3 line. The 3d Marines, which had been meeting little or no resistance, was directed to move its left flank forward 1,000 yards to Bijia Point but to maintain contact with the 21st on the right.

[92] 3d MarDiv OpOrder 11, 3Aug44.

[93] 2/9 SAR, 6.

[94] 3d MarDiv D-3 Jnl; *Tinsley*.

[95] 1/9 SAR, 2.

[96] 1st ProvMarBrig WD, 1 July-10Aug44, 18.

The 9th Marines' plan of attack called for Company A to be attached to the 3d Battalion until the regiment reached O–3. At that time 1/9 would regain control of its unit and the 2d Battalion would pass through the 3d. The regiment would then make the assault with two battalions abreast. Meeting only light resistance, units completed the first phase by 0830 and the 1st and 2d Battalions were in position to carry out the second phase.

On the left Lieutenant Colonel Randall sent Company B back into the line and attached a platoon of tanks to each of the assaulting units. They encountered heavy opposition immediately, and thick brush made the enemy difficult to locate and destroy. It became a blind fight with visibility limited to a few feet on either side of the road. The nature of the fighting and the density of the foliage can be illustrated by an incident that occurred to one of the tanks with 1/9. When it became impossible to proceed farther without checking the road, the tank commander directed one of his men to scout the immediate area. Only 15 yards from his own vehicle, the Marine discovered a camouflaged Japanese medium tank that had been abandoned.[97]

At noon Company C passed through the right unit in an attempt to flank the strongly defended area. Accompanying tanks received heavy AT fire, and the general advance was slow, but by 1800 the two assault companies had crossed the road. A half-track that had been attached late in the afternoon destroyed the one remaining 75mm gun, and Lieutenant Colonel Randall recommitted Company A on the right to close the gap with the 2d Battalion. The latter unit had not met such stiff resistance in its assault, and by 1600 it had reached the road junction in the vicinity of Liguan. Here the battalion received orders to prepare a perimeter defense for the night.[98]

Neither the 3d nor 21st Marines encountered organized opposition during the day. Isolated

pockets of resistance had slowed the advance, but organic weapons quickly silenced these. Before nightfall both regiments had gained their objectives, and by using one company of 3/9 between the 9th and 21st, contact had been obtained throughout the division. No contact existed, however, between the Marines and the Army.

The day's activities had sufficiently uncovered RJ 177 to permit supply trains to move to the forward dump at Dededo. It had been planned to open this distribution point on 4 August, but continuous fighting around Finegayan delayed the move for one day. To help shorten the over-all route, Agana Beach was now ready for use, and UDT's had begun clearing an LVT channel to the shore at Tumon Bay. The opening of these two beaches would give the division close access to incoming supply ships.

In keeping with General Turnage's policy of having service elements well forward, division hospital displaced from the vicinity of Asan to the site of the old U. S. Naval Hospital in Agana on 5 August. About the time this move was complete, 1700, the engineers reported the opening of a water point at Dededo. Its 35,000 gallons per day would be welcomed by those infantry units now making the long run to Agana.[99]

The brigade remained in bivouac in force reserve throughout the day, but General Shepherd received verbal instructions for the employment of his command in the near future. The corps commander intended to pass the brigade through the 3d Marines to attack north along the west coast of Guam. At 1205 Shepherd sent the Reconnaissance Platoon, 4th Marines to reconnoiter routes for the movement of troops and supplies to assembly areas near Dededo. At 1630 the corps' operation plan was received directing the brigade to attack on order, seize successive objectives, and then by aggressive patrolling to clear the enemy from the northern tip of the island.[100]

Although air, naval gunfire, and artillery had been keeping Mt. Santa Rosa under constant

[97] 1/9 SAR, 2. This is no doubt the tank that had been reported knocked out by the armored reconnaissance patrol on the evening of 3 August.

[98] *Ibid.;* 2/9 SAR, 7.

[99] 3d MarDiv D–4 Jnl.

[100] 1st ProvMarBrig WD, 1Jul–10Aug44, 19.

105MM HOWITZER hastily emplaced to support the northern drive of the 3d Division.

bombardment, the Japanese still maintained artillery positions in the area. At least seven guns continued to harass the Americans, and during the night of 5–6 August the weapons increased their activities.[101] The enemy had been firing intermittently throughout the day, but only when rain squalls occurred. This had made detection almost impossible, and when darkness came the guns opened up with the most severe artillery fire encountered during the drive to the north.

Road junctions seemed to be the primary targets and Marine installations located in their vicinity received considerable harassment. The 9th Marines' units near RJ 177 reported the heaviest concentrations. Both division and corps artillery brought fire to bear on the sus-

pected enemy 75mm and 105mm gun positions, but only silenced them temporarily. When the fire shifted to other targets, the Japanese guns immediately resumed their interdiction missions. With the coming of daylight the enemy weapons became silent.[102]

The 3d Division renewed its attack with three regiments abreast at 0630, 6 August. On the right the 9th Marines continued meeting scattered resistance from the remaining Japanese defenders of the Finegayan position. When an enemy patrol led by a tank hit a 2/9 roadblock which had been set up on the division boundary, the tank was destroyed and the infantry scattered. Two platoons of Company G, supported by tanks, pursued the enemy sol-

---

[101] *Japanese Defense of Guam.*

[102] 3d MarDiv D–2 Periodic Rpt 83.

BEER AND SAKE DUMP overrun near Finegayan is checked by Marine supplymen and tallied for eventual issue to troops of III Corps.

diers and killed 15 before breaking off the action at a road junction 1,000 yards inside the 77th Division's zone.[103]

With intelligence agencies indicating the Japanese were establishing delaying forces of infantry and antitank units along the trails and roads only, the division commander decided on a change of tactics. At 0900, General Turnage issued his operation order directing the resumption of the attack by advancing columns along all roads and trails. Each column would search out and mop up enemy resistance for a distance of 200 yards on each side of the road in close country. In open terrain, the edges of the first cover were to be checked. Contact would only be necessary at indicated objectives.[104]

After the remaining enemy positions in the Finegayen defense area had been reduced, the

3d Division encountered little opposition as it moved rapidly forward. At 1155 Marines finally made contact with the 77th Division near RJ 363 when a patrol from the 306th Infantry met a similar patrol of the 9th Marines. By 1300 the head of the 2/9 column had reached RJ 358. Using yellow smoke to mark its position, 2/9 pushed ahead until artillery shells began to fall in the vicinity of the advancing Marines. Commanders later discovered the fire was in support of a 77th Division unit approaching the same road junction on a different trail.[105]

As a result of all units taking to the roads, by nightfall of 6 August the 3d Division had advanced 4,500–5,000 yards all along the front. On the left flank the line extended from Ague along the road to RJ 366; from there it followed the trail to the road that led to RJ 358 where a 300-yard gap existed between the flanking Marine and Army battalions' defense perimeters. (See Map 28, Map Section)

The elimination of 737 Japanese around the Finegayan positions broke the outer ring of the Mt. Santa Rosa defense.[106] The action also cleared the key road junction connecting the highway and trail network to the northeast. This would now permit the movement of equipment and supplies to all corps units with less difficulty. The four days of close, almost hand-to-hand combat, however, had resulted in 18 Marines being killed and 141 wounded.[107]

Of more importance to the individual Marine than the tactical accomplishments, the battle of Finegayan had uncovered a cache of 100 cases of Japanese beer. Division placed guards on the discovery and later moved the supply to dumps for safekeeping until the Guam campaign ended; it was then distributed to units of the division. The presence of the beer in the locality no doubt accounted for the large number of drunken enemy soldiers encountered throughout the action.

Although the Japanese could still harass the Americans with artillery, antitank, and automatic weapons, the effect of the air strikes and

[103] 2/9 SAR, 7.
[104] 3d MarDiv OpOrder 16, 6Aug44.

[105] 3d MarDiv D–3 Jnl.
[106] 3d MarDiv D–2 Periodic Rpts 80–84.
[107] 3d MarDiv WD, August 1944, 3–4.

naval gunfire on these positions was being felt by the enemy. One Japanese officer later wrote:

The enemy airforce seeking our units during the daylight hours in the forest, bombed and strafed even a single soldier. During the night, the enemy naval units attempting to cut our communications were shelling our position from all points of the perimeter of the island, thus impeding our operation activities to a great extent.[108]

While the 3d Division had been moving steadily ahead, the brigade displaced to previously designated assembly areas in the vicinity of Dededo. General Shepherd's forward CP opened at 1410, 6 August, and both regiments were in bivouac prior to darkness. Shepherd received verbal instructions at 1445 ordering his units into the line on 7 August, and when confirmation arrived by dispatch at 1700 the brigade had completed arrangements for the attack.[109] With the commitment of the brigade on the left flank of the corps, General Geiger directed the 3d division to continue the attack and assist the 77th Division on the right.

77th's PRELUDE TO MT. SANTA ROSA

The apparent movement of the Japanese to their main defenses around Mt. Santa Rosa prompted the 77th Division commander to start maneuvering his units into attack position as early as 5 August. At 0700 on that day the 306th Infantry started its move to pass by the right flank of the 307th and extend northwest toward the division boundary. This would pinch out the 307th, allowing it to go into division reserve for a day's rest. (See Map 29)

Although the 306th encountered little resistance, jungle terrain, poor trails, and inaccurate maps slowed the maneuver. Colonel Smith's regiment had covered the 307th by 1600, but the unit was still 1,000 yards short of its objective. Nevertheless, General Bruce instructed the battalions to consolidate their positions for the night, paying particular attention to all-around security.[110]

On the right flank of the 77th Division, the

[108] *Japanese Defense of Guam.*
[109] 1st ProvMarBrig WD, 1Jul–10Aug44, 19.
[110] 306th Inf Unit Rpts.

MOUNT SANTA ROSA, target of the final corps drive, dominated the 77th division zone of action. (Army Photograph.)

305th had continued hacking its way through the dense jungle. With tanks and self-propelled guns beating a trail, the day's activities netted 2,000 yards and put the 2d Battalion on the O–4 line by nightfall. The 1st, about 1,000 yards to the rear, bivouacked in a more or less isolated position. Hard coral underlay about six to nine inches of earth, making the preparation of proper slit trenches and weapons' positions virtually impossible in the time allotted. About 0200 the most destructive Japanese night raid the 77th Division experienced on Guam hit this battalion.

Two Japanese medium tanks with approximately one platoon of infantry broke through Company A, guarding the northern sector of the battalion's defensive area. Troops immediately opened fire all along the line. The enemy infantry scattered, but the vehicles continued on into the rear installations. Once inside the perimeter the tanks separated as if according to plan and sprayed either side of the trail, covering the bivouac area with murderous fire.

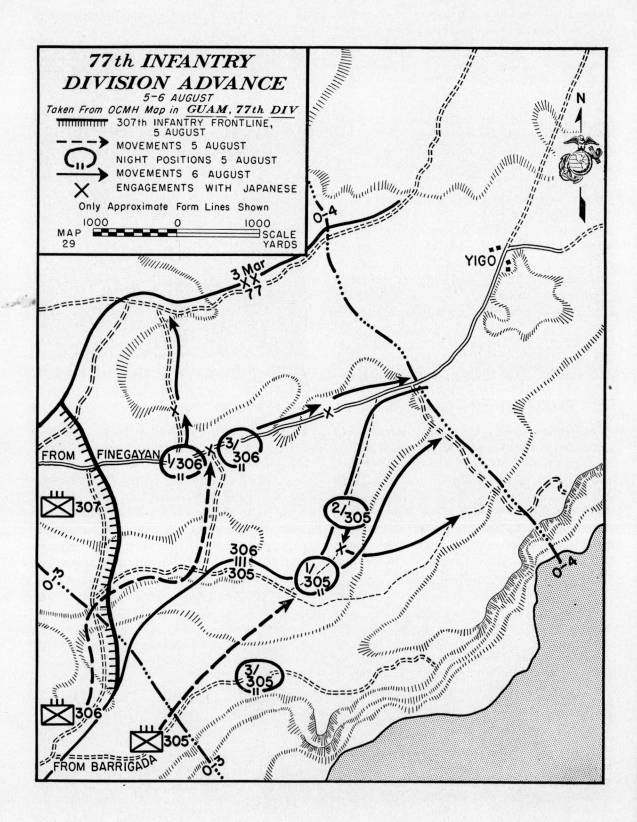

77th INFANTRY DIVISION ADVANCE
5–6 AUGUST
Taken From OCMH Map in *GUAM, 77th DIV*

|||||||||| 307th INFANTRY FRONTLINE, 5 AUGUST
MOVEMENTS 5 AUGUST
NIGHT POSITIONS 5 AUGUST
MOVEMENTS 6 AUGUST
X ENGAGEMENTS WITH JAPANESE
Only Approximate Form Lines Shown

MAP 29

1000   0   1000   SCALE YARDS

N

YIGO

3 Mar
XX
77

O-4

FROM FINEGAYAN

1/306

3/306

2/305

1/305

306
III
305

3/305

307

306

305

FROM BARRIGADA

O-3

O-3

O-4

SOLDIERS of the 307th Infantry advancing past Army tanks as they move up the road from Yigo to Mt. Santa Rosa.

In the excitement that followed, men turned their rifles and automatic weapons on the tanks, but the fire only ricocheted into friendly troops who were shifting to alternate positions. One of the tanks, in trying to rejoin its partner, collided with an Army Sherman, then backed off, smashed a jeep, and continued on its way firing continuously. Joining, the two Japanese mediums charged north toward the perimeter, leaving behind a trail of devastation including 16 killed and 32 wounded. Most of these casualties resulted from the battalion's inability to prepare adequate trenches prior to darkness.[111]

Several hours later men of the 305th encountered these same two tanks again. The 2d Battalion came upon them at 0630 as it retraced its course of the previous day in an effort to find a better route of advance. This time the Japanese in hull defilade covered the narrow trail leading through the dense jungle undergrowth. The ensuing fire fight was a confusing one, involving American medium tanks, heavy machine guns, mortars, and riflemen, all trying to knock out the tank-held position. Finally, when infantry squads pushed through the jungle on either side and moved up on the enemy's rear, they found three dead soldiers; both vehicles had been abandoned. To their previously inflicted casualties the Japanese tankmen added 15 killed and 31 wounded.[112]

Units of the 77th spent most of 6 August in getting into position for the well-planned attack on Mt. Santa Rosa. By nightfall the 306th had reached the division boundary, the 305th had its battalions on the O–4 line, and the 307th was ready to move back into the center of the line. These positions resulted from planning started on 3 August.

Early on the morning of 5 August General Bruce received the corps operation plan ordering the capture of Mt. Santa Rosa and the re-

---

[111] *Landrum.*

[112] *Guam, 77th Div,* 111–113. Official G–1 casualty reports for 6Aug44 do not completely confirm the listed KIA of the Army's monograph account. Only 19 KIA are listed by G–1 for the 305th Inf during the 24-hour period 0001–2400, 6Aug44. 77th InfDiv G–1 Jnl.

mainder of the island to the north. It would be a corps assault with the main effort being made by the 77th Division.[113] Tentative plans had already been worked out by Bruce's staff for the capture of the tactically important Mt. Santa Rosa area, and at 1250 an overlay showing the proposed scheme of maneuver went out to each unit involved. Essentially, the operation would surround the dominating hill, thus cutting off all avenues of escape for the enemy except by the sea (See Map 30, Map Section)

The sweep would be to the left, with the 306th's objective the high ground to the north extending from Lulog to Anao on the coast. Since this regiment would have to cover twice as much ground as the others in the division, it would advance without regard to contact. It would, however, send patrols forward to the division boundary to secure that area. The 307th, supported by the 706th Tank Battalion (less Companies A and B), was to capture Yigo with its important road junction, then turn to the east toward the slopes of the objective. The 305th (less the 3d Battalion which would be in corps reserve) was to continue along the same general avenue of advance the regiment had been following and secure the high ground south of Mt. Santa Rosa. Each regiment would keep one battalion in reserve, to be committed only on authority of the division commander.[114]

Corps had made plans to continue the shelling of the area by warships and further soften enemy positions with air strikes by P-47's and B-25's. In addition, corps artillery would give priority of fires to the 77th on the designated day of the attack. Including the division's own organic artillery, there would not be a shortage of support for the big push.

In the afternoon of 6 August (1720) corps ordered the attack for 0730 the following morning. In anticipation of this move General Bruce had sent his chief of staff forward to reconnoiter for an advance CP earlier in the afternoon. Colonel McNair had selected an area about 600 yards south of Ipapao and was making a last minute check of the position at 1645 when a sniper fired from a hut and killed him instantly.[115]

After the reconnaissance party detected more Japanese, the division reserve (3/305) received instructions to scour the area. Only 500 yards from the proposed site of the CP, Company I encountered an estimated 150 enemy soldiers in well-prepared positions. Many of the individual foxholes were located in the roots of ironwood trees which made them almost impervious to small-arms fire. The job of completely liquidating this pocket took more than six hours and required the major strength of Companies I and K, supported by a platoon of medium tanks.[116]

THE FINAL DRIVE

At 0730 on 7 August all three regiments of the 77th Division left the O-4 line with orders to be in position for the attack at H-Hour, which would be announced later. At about the same time General Bruce authorized the 307th's commander to employ all three of his battalions in the attack on Yigo. In the center of the division zone, 3/307 led the advance toward Yigo, moving in a column toward the line of departure,[117] a road junction 600 yards southwest of the village. On the left, the 306th started cross country to by-pass Yigo on the west. The lead company of 3/307 reached the LD by 0900 without meeting any resistance and halted. As the unit posted its security, sporadic fire started to hit the column. An hour later the snipers had been silenced and the battalion reported its position secure.

The 307th received a message at 1038 fixing H-Hour at 1200, and Colonel Manuel sent for the 706th Tank Battalion commander. But not until 1145, after the artillery preparation had started, did Lieutenant Colonel Charles W. Stokes receive the summons. When he reached the 307th's CP, Manuel informed him of H-

---

[115] 77th InfDiv OpRpt, 5–6. Colonel McNair's father, LtGen Leslie J. McNair, former Commanding General, Army Ground Forces, had been killed only 12 days earlier by an American bomb while watching a battalion in the attack during the St.-Lo breakout in France.

[116] *Chalgren.*

[117] In the true definition of the term, this was not a line of departure, but more of a control point for the column of the 307th.

---

[113] IIIAC OpPlan 8–44, 5Aug44.

[114] 77th InfDiv OpOverlay, 5Aug44.

Hour and directed Stokes to follow the prepared plan of attack. The tank commander immediately radioed for the battalion to come forward from its assembly area a mile to the rear. Hundreds of rounds of 105mm and 155mm shells from seven artillery battalions rumbled overhead as the tanks tried to move on the congested, narrow trail leading into Yigo.[118]

Exactly on schedule, the devastating artillery barrage lifted at 1200, but the tanks and infantry were not yet in position to move into the shelled area. Fifteen minutes later the light tanks reached the head of the 3/307 column that had jumped off from the LD at H-minus three minutes in an attempt to take full advantage of the artillery fire.[119] At this point, 400 yards short of Yigo, the tanks rapidly outdistanced the infantry and fanned out to the right. Overrunning several Japanese machine-gun positions at the edge of the road, the vehicles roared on across the open ground, which rose to a slight crest only 200 yards ahead.

As the tanks swept over the small rise, enemy fire spurted from the left. A call for assistance went out to the mediums. These moved in under an increasing deluge of Japanese machine-gun and antitank fire. Before they could bring their fire to bear on the enemy position, two light tanks were knocked out and one medium set afire. Another stalled and had to be abandoned.

While the tanks continued their searching fires, the infantry tried to make progress through the positions along the road, but it was slow going. On the left, 3/306 led by Lieutenant Colonel Gordon T. Kimbrell met little opposition as it moved through the jungle. On hearing the firing from the vicinity of Yigo, Kimbrell detached the 1st Platoon of Company K and led it toward the action. He located the enemy strong point and proceeded through the underbrush to the rear of the area. The soldiers rushed the unsuspecting Japanese and killed them without loss to the Army unit. Other elements of Company K cleared the enemy from their supporting positions along the edge of the woods further to the north, and the major defense of Yigo was reduced. The

SMASHED JAPANESE TANK near Yigo, one of two that were part of a defensive position that slowed the 307th Infantry advance on 7 August.

enemy position, so skillfully concealed from the front but vulnerable from the rear, was built around two light tanks. Two antitank guns, two 20mm guns, six light and two heavy machine guns, plus about a makeshift battalion of infantry added their fire to make the Yigo defense formidable.[120]

This tank action had been fast and furious, and by 1325 leading elements of the 307th had reached the high ground northeast of the village. There was little sign of the enemy the rest of the afternoon as the three battalions of the 307th jockeyed into their respective positions for the attack on Mt. Santa Rosa. But by the time this had been completed, it was too late to renew the assault, and the regiment dug in along the road from Yigo to a point a half-mile east of the village. (See Map 31, Map Section) The 306th prepared a defense 1,000 yards to the north of RJ 415; the forward battalion of the 305th had beaten its way through the jungle to within 600–800 yards of the day's objective.

In the center of the corps zone the 3d Marine Division, now attacking to the northeast, had jumped off on time the morning of 7 August

[118] 77th InfDiv G–3 Jnl.
[119] 307th Inf S–2, S–3 Jnl.

[120] *Guam, 77th Div,* 124–125.

MARINE CORSAIRS of MAG–21 lined up on Orote Airfield in readiness to fly close support missions during the last days of organized fighting on Guam.

and moved ahead against light resistance. However, the dwarf jungle terrain made progress slow, and bulldozers had to be employed to clear roads for the advance. On the left flank the 3d Marines encountered antitank guns at a roadblock in the vicinity of RJ 390, but the regiment quickly destroyed the weapons without suffering a casualty. Of great assistance in reducing any strong point encountered was the immediate action taken by the now mobile command post.[121] This system of having the CP mounted permitted commanders to keep abreast of the fighting and to employ the necessary weapons without delay.

Elements of the Marine division, inspired by the enemy's apparent disorganization, pushed through 6,000 yards of dense vegetation to the corps' objective (O–5) by 1530. The only halt during the day had been at the O–4 line, and that to enable all units to coordinate and make contact. So well had the attack progressed throughout the day that General Turnage sent instructions at 1515 to prepare to advance the center and left of the line another 1,000–1,500 yards. However, 45 minutes later Turnage rescinded the order, and the division prepared defensive positions for the night along the O–5 line.[122]

The 1st Brigade had started its advance along the coast at 0730 on 7 August by passing the 4th Marines through the 1st and 2d Battalions of the 3d Marines. When the maneuver was complete, 1/3 passed to corps reserve and the 4th Marines surged ahead toward the O–4 line. Progress had ben sod rapid by 0910 that General Shepherd ordered his reserve regiment, the 22d Marines, to move forward to a new assembly area in the vicinity of Ague. He also directed the assault unit to continue the attack to a new objective approximately 1,000 yards beyond the O–4.

An hour later, with the first objective secured, Lieutenant Colonel Shapley's 4th Marines made preparations to push forward as rapidly as possible. Shortly after noon Shepherd issued another operation order which directed the seizure of O–5. This plan called for the 22d Marines to pass through the left battalion of the 4th Regiment and continue the attack in junction with Shapley's unit.[123] By 1600 the 4th Marines had reached its objective and the 22d was in position to carry out the passage of lines, but General Shepherd decided not to execute the maneuver until 0730 the following morning.[124]

During the day the corps lines had moved ahead as much as 6,000 yards in some zones and the Yigo area had been reduced without too much delay. The 77th Division was ready to attack Mt. Santa Rosa while the 1st Provisional Brigade and the 3d Division were in position to drive to the end of the island. The day had also seen the first Marine planes (VMF–225) based on Orote airfield flying combat missions over Guam.[125] In the south, patrols of 1/22 continued to cover their zones while troops not so engaged started regular camp routine under their new battalion commander, Major Crawford B. Lawton.[126]

During the night of 7–8 August, the Japanese tried another of the tank-infantry raids that had proved so successful against the 305th Infantry only two nights before. This time they chose to hit the 306th. Before midnight two infantry infiltration attempts had been repulsed, and all front line troops alerted for fur-

---

[121] 3d MarDiv D–3 Jnl.
[122] *Ibid.*

[123] 1st ProvMarBrig OpOrder 38, 7Aug44.
[124] 1st ProvMarBrig WD, 1Jul–10Aug44, 19.
[125] MAG–21 WD, August 1944, 4.
[126] LtCol Walfried H. Fromhold was evacuated on 6Aug44 with filariasis.

ther action. At 0300 outposts heard tanks approaching from the north. The lead tank, followed closely by a second, opened fire as it drew near, but as the Japanese infantry tried to move in small-arms and machine-gun fire forced them to withdraw. Rifle grenades destroyed one tank and heavy machine guns halted the second, but a third appeared and pulled the disabled tank away. In the morning 18 dead Japanese, including three officers, lay in front of the 3d Battalion, 306th, which had suffered six killed and 13 wounded during the night's activities.[127]

All units were organized to renew the attack on Mt. Santa Rosa by 0730. The 305th and the 307th were to close in on the objective while the 306th captured Lulog to the north. This would put pressure on the defenders from the south and west and at the same time cut off the escape route to the north.

In its drive toward Lulog, 3/306 led the regiment and met only slight opposition from scattered enemy troops, many still too dazed from the artillery and air bombardment to fight. The battalion continued to press rapidly forward, and as it neared its objective new orders directed a change in the regiment's mission. The 3d Battalion would take the previously assigned objective and continue on to the east coast; the 2d would go to Pati Point in the extreme northeast corner of the division's zone; the 1st was to proceed on the trail leading to Salisbury and set up a blocking position in the vicinity of the junction of that trail and the one going to Chaguian.[128] (See Map 31, Map Section)

By 1040, 3/306 had taken its objective and the 307th had captured Mt. Santa Rosa, having killed 35 Japanese on the approaches to the mountain. Soldiers did not encounter any opposition on the bare slopes of the hill mass itself, and by 1400 a line had been consolidated across the summit. Patrols were sent to the sea with instructions to investigate all caves and other possible hiding places.

Meanwhile, in attempting to execute its part of the new plan, 2/306 converged on the 9th Marines near the Salisbury Road. During the movement, Marine artillery shells fired in support of the 9th fell on the Army column causing several casualties.[129] This incident grew out of a misunderstanding of the division boundary along the Salisbury Road.[130]

The corps order of 5 August established the boundary from the trail junction near Mataguac to the junction of the roads leading to Salisbury and Chaguian and thence along the Salisbury Road. Responsibility for this road was given to the 77th Division, but both the Army and Marine divisions had equal priority on movement over the road. The 77th Division overlay of 5 August being used by lower units of the Army, however, gave the boundary as running from the trail junction near Mataguac along the trail to the road leading to Chaguian and then *cross country* to the Salisbury Road at that village.[131] (See Map 30) When units discovered the difference, the respective regimental commanders soon took the necessary measures to prevent further confusion.[132]

When a POW report indicated the presence of 3,000 Japanese in the area, General Bruce issued another change of orders to the 306th. One company of the 1st Battalion received instructions to follow behind the 9th Marines to maintain contact while the rest of the battalion moved to Lulog to join the 3d Battalion. The 2d would be held in reserve about 1,200 yards northeast of Yigo, with the possibility of being committed on the left flank of the 307th.

Shortly thereafter Colonel Smith decided to commit the 2d Battalion as a precaution against the possibility of the 3,000 enemy being an actuality. He ordered the unit to move to the north of Mt. Santa Rosa and tie in with the 3d. Later in the afternoon the 1st marched cross country and made contact with the rest of the regiment near Lulog.

That night (8 August), as units began to take up defensive positions, the difficulties of coordination in jungle terrain were once again demon-

[127] 306th Inf OpRpt, 4.

[128] 77th InfDiv G-3 Jnl.

[129] Ltr Col J. A. Remus to CMC, 4Dec52; 77th InfDiv G-3 Jnl.

[130] 9th Mar R-2 Jnl.

[131] IIIAC OpOrder 8-44, 5Aug44; 77th InfDiv OpOverlay, 5Aug44.

[132] Ltr BrigGen W. A. Wachtler to author, 24Apr52; *Craig 1952.*

strated. Men of the 306th and 307th mistook each other for the enemy, and a heavy fire fight ensued. Mortars and tanks added to the confusion, and before the fracas could be halted at least ten men had been wounded.[133]

With the end of the battle for Mt. Santa Rosa, all effective resistance ceased in the zone of action of the 77th Division. In the two-day engagement Army infantry and tank units suffered 30 KIA, 104 WIA, and 11 MIA,[134] but these casualties proved to be somewhat lighter than had been anticipated because of the lack of determined resistance on the objective. The terrific shelling from artillery and naval gunfire, along with air strikes accounted for this light opposition in reducing what had been the enemy's last strong defensive position on the island. Japanese sources indicate their strength in the vicinity of Mt. Santa Rosa at the start of action at 1,500 Army troops, 1,000 Navy, and 2,500 laborers. Seven medium caliber guns and ten medium and three light tanks supported the rifles, machine guns, and other automatic weapons in the position.[135] Only 528 enemy bodies were counted during the two-day period of the action. Elements of the 77th Division either captured or destroyed all guns, but put only five of the 13 tanks out of action.[136] It was now evident that the maneuver had failed to seal the Japanese in the Mt. Santa Rosa area, and other steps would have to be taken to ferret them from their hiding places.

Small groups of the enemy, trying to escape through the jungle, drifted into the zone of action of the 9th Marines, and slowed that unit's advance on 8 August. Opposition had been encountered immediately after the regiment started its drive at 0730 to capture the remainder of the island in its sector. After reducing these scattered pockets of resistance, which took most of the day, elements reached the intermediate objective at 1615. Here units dug in for the night with the most forward battalion (3/9) set up in a perimeter defense

1,000 yards northwest of the 2d Battalion, located around Salisbury. The 1st, in reserve, during the day, continued patrolling around the road junction near Mataguac and contributed 25 enemy killed to the 128 total reported by the regiment.[137]

Although Colonel Craig did not know it at the time, his CP was set up approximately 300 yards from General Obata's headquarters. Patrols from the 9th Marines had noticed a small jungle-covered hill within the zone of action of the 77th Division and when scouts tried to investigate the area they immediately drew fire. Craig notified Army units charged with the responsibility of the sector and withdrew his patrols so the 77th's battalion could operate against the strong point.[138]

The 3d Marines, on the division's left flank, fought thick, tangled jungle instead of the Japanese as Colonel Stuart's regiment pushed northeast toward the sea. The 2d Battalion had passed through the 3d Battalion at 0730 and proceeded on an unimproved road that was the axis of advance. At about noon the trail ended abruptly, and a search started for a road extending from Salisbury northwest across the regimental front and over the cliff to the sea, which the map indicated lay only a short distance to the front. Actually it was found 1,300 yards away and with no approaches from the direction of advance.[139]

The battalion did not get on the road until 1700, and since it had to cut its way through the dense jungle, arrived without its supporting weapons. These followed behind tanks and bulldozers, which had to cut a usable road. Meanwhile, in an effort to contact the 9th Marines, 2/3 extended to the right along the trail. While carrying out this mission, the Marines encountered a Japanese roadblock held by 19 enemy soldiers. All were killed in the action that followed but the fight delayed 2/3 so that a juncture could not be made with the 9th before

[133] 77th InfDiv G–3 Jnl.
[134] 77th InfDiv G–1 Casualty Rpts for 7–8Aug44.
[135] *Japanese Defense of Guam.*
[136] IIIAC C–2 Periodic Rpts 17–19.

[137] 3d MarDiv D–2 Periodic Rpt 86.
[138] *Craig 1952.*
[139] 3d Mar SAR, 4. The map, with corrections up to April 1944, shows this road as a trail and, if little used, the fast-growing vegetation indigenous to this part of the island would completely cover it in a few months.

DENSE JUNGLE crowds in on men of the 3d Marines moving up the Salisbury-Tarague Trail, scene of the last tank action on Guam.

darkness. Colonel Stuart then ordered the battalion to set up a perimeter defense two miles north of Salisbury along the road to Tarague.

The rest of the 3d Marines, less 1/3 in corps reserve, had followed behind the 2d Battalion meeting little or no resistance during the day. When these elements reached a point 1,500 yards beyond RJ 462, they started to prepare night defense positions. Patrols examined the low ground below the cliffs overlooking the sea, but made no contact with the enemy.[140]

The 21st Marines, placed in division reserve prior to the start of the attack in the morning, had spent the day (8 August) patrolling. This regiment had been assigned the mission of searching the area between the 3d and 9th Marines, at the same time being prepared to support the division if so ordered. It had regained

control of its 2d Battalion at 0730, but at 1800 it lost the 1st to the 3d Marines.[141] Patrols returned late in the afternoon and reported few enemy contacts, but one such unit from 3/21 had discovered a Japanese truck containing the bodies of 30 native men who had been beheaded. According to the official account of the incident, the Guamanians, found near Chaguian, had not been dead more than 24 hours. The next morning another patrol found an additional 21 bodies in the jungle near the same village.[142]

General Shepherd's brigade had started its advance along the west coast at 0730 to seize the O-5 line. The 22d Marines had moved into the

[140] *Ibid.*, 5.

[141] 21st Mar SAR, 9.

[142] 3/21 Bn–2 Jnl. Investigators from corps and division were able to identify the bodies and concluded that the men were among those who had been brought from the Yona concentration camp to work on the Yigo defense area. IIIAC C–2 Jnl.

RITIDIAN POINT served as the patrol base of one of the many small units spread out through Northern Guam when the mopping up of Japanese survivors began.

line on the left of the 4th, and the two regiments began the coordinated attack designed to carry them to the end of the island. The infantry encountered only moderate resistance, but when an air strike hit Mt. Machanao and Ritidian Point pilots reported receiving enemy antiaircraft and small-arms fire.[143] Corps artillery and naval gunfire soon neutralized this Japanese activity. Nevertheless, corps requested that surface craft make a search of the beach area during daylight hours to observe any Japanese movements. As an added precaution, General Shepherd directed the 2d Battalion, 22d Marines to send a patrol to Ritidian Light.

After leaving a roadblock at RJ 530, 2/22 advanced in column of companies toward the northern coast of Guam. Air strikes hit each road junction to the front, and by 1500 that unit had reached Ritidian Point. A patrol of Company F that had been sent down a trail leading to the beach encountered the only enemy resistance. The Marines easily overcame the oppo-

sition, an ambush, and accomplished the mission without further incident.[144] This gave General Shepherd's units the distinction of being the first to reach both the northernmost (Ritidian Point) and southernmost (Liguan Point) parts of Guam.[145]

The 4th Marines had secured O–5 in its zone and had contact with the 22d along that line at RJ 470 by 1600. The regiment had also sent units along the road toward Tarague to tie in with the 3d Battalion, 3d Marines. After locating 3/3, the 2d Battalion, 4th set up for the night about 700–800 yards east of RJ 462. To the north 800–1,000 yards along the trail, 3/4 prepared a perimeter defense, paying particular attention to the northeast sector. (See Map 31, Map Section)

The 22d Marines had also taken its objective easily, and after the 2d Battalion had returned

[143] 1st ProvMarBrig Jnl.

[144] 2/22 Jnl.

[145] The 6th MarDiv under Gen Shepherd accomplished the same feat on Okinawa by securing both ends of that island.

from Ritidian Point it established a roadblock at RJ 580. The remainder of the unit organized positions that could counter any threat from Mt. Machanao. The 3d Battalion set up two roadblocks, one at RJ 530 and another at RJ 470, with its main elements on O–5 between the two junctions.

Fighting on the corps front during the day had not been spectacular, but the enemy had been driven into the extreme northeastern part of the island. In addition, the thrust in the center of the line by the 3d and 4th Marines had divided the enemy remnant into two groups. It was now evident, even to the Japanese, that their remaining strength had little fighting power, and Radio Tokyo began preparing the population of the homeland for the inevitable announcement of the fall of Guam. On the evening of 8 August an enemy announcer stated that the Americans now held nine-tenths of the island and that the enemy was patrolling the area still held by the Japanese.[146]

About the time Tokyo released this news, corps issued its operation order directing all units to continue the pursuit with utmost vigor. General Geiger set the time for the attack to capture the remainder of Guam for 0730 the following morning (9 August).[147]

During the night, only one corps unit reported organized enemy activity. At about 0130, the 2d Battalion, 3d Marines, still without its antitank guns and other supporting weapons, notified division headquarters that it was under attack. (See Map 32) Five Japanese medium tanks followed by an undetermined force of infantry ran headlong into the Marines' perimeter. By 0330 the men of 2/3 had destroyed or dispersed the enemy foot soldiers but the armor still remained a threat. The battalion commander ordered a withdrawal into the jungle and 15 minutes later all companies had pulled out without the tanks firing a shot. Whether the tankmen ran out of ammunition and fuel is purely speculative, but in any case 2/3 after completing its reorganization found to everyone's amazement that the battalion had

not suffered a single casualty during the night's activity.[148]

When daylight came, regiment directed all efforts toward getting tanks and antitank guns through the jungle to close with the Japanese. By noon, bulldozers, closely followed by tanks, had broken through to the trail to Salisbury. Hoping to trap the enemy armor before it escaped to the north, a task force composed of 3/3 and supporting elements turned down the trail toward Salisbury, after leaving a blocking force at the new trail junction.

Meanwhile, 2/3 was extricating itself from a dangerous situation. Scouts had located the Japanese tanks near the battalion's night perimeter, but Major Culpepper still had no weapons suitable to cope with the enemy tanks. Under cover of a rear guard Culpepper ordered his men to withdraw. They cut their way through the jungle undetected and eventually reached the area occupied the night before by 3/3 near RJ 462. Men of the rear guard were the last Marines to see the enemy tanks on 9 August. Before the 3d Battalion task force could block the trail, the Japanese had escaped unseen toward the coast.

At 1500 the 1st Battalion, 21st, still attached to the 3d Marines, followed 3/3 over the newly cut track to the Salisbury-Tarague trail and turned to the north. When division headquarters passed the word to dig in for the night, 1/21 had moved to within 1,500 yards of the northeast coast.[149]

During the day's activities, the 3d Marines had killed an estimated 55–60 Japanese stragglers and destroyed a 37mm gun, but the whereabouts of the five tanks was now unknown. Although there had been much maneuvering and a somewhat confused situation throughout the night and day, the evening of 9 August found Colonel Stuart's units in position to continue the search for the elusive enemy the following morning.

Even though there had been little opportunity for the 3d Marines to use artillery support during the day, such was not the case in the 9th's zone. The attack toward the northeastern

[146] IIIAC C–2 Periodic Rpt 19.
[147] IIIAC OpOrder 10–44, 8Aug44.

[148] 2/3 Jnl.
[149] 3d Mar SAR, 5.

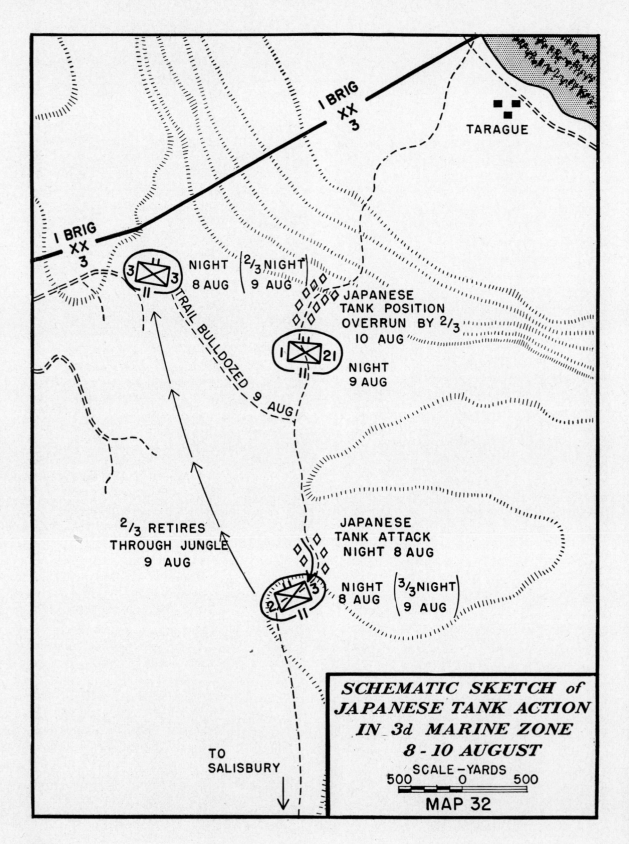

I BRIG
XX
3

TARAGUE

I BRIG
XX
3

NIGHT
8 AUG

2/3 NIGHT
9 AUG

3 ⊠ 3

TRAIL BULLDOZED 9 AUG

JAPANESE
TANK POSITION
OVERRUN BY 2/3
10 AUG

1 ⊠ 21

NIGHT
9 AUG

2/3 RETIRES
THROUGH JUNGLE
9 AUG

JAPANESE
TANK ATTACK
NIGHT 8 AUG

2 ⊠ 3

NIGHT
8 AUG

3/3 NIGHT
9 AUG

TO
SALISBURY

SCHEMATIC SKETCH of
JAPANESE TANK ACTION
IN 3d MARINE ZONE
8 - 10 AUGUST

SCALE — YARDS
500   0   500

MAP 32

coast started on time and made rapid progress until 0935 when Colonel Craig received orders to stop the main effort and send patrols to Savana Grande. Investigation showed that a native telling of 2,000–3,000 Japanese located in the northern cliff area had caused the sudden halt.[150] Corps artillery was notified to place all fire possible in that region. With the 7th 155mm Gun Battalion being the only corps unit that could reach the suspected enemy concentration, it received orders to cover the densely forested terrain. In two and a half hours of uninterrupted firing, the 7th hurled an unprecedented 1,000 rounds into the area from the 12 guns of its battalion.[151] Division artillery batteries added 2,280 75mm and 105mm shells to the same target.

No resistance met the 9th Marines when it moved in, but neither were there many Japanese bodies. As the Corps Artillery A–3 later wrote:

> The intelligence information on which all the firing had been based was wrong, and we had made this great effort for nothing. However, it did provide a bang-up end to the campaign.[152]

By 1800, the company from 3/9 which had been assigned the mission of protecting the right flank of the regiment reached Pati Point. Farther to the north, advance elements of the 9th had passed through the heavy vegetation to the cliff overlooking the beach.

Units from both the other major components of the corps also gained the northern beaches on 9 August. Patrols from the 22d Marines descended the cliffs in the vicinity of Ritidian Point while those from the 4th reached the coastal plain just south of Mergagan Point. Only scattered opposition met these mopping-up details, and at 1800 General Shepherd announced that all organized resistance had ceased in the brigade zone.[153]

Infantrymen of the 77th Division continued their mission of searching out individual Jap-

LIEUTENANT GENERAL HIDEYOSHI OBATA, 31st Army Commander, who took command of the defense of Guam after General Takashina's death, was killed by men of the 306th Infantry who overran the Mataguac command post on 11 August.

anese, and early in the day the 306th reported it had hit the coast in its zone. With resistance lacking, General Bruce felt there was need for only one regiment north of Mt. Santa Rosa. He selected the 306th to remain in position and continue patrolling and directed the 305th (less 3d Battalion) to move to the vicinity of Barrigada. This would leave the 307th on Mt. Santa Rosa with the additional responsibility of clearing the snipers from along the supply route to Yigo.

By nightfall of 9 August the end of the Guam campaign was in sight, and all units of the corps prepared to comply with General Geiger's directive to "Push all Japanese from Guam."[154] With both the 77th Division and

---

[150] 9th Mar R–2 Jnl.

[151] Each gun crew in this mission would be required to handle approximately four tons of shells and a ton of propelling charges.

[152] Henderson.

[153] 1st ProvMarBrig Jnl.

[154] 77th InfDiv G–3 Jnl.

the Marine brigade declaring their zones cleared of organized resistance, the only potential source of enemy trouble seemed to be the five tanks last seen by the 3d Division.

In an attempt to keep the tanks from operating during the night, the 12th Marines fired 1,239 rounds on possible bivouac areas and along trails leading into the division's defenses.[155] On 10 August the 2d Battalion, 3d Marines passed through 1/21 at 0730 in a renewal of the previous day's efforts and made the desired contact only 400 yards up the trail. Two tanks opened fire, but the platoon of Marine armor following directly behind the infantry point quickly disposed of the opposition. The advance continued, and by 1030 seven more medium tanks, which had been abandoned, were within friendly lines.[156] The destruction and capture of these, the last reported on Guam, brought the total number of Japanese tanks claimed to have been put out of action by IIIAC units to 59.[157]

At about the same time as this last important action in the north, the USS *Indianapolis* steamed into Apra Harbor with Admiral Spruance and General Holland Smith on board. Although the expected arrival of Admiral Nimitz and General Vandegrift prompted the visit, it coincided with another event of 10 August 1944 of even greater importance. As if the occasion had been planned for all the dignitaries, General Geiger announced at 1131 that organized resistance on Guam had ended.[158] (See Map 33, Map Section)

This information was welcome news to the Commander in Chief, Pacific Ocean Areas and the Commandant of the Marine Corps, who landed at Orote Airfield at 1635. After a night on the USS *Indianapolis*, they spent the next day inspecting front line units and installations on Guam. Also, before leaving, commanders held top-level conferences concerning the future role the island would play in the advance to Tokyo.

Even though officially the island had been secured, corps issued an operation order at 1423 on 10 August outlining the future activities of the units. General Geiger directed the 77th and 3d Divisions to establish a line across the island from Fadian Point to a point northwest of Tumon Bay. Emphasis was then to be placed on mopping up the estimated 7,500 Japanese still remaining on the island and to prevent them from moving south of the straggler line.[159]

With the message sent at 1324 on 10 August to Fifth Fleet confirming the announcement of the fall of Guam went a casualty summarization for the 20-days' fighting. Totals for all corps units showed 1,214 KIA, 5,704 WIA, and 329 MIA. For the same period, 10,971 Japanese dead had been counted.[160]

The Japanese considered they still maintained an organization until 11 August when the Mt. Mataguac command post fell to units of the 306th Infantry. (See Map 30, Map Section) On 8 August, after the 9th Marines substantiated civilian reports of the enemy underground headquarters, a unit from the 77th Reconnaisance Troop moved in to check the area. The patrol encountered numerous ambushes and concluded the job required a stronger force. Two days later, 10 August, 1/306 reconnoitered the sector and found a brush-covered hollow about 100 yards long and 40 feet deep. As a patrol tried to get into position to

---

[155] 3dMarDiv D-3 Periodic Rpt 22.

[156] 2/3 Jnl. Capt Hideo Sato, IJA, Commanding Officer, 24th TkCo, 29th InfDiv, reported these tanks as being "scuttled" rather than abandoned because of lack of fuel or mechanical failure. 3d MarDiv POW Interrogation Rpt 396, 7Oct44.

[157] IIIAC C-2 Periodic Rpt 21. The interrogation of Capt Sato mentioned above indicates a much lower figure. CinCPac-CinCPOA Item 9956, translation of the notebook of a Japanese staff officer found on Saipan, lists 38 Japanese tanks on Guam as of 29May44. This agrees with the figure listed in CinCPac-CinCPOA Item 9304 giving the order of battle of the 9th TkRegt on 15May44. This discrepancy between Japanese and American figures is no doubt due to the duplication of units claiming tank "kills" plus the reporting of hit or damaged tanks as being destroyed

[158] ComFifthFlt WD, August 1944, 11–12.

[159] IIIAC SAR, OpRpt, 8.

[160] CTF 53 dispatch to ComFifthFlt, dtd 10Aug44. The above figures include only those casualties suffered during the period from the initial landing to the time that the island was declared secure. For a complete, corrected tabulation of the Guam campaign casualties see Appendix III.

MAJOR GENERAL GEIGER'S HEADQUARTERS was the scene of a top level conference on 11 August attended by leaders of the Pacific War. Left to right: General Geiger, Admiral Spruance, General Smith, Admiral Nimitz, General Vandergrift.

cover a flame thrower attempting to fire into the caves that lined the depression, enemy soldiers opened up with rifles and machine guns. The battalion lost eight men killed and 17 wounded in the fight that followed before 1/306 withdrew for the night.

In the morning the same unit launched a carefully prepared attack behind tanks and a mortar barrage. The Japanese were momentarily stunned, but as Army troops started to investigate the various entrances into the caves the defenders once more began firing. Soldiers tossed pole charges and white phosphorus hand grenades into the openings and later in the day 400-pound blocks of TNT, placed in the entrances, closed the underground cavern. Four

days later, when demolition men reopened the caves, over 60 bodies filled the inside of the elaborately constructed command post.[161]

The fighting around this installation took the life of the top enemy commander, Lieutenant General Obata. After this engagement the enemy considered his defensive power on the island broken.[162] But, even with both the Americans and the Japanese declaring organized resistance at an end, intensive patrolling by the garrison forces on Guam continued through the rest of the year under the close scrutiny of Island Command.

---

[161] *Guam, 77th Div*, 131; *77th InfDiv History*, 122.
[162] *Takeda*.

CHAPTER VII   The Finish in the Marianas

ISLAND COMMAND TAKES OVER

The declaration of the end of organized resistance on Guam brought to a close the assault phase of the Marianas operation. In anticipation of the finish, Admiral Nimitz, on 8 August, had directed a reshuffling of commands to take place as soon as practicable after the island was secured. The order called for General Geiger and key staff members to report to Guadalcanal to take charge of the Palau landing;[1] General Holland Smith to be relieved as Commanding General, Expeditionary Troops, Marianas and return to Pearl Harbor to continue his duties as Commanding General, Fleet Marine Force, Pacific.[2]

All assault troops remaining in the Marianas were to be assigned to V Amphibious Corps, and when the situation warranted, the corps commander, Major General Harry Schmidt, was to transfer operational control of the units to the various island commanders. He would, however, retain authority to direct the training, re-

habilitation, and evacuation of assault troops. His immediate superior, Vice Admiral John H. Hoover, Commander, Forward Area Central Pacific, would assume responsibility for the defense and development of the Marianas.[3]

At 1500, 10 August, Admiral Conolly hauled down his flag on board the *Appalachian* and transferred command of TF 53 and duties of Senior Officer Present Afloat (SOPA) to Admiral Reifsnider. By evening of this day no combat ships larger than destroyers, excluding Admiral Spruance's flagship, USS *Indianapolis*, remained in the Marianas area.[4] Most of the ships that had supported the Guam assault were en route to the South Pacific to join the Third Fleet for future strikes against the Japanese. TF 53 was formally dissolved on 20 August 1944 after Admiral Reifsnider turned over his SOPA duties to the Deputy Commander, Forward Area Central Pacific (Commodore W. R. Quigley). The last of the naval commanders of the Guam assault left the Marianas on 26 August. On that date, after transferring responsibility for the Central Pacific to Admiral William F. Halsey, Commander, Third Fleet, Admiral Spruance departed for Pearl Harbor.

Earlier in the month, 12 August, General Geiger, his mission accomplished, left Guam by air for Guadalcanal. General Turnage as-

---

[1] For a complete discussion of the Palau operation see Maj F. O. Hough, *The Assault on Peleliu*, MC Historical Monograph, (Washington, 1950).

[2] On 12Jul44 Gen H. M. Smith turned over command of VAC and NTLF to MajGen Harry Schmidt and assumed command of the newly activated Fleet Marine Force, Pacific (FMFPac). This headquarters took control of both IIIAC and VAC and became the top Marine Corps echelon in the field. Until the end of the Guam campaign Gen Smith served concurrently as CG, ExTrps and CG, FMFPac.

[3] ComFifthFlt WD, August 1944, 13.
[4] *Ibid.*, 14.

sumed temporary command of the Southern Troops and Landing Force, but was relieved at 1200, 12 August when General Schmidt, at sea en route to Guam, reported by dispatch to take control of assault troops. At 0700, 13 August, the CP of IIAC closed on Guam, reopening at the same time on Guadalcanal. Headquarters detachments of VAC set up their CP near Agana at 1430 and took command of the remaining III Corps elements.

With the establishment of General Schmidt's command post, his staff started to direct cleanup activities, coordinating their efforts with those of the Island Command operations section under Lieutenant Colonel Shelton C. Zern.[5] In accordance with Nimitz' directive, the island commander, General Larsen, took control of Guam at 1200, 15 August. "At this time, except for patrolling, the combat phase was completed; the huge task of relief and rehabilitation, construction and repair, and housing and feeding was ahead."[6]

MOPPING-UP ACTIVITIES

General Larsen held conferences with Admiral Nimitz and top-ranking Marine officers on 11 August to acquaint them with the progress of the base development and defense plan for Guam. Island Command had already taken over all extended radio circuits and the joint communication center on 7 August. Two days later all unloading activities came under its control. Units of the advance naval base, Lion 6, commanded by Captain Adolph E. Becker, Jr., USN, began the extensive work necessary to convert Apra Harbor into the hub of a projected naval operating base.

Seabees of the 5th Naval Construction Brigade under Captain William O. Hiltabiddle (CEC), USN, were busily engaged in their assigned tasks of airfield construction and road improvement and repair. The Seabees also undertook the expansion of the island's existing water facilities to meet the requirements of the thousands of troops present. Some indication

MAJOR GENERAL LARSEN, Island Commander, confers with General Shepherd at the close of the campaign while two natives who returned to the island with the assault forces look on.

of the broad scope of the work planned for the construction brigade was the assignment of nine naval and three special (stevedore) naval construction battalions, one Marine special engineer battalion, and four Army aviation engineer battalions to its initial complement.[7]

Since 10 August assault units had been engaged in mopping-up activities. Strong patrols and reinforced ambushes accounted for an average of over 80 Japanese killed or captured daily.[8] Elements of the 3d Marine Division, flushing its sector of the northern jungles, added the greatest number to this score. On 14 August V Corps had established a line, Na-

---

[5] Col B. W. Atkinson, IsCom A–3 through the planning and assault phases of the operation, had become island provost marshal on 8 August.

[6] IsCom WD, 1Apr–15Aug44, 8.

[7] *Ibid.*, Enclosure N.

[8] IsCom WD, 15–31Aug44, Enclosure A. This figure is the average of the period from 10 August to the end of that month.

ton Beach to Sassayan Point, above which the 3d and 77th Divisions received orders for each to maintain one infantry regiment and one artillery battalion to seek out and destroy all hostile elements within their respective zones.

The corps commander directed the remainder of both divisions to proceed immediately to camp sites to reorganize and prepare for future operations. Island Command assigned the east coast road between the Pago and Ylig Rivers to the 3d, and the hills east of Agat along Harmon Road to the 77th. The 1st Provisional Marine Brigade, because of its imminent departure, was instructed to remain in its former combat zone above the designated line and continue vigorous patrolling to eliminate the remaining Japanese.[9]

The 21st Marines and the 306th Infantry, which drew the assignment to comb the northern jungle, encountered for the most part only disorganized remnants of the Imperial forces. Occasionally small groups of 10 or 15 forced a fire fight, but the results were invariably in favor of the Americans. A large proportion of the Japanese were defenseless; a few still had rifles, others only grenades or bayonets. The majority were also beginning to feel the pinch of hunger and thirst; captured diaries show the need for food as a gradually overwhelming obsession. Typical entries from the log of a Japanese Navy Corpsman killed in November 1944 by a garrison force patrol reveal the nature of most comments:

12 August—Fled into a palm grove feeling very hungry and thirsty. Drank milk from five coconuts and ate the meat of three.

15 August—Tried eating palm tree tips but suffered from severe vomiting in the evening.

23 August—Along my way I found some taro plants and ate them. All around me are enemies only. It takes a brave man, indeed, to go in search of food.

10 September—This morning I went out hunting. Found a dog and killed it. Compared with pork or beef it is not very good.

19 September—Our taro is running short and we can't afford to eat today.

2 October—These days I am eating only bread fruit. Went out in search of some today but it is very dangerous.

15 October—No food.[10]

[9] VAC WD, August 1944, Enclosure I.
[10] IsCom A–2 Periodic Rpt 87.

Outposts and patrols in the vicinity of ration dumps killed or captured a steady stream of starved men who had forgotten caution.[11] The fortunate minority who could sustain themselves showed little or no offensive spirit, desiring only to avoid the probing patrols. All indications pointed to a long and exhausting hunt for the thousands of surviving enemy troops.

Gradually the burden of the task of seeking out the hidden Japanese fell to the 3d Marine Division. Operational control of the division passed to Island Command on 23 August, and 1/306 and 3/306, which had been cleaning out the area above the V Corps line, were assigned to the 3d Division. When these battalions reverted to the 77th's control on 26 August, the mop-up zones of both units came under the Marine division. In the brigade area, advance elements had begun to reembark on 21 August, and eight days later General Turnage's units took over responsibility for patrolling all of northern Guam.[12] The last elements of the brigade were afloat by 31 August and the conquerors of Orote sailed for Guadalcanal. Island Command assumed control of all forces remaining on Guam on 1 September 1944.

One of General Larsen's major problems, besides Japanese survivors and the military development of Guam, was the relief and rehabilitation of the Guamanians. A census conducted by the Japanese civil government in January 1944 had listed 23,915 natives as being on the island.[13] During the early part of August, civil affairs officers attached to Island Command and the assault units estimated that over 18,000 of these civilians were being cared for in the three refugee camps near Anigua, Agat, and Yona.[14] As soon as patrols declared an area free of

[11] How very desperate the food situation became is revealed by an authenticated case of cannibalism which took place in January 1945 among a group of Japanese soldier and civilian holdouts. IsCom A–2 Periodic Rpt 196.

[12] As an example of the extent of the patrolling, one battalion (3/21) remained in northern Guam until January 1945, operating out of a bivouac near Yigo, and hunting down the surviving Japanese. Duplantis.

[13] IIIAC C–2 Periodic Rpt 10.

[14] IsCom WD, 1Apr–15Aug44, Enclosure K.

NEW SINAJANA, one of several large towns set up by Civil Affairs Section of Island Command to house the natives displaced by the fighting on Guam.

Japanese stragglers, natives were encouraged to return to their villages and farms and begin raising crops to help feed the non-military population. However, military preemption of increasingly larger areas of the island for airfields, combat firing ranges, training areas, camp sites, and supply depots prevented the natives from occupying many of the places where they had lived before the landing.

The establishing of new villages outside the areas occupied by American installations remedied this situation to some extent. The aim of the Island Command Civil Affairs Section under Colonel Charles I. Murray was to restore the native economy as soon as possible and repair the damage wrought by the enemy occupation and the recapture of the island. The section made extensive efforts to revive the copra and soap industries, provide a market for native handicraft among the troops, and employ the able-bodied in building up the Guam base. The Americans encouraged offshore fishing, which had been forbidden under the Japanese, in an attempt to increase the civilian larder. Preliminary steps were taken to reinstitute governmental agencies and arrangements made to compensate the Guamanians for their land and labor.[15]

The native guides who accompanied many of the Marine and Army patrols during the campaign proper and the mop-up period performed invaluable service in ferreting out Japanese

---

[15] IsCom WD, 15–31Aug44, Enclosure F.

PATROL FIGHTERS of the native military government proceed along one of the many jungle trails seeking enemy holdouts. (Navy Photograph.)

troops and equipment. After being supplied with arms and ammunition, most of these men functioned as regular patrol members.

The loyalty of the overwhelming majority of the Guamanians to the United States was as definite as that of the patrol guides. Investigation of reported collaborators and screening of all the natives to detect the few Japanese sympathizers revealed that most of those who aided the enemy had been forced to do so by lack of any alternative. The necessity of protecting and supervising the native population had been recognized by Admiral Nimitz, who authorized the formation of a successor to the prewar Insular Patrol Force.[16] Headed by a Marine police chief, this Local Security Patrol Force was organized in August, its nucleus consisting of former members of the Insular Patrol and Marines from Island Command. In addition to normal police functions, the force participated in many Japanese-hunting patrols until 15 August 1945.

_____

[16] ComFifthFlt WD, August 1944, 17.

By the end of the war the entire face of Guam had been changed. A busy naval operating base occupied Apra Harbor, and Navy planes crowded the fields at Agana and on Orote Peninsula. On the northern plateau, B–29's of the Twentieth Air Force rested on fields bulldozed from the jungle that had impeded the advance of the III Amphibious Corps. On the heights above Agana was the advance headquarters of the Pacific Fleet, nerve center of Nimitz' strikes against the Japanese homeland. Scattered throughout the island were vast naval and military supply installations. Encamped in the south, reunited for the first time since August 1944, were the Marine elements of the assault forces that had taken Guam. A crowded year of training and battle had seen the 3d Marine Division fighting on Iwo Jima and the 6th Marine Division [17] a leading participant in the Okinawa campaign.[18] The island population on 31 August 1945 had swelled to over 220,000, with 21,838 natives, 65,095 Army, 77,911 Navy, and 58,712 Marine troops.[19]

_____

[17] On 7Sept44 the 1st ProvMarBrig had been redesignated the 6th MarDiv with Gen Shepherd in command.

[18] The 77th InfDiv had fought again beside the 6th MarDiv in the Okinawa operation, after participating in the battles on Leyte in the Philippines.

[19] IsCom WD, 15–31Aug44, Enclosures B and F.

ENEMY HOLDOUTS accompanied by their mascot are brought in to surrender after intensive preparations by the Island Command Psychological Warfare Unit.

At the end of August 1945, a little over a year after General Geiger had declared organized resistance over on Guam, a recapitulation of Japanese casualties showed that 18,377 enemy dead had been counted and 1,250 prisoners taken.[20] More than 8,500 Japanese had been killed or captured since 10 August 1944. The efficiency of the organized campaign to eliminate the survivors was recognized by Colonel Takeda, who said:

Since August 11, [1944] the troops which had lost the center of command, and their commanders and men, entered, one by one, into the jungle to wait for the chance of counterattack. During this period LtCol H. Takeda in the north and Maj S. Sato in the south planned guerilla warfare, assembling the survivors living in the jungle, but owing to the loss of men and weapons and the shortage of food under successive subjugations, accompanied by skillful psychological warfare, their men dropped gradually into the hands of the Americans. Their objective failed. Thus it came the end of the war.[21]

Before the war's end the psychological warfare unit under Island Command had been successful in convincing Major Sato of the futility of further resistance. He surrendered on 11 June 1945 bringing in with him 34 men.[22]

After the Emperor issued his rescript at the end of the war, ordering Japanese troops to cease fighting, Lieutenant Colonel Hideyuki Takeda sent emissaries to General Larsen to arrange for his surrender. On 4 September 1945 he left his "division command post," which had been located in the jungle about a mile and a half southwest of Tarague since the end of the organized fighting,[23] and led a group of 67 officers and men in to surrender. When he ordered in an additional 46 men from the same area on 11 September, the last unified element of the Japanese defenders of Guam was in American hands.[24]

PRISONERS OF WAR in a stockade on Guam stand with bowed heads as they are read Emperor Hirohito's announcement of unconditional surrender. (Navy Photograph.)

MARIANAS CAMPAIGN SUMMARY

The capture of Guam was but the final phase of a much larger and more ambitious undertaking that included the seizure of Saipan and Tinian. It was the possession of all three islands that gave the United States such an overwhelming strategical advantage in the remaining year of the war. Therefore, the discussion here of the effect on future operations of the lessons learned in the Marianas will be concerned with the total effort rather than the parts.[25]

To the Japanese high command the loss of control of the Marianas proved to be a heavy spiritual as well as material blow. Many felt as did the Emperor's chief naval advisor that "Hell is on us."[26] In fact, the majority of military leaders agreed that there remained "no chance of ultimate success."[27] Again and again, the bitter memories of defeated men

---

[20] *Ibid.*, Enclosure C. These figures include about 500 Japanese civilians that were on the island at the time of the American landing.

[21] *Takeda.*

[22] IsCom WD, June 1945, Enclosure C.

[23] *Takeda Letter.*

[24] IsCom WD, September 1945, Enclosure C.

[25] For a discussion of innovations peculiar to each campaign see *Saipan*, Chap VII; *Tinian*, Chap V, and Chap V of this monograph.

[26] USSBS(Pac) Interrogation No. 392 of Fleet Admiral Osami Nagano, IJN; Chief of Naval General Staff, Apr41–Feb44; Supreme Naval Advisor to Emperor, Feb44–20Nov45.

[27] *Fukudome.*

turned to that fateful June of 1944 when Marines stormed ashore at Saipan. Decisive victory on that island and the accompanying destruction of Japanese naval air in the Battle of the Philippine Sea ensured the subsequent capture of Tinian and Guam.

Over 50,000 Japanese fighting men [28] gave their lives in frantic but futile defense of the three islands. A hard core of 30 infantry battalions composing the main strength of the 29th and 43d Divisions, 47th and 48th Independent Mixed Brigades, and 5th Naval Base Force was utterly destroyed.[29] But the death of these men remained secondary in importance to loss of the Marianas.

Now, from their blocking positions astride the inner ring of Imperial defenses, American hunter-killer teams could choke off the trickle of supply ships and submarines that had previously reached outlying enemy garrisons. Dominance of the Marianas meant "submarine operations were completely shut out," [30] in the words of the Japanese undersea fleet commander. For the thousands of enemy troops purposely by-passed in the island-hopping drives through the South and Central Pacific, the last hope of rescue faded. To the end of the war their only visitors were watchdog planes and ships of American rear area commands.

This stranglehold imposed on Japan's extended positions, however, was not the most dangerous threat to her security. The naval base developed at Guam, capable of supporting one-third of the Pacific Fleet,[31] and the tremendous forward supply depots maintained on that island posed a threat of quicker attacks on the Japanese home islands. Of primary importance were the B–29 fields developed on all the islands captured by TF 51. Raids launched from these airstrips brought the full impact of

total war to the Japanese people in the punishing rain of explosives and fire dropped on their homeland.

On 24 November 1944 one hundred B–29's left Saipan to hit Tokyo. Before the end of the year, stronger raids had hit the enemy capital three more times and demolished the Mitsubishi Aircraft Plant at Nagoya. The number of B–29's and the frequency of their attacks increased steadily. At the war's end almost a thousand of the giant planes based on Saipan, Tinian, and Guam were blasting targets on the Japanese home islands.[32] The climax came in August of 1945 when two B–29's rose from Tinian's fields to carry atomic death and devastation to hapless Hiroshima and Nagasaki.

There had been a tremendous outpouring of national effort involved in the capture of Saipan, Tinian, and Guam. Shipyards, factories, farms, arsenals, and training camps had funnelled the men and equipment necessary to maintain the attack force into the long supply line stretching from the United States through Pearl Harbor and Eniwetok to the fighting front. More than 600 ships from carriers to tankers, in excess of 2,000 planes of all types, and over 300,000 men from all services took part in FORAGER.[33] The actual assault echelon numbered 54,891 at Guam and 67,545 at Saipan, from which force 42,290 men were drawn for the Tinian landing.[34] Expeditionary Troops' records show that more than a fifth of the total assault troops became casualties in the 54 days of organized combat between 15 June and 10 August 1944. Of the 24,439 killed, wounded, or missing in action, 4,679 men died as a result of action on the three islands. However, for each American killed, ten Japanese lost their lives.[35]

It is interesting to speculate how much the casualty figure might have been whittled down, if the forces had been available, by an assault on the Marianas prior to June 1944. If the Americans had attacked earlier in the year with

---

[28] TF 56 G–2 Rpt, 58–59.

[29] *Ibid.*, 41–47.

[30] USSBS(Pac) Interrogation No. 366 of VAdm Shigeyosh Miwa, IJN; successively Director, Naval Submarine Department and CinC, 6th (Submarine) Fleet.

[31] Fleet Admiral E. J. King, *Third Official Report to the Secretary of the Navy*, 8Dec45.

[32] *Global Mission*, 540.

[33] Fleet Admiral E. J. King, *Second Official Report to the Secretary of the Navy*, 12Mar45.

[34] TF 56 G–1 Rpt, 3–23.

[35] TF 56 MedRpt, Annex A.

APRA HARBOR had become one of the world's busiest ports by the war's end with an average of 1,700 vessels standing in or out every month. (Navy Photograph.)

a force the same size as that which took the Marshalls (60,000), at least one Japanese admiral stated:

> . . . it is certain that, the defense preparations having only started in March, successful resistance would have been impossible. In other words, such a force would have been overwhelming.[36]

What is certain, however, is that the attack, when launched, caught the enemy off balance. Confirmation of this viewpoint comes from Admiral Kichisaburo Nomura, IJN, Ambassador to the United States at the time of the Pearl Harbor attack, who recalled, "Everywhere, I think, you attacked before the defense was ready. You came far more quickly than we expected."[37]

During FORAGER the Americans learned several valuable lessons in amphibious tactics. The most important of these proved to be in the fields of naval gunfire support, close air support, and ship-to-shore supply operations.

At Saipan, the heavy casualties on the beach gave proof of the ineffectiveness of the two-day NGF preparation there. On the other hand, the lengthy pounding given Tinian and Guam disrupted enemy defense preparations, knocked out most coast defense guns, and insured landings with relatively light losses. The inference was obvious, and with the added weight of evidence from NGF results at Peleliu and Iwo Jima, the Pacific Fleet conducted a preinvasion bombardment schedule of eight days at Okinawa in 1945.[38]

Admiral King, reviewing the effectiveness of naval gunfire during the FORAGER campaign, observed:

> In the Marianas operation, though heavy and prolonged concentrations of naval gunfire succeeded in neutralizing immediate beach defenses, mortar and artillery positions located in the rear of beaches were not silenced, thus demonstrating the need for continuous

[36] *Fukudome.*

[37] USSBS (Pac) Interrogation No. 429 of Adm Kichisaburo Nomura; former Ambassador to the United States (1941); appointed member of the Privy Council, 26May44.

[38] *Turner.*

supporting fires from seaward to a distance of approximately 5,000 yards inland.[39]

This lack of protective fire for initial assault troops before artillery fire control agencies could be set up ashore had been duly noted by senior troop commanders at both Saipan and Guam.[40] By the time the Tenth Army hit Okinawa on 1 April 1945, the period during which the Navy supplied continuous fire support after H-Hour had been increased to four hours from a previous high of 90 minutes at Guam.[41]

Close air support operations during the remainder of the war also became more effective as a result of FORAGER.[42] The system initiated at Guam of limiting gunfire maximum ordinates and controlling plane pull-out levels to permit simultaneous air and NGF bombardment of the same area became standard practice. This method resulted in a terrific combination of flat trajectory and plunging fires more devastating in effect than any concentration laid down by only one of the supporting arms.

In another field of air operations, the recommendations of troop commanders, championed by Generals Schmidt and Geiger and approved by General Holland Smith, won acceptance by the Navy. On 30 December 1944 Admiral King announced that:

Four CVE's have been designated for close troop support and will embark Marine aircraft squadrons. It is not anticipated that Marine squadrons will furnish all close air support but they will be used with Marine divisions when the situation permits. In addition a certain number of Marine aviators are being assigned to the various amphibious force flagships to assist in control of support aircraft.[43]

In general, supply operations proceeded smoothly at each of the objectives in the Marianas. Even the hurried commitment of the 77th Infantry Division at Guam, which presented some problems, did not jeopardize the mission of the attack force. However, there

was sufficient evidence of confusion at offshore cargo transfer points and on board landing control vessels to warrant Admiral Turner recommending that only "the most experienced personnel available should be used in the Control Parties for assault landings." [44] Certainly the haphazard way in which III Corps Artillery was landed and supplied during the initial stages at Guam had quite a bit to do with the above directive. The strong protest registered by General del Valle bore fruit in other fields too, as his operations officer has noted:

. . . the various high commanders involved realized the tremendous problem involved in landing the heavy Corps Artillery ammunition in an amphibious operation. As a result, a definite artillery ammunition unloading plan was prepared for Okinawa which brought our ammunition ashore smoothly and properly.[45]

In order to speed up the flow of equipment ashore and expedite handling on the beach and in dumps, most unit supply officers of Expeditionary Troops recommended that initial assault items of supply be palletized.[46] Positive results followed increased use of this efficient supply method in landings following FORAGER. As foreseen by Admiral King, there was a reduction in the number of shore party personnel required to handle the palletized equipment and a corresponding increase in assault troops.[47]

Unfortunately, the Japanese as well as the Americans profited from experience in the Marianas. Enemy headquarters on each island had contact with Tokyo and submitted daily action reports until the end of organized resistance. According to a captured message file of the 31st Army, plus reliable comments

---

[39] *CominCh P-007*, Chap 3, 14.

[40] The proximity of Saipan to Tinian permitted artillery emplaced on the former island to support the Tinian landing. As a result, continuous protective fire was available to assault troops of the 4th MarDiv.

[41] *Gilliam*.

[42] See discussion of air support in *Saipan*, 248–250, and *Tinian*, 126–130.

[43] *CominCh P-007*, Chap 2, 8.

[44] CTF 51 OpRpt, Recommendations, 2.

[45] *Henderson*.

[46] Palletization is the process of arranging a quantity of any item, packaged or unpackaged, upon a wooden pallet (platform on which supplies are stored). The load is then securely strapped or lashed to the pallet so that the whole is handled as a unit. At Guam, a good portion of 77th Div gear was palletized, but the lack of landing vehicles forced the breakup of unit loads, adding considerably to the difficulties of maintaining division supply levels.

[47] *CominCh P-007*, Chap 5, 11.

and reports available following the war, strengths and weaknesses of both the attackers and defenders were analyzed and continually reported. From this information, the enemy high command concluded that the punishing effectiveness of the American air-NGF-artillery team in supporting the infantry dictated a change in Japanese tactics.

Battle studies distributed from Tokyo stressed the need to dig in troops and guns and underground all supplies and communication lines. To counter the power of American fire support, which enabled a force to penetrate any single thin defensive line, Japanese commanders gave instructions to organize defenses in depth.[48]

There were to be no more field days for

[48] Maj Y. Horie, IJA, "Explanation of Japanese Defense Plan and Battle of Iwo Jima," 25Jan46; CinCPac-CinCPOA Translation B–14986, 32d Army Battle Instructions, 15Feb45.

SUPERFORTRESSES of the Twentieth Air Force return from a 3,000-mile mission over Japan to their home base at North Field, Guam. (Air Force Photograph.)

American gunners pouring their fire on inviting targets of thousands of men charging in all out *banzai* attacks, as had happened in the Marianas. Until the end of the war the average enemy soldier stuck to his assigned defensive position like a leech, firing from cover and doing his best to take as many Americans as possible to the grave with him. At least two Japanese commanders, those at Iwo Jima and Okinawa, issued orders against expending everything in one frenzied counterattack. The extensive casualty lists and the lengthy campaigns necessary to capture the islands of Peleliu, Iwo Jima, and Okinawa furnish mute testimony to the efficiency of the new enemy defensive techniques.

To the average American participant in the Marianas campaign, the war was on a minute-to-minute basis. Big picture strategy had no place in his personal struggle to survive, and even today his picture of the operation is a compound of individual memories that probably missed this history and many others. Yet no matter how small a part an individual took in capturing these islands, he is justified in feeling he helped shorten the war. For it was from the Marianas that ships, planes, and men struck out to bring defeat to Japan.

Bibliography

APPENDIX I

THE RECAPTURE OF GUAM

The narrative of the Guam operation has been written only after careful examination of a wide variety of sources. Chief among these have been the reports, journals, war diaries, orders, and plans of the units involved. Descriptions of specific actions have been based mainly on the reports of the units most directly concerned. In general, the lowest echelons have been considered the best source for details, while reports of higher units familiar with the overall picture have been used in evaluating results.

More than 200 of the key participants in the Guam campaign have commented by interview or letter on preliminary drafts of this monograph or have replied to specific questions regarding various aspects of the operation. In many cases individuals have furnished information that is not contained in available records. For the most part, however, these comments have been used only to supplement existing official reports.

Since much of the material consulted had only a very general or indirect bearing on the campaign, this bibliography does not constitute a complete listing. Only the most useful sources, including all those cited in the text, have been included below. Unless otherwise noted all material listed is available in the records of the Historical Branch, G–3 Division, Headquarters, U. S. Marine Corps.

DOCUMENTS

CominCh P–007, Amphibious Operations—Invasion of the Marianas, dtd 30Dec44.

Joint Chiefs of Staff Directive to CinCPOA and CinCSoWesPac, Future Operations in the Pacific, Serial JCS 713/4, dtd 12Mar44. Filed at ONRL.[1]

CinCPac-CinCPOA Intelligence Items and Translations.

JICPOA Intelligence Items and Bulletins.

Military Intelligence Service, War Department, Survey of Guam, Serial S30–601, dtd June 1943. Filed at Record Section, Marine Corps Schools.

Military Intelligence Division, War Department, Order of Battle for the Japanese Armed Forces, dtd 1Mar45.

Office of Naval Intelligence—99, Strategic Study of Guam, dtd 1Feb44.

Commander, Fifth Fleet, Final Report on the Operation to Capture the Marianas Islands, dtd 26Oct44.

Commander, Amphibious Forces, Pacific Fleet, Comments and Remarks on the Marianas Operation, dtd 5Mar45.

Commander, Support Aircraft, Pacific Fleet, Report of Support Aircraft Operations, Marianas, Serial 012, dtd 11Sept44. Filed at ONRL.

Task Force 58 Action Report of Operations in Support of the Capture of the Marianas, 2 vols., dtd 11Sept44.

Task Force 51 Operations Report, dtd 25Aug44.

Task Force 56 Report on FORAGER, 7 vols., contains separate reports from planning, operations, intelligence, logistics, personnel, and special staff officers, dtd 2Oct44.

Task Force 53 Operation Plan No. A162–44, dtd 17May44.

[1] The Office of Naval Records and Library, Navy Department, Washington 25, D. C.

Task Force 53 Operations Report, dtd 10Aug44.

Task Group 53.2 Operations Report, dtd 11Sept44.

Task Unit 53.7.2 Report of Carrier Operations in Close Support of Amphibious Operations at Guam, 17Jul–1Aug44, dtd 8Aug44. Filed at ONRL.

III Amphibious Corps Operation Orders Nos. 1–11, 11May–10Aug44.

III Amphibious Corps Special Action Report, contains separate reports of planning, operations, intelligence, supply, personnel, air, naval gunfire, ordnance, signal, medical, and service group officers, dtd 3Sept44.

III Amphibious Corps Artillery Special Action Report, dtd 2Sept44.

III Amphibious Corps C–1 Journal, 20Jul–14Aug44.

III Amphibious Corps C–1 Periodic Reports, 31Jul–10Aug44.

III Amphibious Corps C–2 Journal, 21Jul–13Aug44.

III Amphibious Corps C–2 Periodic Reports Nos. 1–23, 21Jul–13Aug44.

III Amphibious Corps Prisoner of War Interrogations Nos. 17–24, dtd 28Jul44.

Task Group 56.2 Prisoner of War Interrogations Nos. 25–53, 31Jul–10Aug44.

III Amphibious Corps C–3 Journal, 12Jun44–24Feb45.

III Amphibious Corps C–3 Periodic Reports Nos. 1–24, 21Jul–14Aug44.

III Amphibious Corps C–4 Periodic Reports Nos. 1–23, 21Jul–14Aug44.

3d Marine Division Operation Plan No. 2–44, dtd 13May44.

3d Marine Division Operation Orders, 29Jul–30Oct44.

3d Marine Division Administrative Plan No. 2–44, dtd 13May44.

3d Marine Division Special Action Report, dtd 19 Aug44, contains comments and reports from all division special staff officers plus a special action report from each of the following units:

   3d Marines

   9th Marines (each battalion)

   12th Marines

   19th Marines (each battalion)

   21st Marines

   3d Service Battalion

   3d Medical Battalion

   3d Motor Transport Battalion

   3d Headquarters Battalion (each company)

   3d Tank Battalion

   3d Joint Assault Signal Company

   3d Amphibian Tractor Battalion

   14th Defense Battalion (includes battalion journal)

   IIIAC Motor Transport Battalion

3d Marine Division D–1 Journal, 21Jul–10Aug44.

3d Marine Division D–2 Journal, 3Jun–29Jul44.

3d Marine Division D–2 Journal, 29Jul–10Aug44.

3d Marine Division D–2 Periodic Reports Nos. 72–171, 25Jul–2Nov44.

3d Marine Division Prisoner of War Interrogations Nos. 396–485, 7Oct–4Nov44.

3d Marine Division D–3 Journal, 21Jul–22Oct44.

3d Marine Division D–3 Periodic Reports Nos. 1–73, 20Jul–30Sept44.

3d Marine Division D–4 Journal, 21Jul–10Aug44.

3d Marines Operation Plan No. 3–44, dtd 27May44.

3d Marines Journal, 21Jul–12Aug44.

1st Battalion, 3d Marines Journal, 21Jul–16Aug44.

2d Battalion, 3d Marines Journal, 21Jul–24Aug44.

3d Battalion, 3d Marines Journal, 21–31Jul44.

9th Marines R–2 Journal, 21Jul–31Aug44.

9th Marines R–3 Journal, 22Jul–26Aug44.

9th Marines Unit Reports, 21Jul–19Sept44 (Fragmentary).

12th Marines Special Action Report for 26Jul44, dtd 15Aug44.

12th Marines Journal, 21Jul–15Oct44.

12th Marines Operation Summaries, 29Jul–1Nov44 (Fragmentary).

21st Marines Unit Reports, 22Jul–3Nov44 (Fragmentary).

3d Battalion, 21st Marines Journal, 21Jul–1Nov44.

3d Tank Battalion Special Action Report, dtd 19Apr45.

2d and 3d War Dog Platoons' Special Action Report, dtd 17Sept44.

77th Infantry Division Operation Orders and Overlays, 25Jul–16Aug44.

77th Infantry Division Operation Report, 21Jul–16Aug44, contains reports from all major component and attached units, Serial 377–0.3(7055). Filed at AGOKC.[2]

77th Infantry Division G–1 Journal, 1Jul–13Aug44, Serial 377–1.2(7364). Filed at AGOKC.

77th Infantry Division G–1 Daily Consolidated Report of Casualties, 1Jul–13Aug44, Serial 377–1.16 (21589). Filed at AGOKC.

77th Infantry Division G–3 Journal, 6Jun–10Aug44, Serial 377–3.2(7008). Filed at AGOKC.

77th Infantry Division G–3 Periodic Reports, 23Jul–11Aug44, Serial 377–3.1(21591). Filed at AGOKC.

77th Infantry Division Artillery After-Action Report, 21Jul–10Aug44, Serial 377–ART–0.3(7333). Filed at AGOKC.

305th Infantry After-Action Report, 18Jun–9Aug44, Serial 377–INF(305)–0.3(28961). Filed at AGOKC.

305th Infantry Journal Record Book, 1Jul–8Sept44, Serial 377–INF(305)–0.7(28962). Filed at AGOKC.

306th Infantry Operations Report, 1Apr–10Aug44, Serial 377–INF(306)–0.3(28945). Filed at AGOKC.

306th Infantry Journal File, 23Jul–10Aug44, Serial 377–INF(306)–0.8(12218). Filed at AGOKC.

306th Infantry Unit Reports, 23Jul–10Aug44, Serial 377–INF (306)–0.9(28951). Filed at AGOKC.

307th Infantry Historical Records, 7Jul–10Aug44, contains Operations Report and S–2, S–3 Journal, Serial 377–INF(307)–0.3(28960). Filed at AGOKC.

305th Field Artillery Battalion After-Action Report, 21Jul–10Aug44, Serial 377–FA(305)–0.3(7339). Filed at AGOKC.

[2] The Adjutant General's Office, Kansas City Records Administration Center, Kansas City, 24, Missouri.

1st Provisional Marine Brigade Operation Plan 7–44 (Preferred), dtd 11Jul44.

1st Provisional Marine Brigade Operations and Special Action Report, contains summary of events prior to 1Jul44, War Diary 1Jul–10Aug44, Operations Journal, and Operations Plans and Orders, dtd 19Aug44.

1st Provisional Marine Brigade Unit Reports Nos. 1–12, 21Jul–1Aug44.

22d Marines Journal, 21Jul–16Aug44.

22d Marines Unit Reports, 21Jul–21Aug44 (Fragmentary).

1st Battalion, 22d Marines Journal, 21Jul–9Aug44.

2d Battalion, 22d Marines Journal, 21Jul–21Aug44.

6th Tank Battalion Guam Action Report, contains the reports of the 4th and 22d Marines Tank Companies, dtd 30Mar45.

1st Armored Amphibian Group Action Report, dtd 1Aug44. From personal files of LtCol R. G. Warga.

Island Command A–2 Periodic Reports Nos. 4–127, 27Aug–28Dec44.

48th Bombardment Group (Medium), VII Bomber Command, Seventh Air Force Organizational History, August 1944. Filed at the Air University, Maxwell Field, Alabama.

318th Fighter Group, VII Fighter Command, Seventh Air Force Organizational History, August 1944. Filed at the Air University, Maxwell Field, Alabama.

WAR DIARIES

Monthly war diaries for the period April 1944 through August 1944 have been consulted for all of the following organizations; these are listed overall rather than separately for purposes of convenience and simplicity.

Pacific Fleet
Fifth Fleet
V Amphibious Corps
III Amphibious Corps Artillery
3d Marine Division
1st Provisional Marine Brigade
Marine Air Group 21
5th Field Depot
1st Battalion, 4th Marines
2d Battalion, 4th Marines
1st Armored Amphibian Battalion
3d Amphibian Tractor Battalion
4th Amphibian Tractor Battalion
9th Defense Battalion
10th Antiaircraft Battalion
14th Defense Battalion
Island Command, Guam (through September 1945)

BOOKS, PAMPHLETS, PERIODICALS

Arnold, General of the Air Force Henry H., *Global Mission*. New York: Harper and Brothers, 1949.

Aurthur, 1stLt R. A. and Cohlmia, 1stLt K., *The Third Marine Division*. Washington: Infantry Journal Press, 1948.

Bridgewater, LtCol F. Clay, "Reconnaissance on Guam," *The Cavalry Journal*, May–June 1945.

Bruce, MajGen Andrew D., "Administration, Supply, and Evacuation of the 77th Infantry Division on Guam," *Military Review*, December 1944.

Callaway, Cdr Raymond R. (MC), "The Third Medical Battalion in Action: Bougainville and Guam," Historical Study, Marine Corps Schools Senior Course (1948–49). Filed at Record Section, Marine Corps Schools.

Carleton, Capt Philips D., "The Guam Operation," *Campaign for the Marianas*. Washington: Historical Division, USMC, 1946.

Cass, Bevan G., ed., *History of the Sixth Marine Division*. Washington: Infantry Journal Press, 1948.

Cushman, LtCol Robert E., "The Fight at Fonte," *Marine Corps Gazette*, April 1947.

del Valle, MajGen Pedro A., "Guam, the Classical Amphibious Operation," *Military Review*, April 1947.

del Valle, BrigGen Pedro A., "Massed Fires on Guam," *Marine Corps Gazette*, December 1944.

Fink, PFC Stanley, "Co-Prosperity on Guam," *Marine Corps Gazette*, October 1944.

Frances, 1stLt Anthony A., "The Battle of Banzai Ridge," *Marine Corps Gazette*, June 1945.

Guam: Operations of the 77th Division; American Forces in Action Series. Washington: Historical Division, War Department, 1946.

Hoffman, Maj Carl W., *Saipan: The Beginning of the End*, Marine Corps Historical Monograph. Washington: Government Printing Office, 1950.

Hoffman, Maj Carl W., *The Seizure of Tinian*, Marine Corps Historical Monograph. Washington: Government Printing Office, 1951.

Hough, Maj Frank O., *The Island War*. Philadelphia and New York: J. B. Lippincott Company, 1947.

Isely, J. A. and Crowl, P. A., *The U. S. Marines and Amphibious War*. Princeton: Princeton University Press, 1951.

Johnson, Capt Lucius W. (MC), "Guam Before December 1941," *U. S. Naval Institute Proceedings*, July 1942.

McMillian, Cdr I. E., "Naval Gunfire at Guam," *Marine Corps Gazette*, September 1948.

Nelson, LCdr F. J., "Guam—Our Western Outpost," *U. S. Naval Institute Proceedings*, January 1940.

Nelson, Lt. F. J., "Why Guam Alone Is American," *U. S. Naval Institute Proceedings*, August 1936.

Ours To Hold it High: The History of the 77th Infantry Division in World War II. Washington: Infantry Journal Press, 1947.

Pratt, Fletcher, *The Marines' War*. New York: William Sloane Associates, 1948.

Rentz, Maj John N., *Bougainville and the Northern Solomons*, Marine Corps Historical Monograph. Washington: Government Printing Office, 1948.

Robson, R. W. *The Pacific Islands Handbook—1944*. New York: The MacMillan Company, 1945.

Rosinski, Dr. H., "The Strategy of Japan," *Brassey's Naval Annual, 1946*. New York: The MacMillan Company, 1946.

Rowcliff, RAdm G. J., "Guam," *U. S. Naval Institute Proceedings*, July 1945.

Smith, Cdr H. E. (CEC), "I Saw the Morning Break," *U. S. Naval Institute Proceedings*, March 1946.

Smith, Gen Holland M., *Coral and Brass*. New York: Charles Scribner's Sons, 1949.

Thompson, Laura, *Guam and its People*. Princeton: Princeton University Press, 1947.

United States Strategic Bombing Survey (Pacific), Naval Analysis Division, *Interrogations of Japanese Officials*, 2 vols. Washington: Government Printing Office, 1946.

United States Strategic Bombing Survey (Pacific), Naval Analysis Division, *Campaigns of the Pacific War*. Washington: Government Printing Office, 1946.

Walker, Maj Anthony, "Advance on Orote Peninsula," *Marine Corps Gazette*, February 1945.

The War Reports of General of the Army George C. Marshall, General of the Army Henry H. Arnold, and Fleet Admiral Ernest J. King. New York and Philadelphia: J. B. Lippincott Company, 1947.

Yanaihara, Todao, *The Pacific Islands Under Japanese Mandate.* New York: Oxford University Press, 1940.

MISCELLANEOUS

Cohlmia, 1stLt K., Preliminary Draft of the 3d Marine Division History.

Horie, Maj Yoshitaka, Explanation of Japanese Defense Plan and Battle of Iwo Jima, dtd 26Jan46.

Japanese Studies In World War II: Operations in the Central Pacific; Guam Operation, Serial 8–5.1 AC 55. Filed at the Office of the Chief of Military History, United States Army.

McMillan, Capt George J., Official Report to the CNO on the Surrender of Guam to the Japanese, dtd 11Sept45.

Takeda, LtCol Hideyuki, Letter to the Director of Marine Corps History, dtd 20Feb52.

Takeda, LtCol Hideyuki, "The Outline of Japanese Defense Plan and Battle of Guam," dtd 4Oct46.

APPENDIX II

Chronology

1944

2 January_____ U. S. Army troops land at Saidor, beginning drive up New Guinea coast.

30 January–
7 February_____ U. S. forces assault and capture Kwajalein Atoll, Marshall Islands.

16–17 February_____ Task Force 58 strikes Truk, revealing weakness of that base.

18–23 February_____ U. S. forces assault and capture Eniwetok Atoll, Marshall Islands, completing the breach of the Japanese outer defenses in the Central Pacific.

22–23 February_____ Task Force 58 strikes Southern Marianas.

29 February–
28 March_____ U. S. forces assault and capture the main islands of the Admiralties group.

6 March_____ 1st Marine Division lands near Talasea on New Britain.

12 March_____ Joint Chiefs of Staff direct that Southern Marianas be seized, target date 15 June.

22 March_____ 1st Provisional Marine Brigade activated.

23 March_____ CinCPOA issues operation order for FORAGER directing capture of Saipan, Tinian, and Guam.

23–25 March_____ 77th Infantry Division departs U. S. for Hawaiian Islands.

30 March–1 April__ Task Force 58 strikes Western Carolines.

16 April_____ BrigGen Lemuel C. Shepherd, Jr. assumes command of the 1st Provisional Marine Brigade.

22 April_____ U. S. Army troops invade Northern New Guinea, landing at Aitape and Hollandia.

26 April_____ Expeditionary Troops Headquarters issues operation order for FORAGER.

11 May_____ Southern Troops and Landing Force issues operation order for capture of STEVEDORE (Guam), second phase of FORAGER.

17 May_____ Task Force 53 issues operation order for STEVEDORE with tentative landing date (W-Day) of 18 June.

23–27 May_____ Task Force 53 conducts final rehearsal on beaches near Cape Esperance, Guadalcanal.

1 June_____ LST groups carrying assault elements of Southern Troops and Landing Force depart Solomons for staging area at Kwajalein.

4 June_____ Remainder of Task Force 53 with IIIAC Headquarters on board departs Solomons for Kwajalein.

6 June_____ Allied troops invade the continent of Europe in Normandy.

9–12 June_____ Elements of Task Force 53 leave Kwajalein for Southern Marianas.

15 June_____ China-based B–29's attack Kyushu Island in first Superfort raid on Japan.

15 June_____ 2d and 4th Marine Divisions land on Saipan in first phase of FORAGER.

16 June_____ 27th Infantry Division, Expeditionary Troops Reserve, begins landing on Saipan.

16 June_____ Fifth Fleet Commander cancels 18 June as W-Day for STEVEDORE, directs Task Force 53 to remain off Saipan as floating reserve, and orders Task Force 58 to engage approaching Japanese Fleet.

19–20 June_____ Battle of the Philippine Sea. Japanese naval air arm suffers decisive defeat.

25 June_____ 3d Marine Division released from floating reserve off Saipan and directed to return to Eniwetok.

30 June_____ 1st Provisional Marine Brigade released from floating reserve off Saipan and directed to return to Eniwetok.

30 June–4 July_____ Conference of top commanders on Saipan regarding STEVEDORE. Decision to commit 77th Infantry Division on Guam.

1–8 July_____ 77th Infantry Division departs Pearl Harbor to join Task Force 53 at Eniwetok.

2–7 July_____ U. S. Army troops assault and capture Noemfoor Island off Dutch New Guinea.

8 July_____ Commander Fifth Fleet sets W-Day as 21 July.

8 July_____ Ships and planes of Task Forces 53 and 58 commence intensive preinvasion bombardment of Guam.

9 July_____ All organized resistance ceases on Saipan; mop-up begins.

10 July_____ 305th Regimental Combat Team joins Task Force 53 at Eniwetok, assigned to 1st Provisional Marine Brigade.

14 July_____ Admiral Conolly, embarked in the *Appalachian*, arrives off Guam to assume personal control of the bombardment program.

15–17 July_____ Tractor and transport groups of Task Force 53 depart Eniwetok for Guam.

17 July_____ Remainder of 77th Infantry Division arrives at Eniwetok.

18 July_____ Japanese Premier Hideki Tojo and Cabinet resign as a result of the capture of Saipan.

21 July_____ 3d Marine Division and 1st Provisional Marine

Brigade land on Guam in second phase of FORAGER.

22 July_____77th Infantry Division begins landing on Guam.

24 July_____4th Marine Division lands on Tinian in third phase of FORAGER.

25 July_____2d Marine Division lands on Tinian.

25–26 July_____Japanese counterattack against Marines on Guam repulsed with crippling losses to enemy.

27 July_____American sovereignty over the island of Guam is proclaimed.

29 July_____United States flag raised over ruins of former Marine Barracks on Orote Peninsula, Guam.

1 August_____All organized resistance ceases on Tinian; mop-up begins.

10 August_____All organized resistance ceases on Guam; mop-up begins.

21–22 August_____Units of 1st Provisional Marine Brigade begin leaving Guam.

1 September_____Island Command takes control over all forces remaining on Guam; intensive mop-up continues.

15 September_____U. S. Army troops assault and capture Morotai Island, Netherlands East Indies.

15–30 September____U. S. forces assault and capture Peleliu and Angaur, Palau Islands.

23 September_____U. S. Army troops seize Ulithi Atoll in Western Carolines.

20 October_____U. S. Army troops invade Leyte Island in the Philippines.

23–26 October_____Battle of Leyte Gulf. Elimination of Japanese surface fleet as a major threat.

3 November_____77th Infantry Division departs Guam.

24 November_____Saipan-based B–29's bomb Tokyo in first attack on enemy capitol by land-based planes.

15 December_____U. S. Army troops invade Mindoro Island in the Philippines.

APPENDIX III

Southern Troops and Landing Force Casualties

Marine Organizations [1]	KIA		DOW		WIA		Total	
	OFF	ENL	OFF	ENL	OFF	ENL	OFF	ENL
IIIAC Trps								
H&S Bn		3		1	1	2	1	6
Med Bn								
MT Bn					2	12	2	12
Sig Bn		2		1	1	12	1	15
1st Armd Amph Bn	2	25		4	6	60	8	89
2d Sep Eng Bn		5		1		26		32
2d Mar Ammo Co						2		2
3d Amph Trac Bn	1	9		2	1	41	2	52
4th Amph Trac Bn	2	14		2	1	35	3	51
4th Mar Ammo Co				3				3
IIIAC Arty								
H&S Btry						2		2
1st 155mm How Bn		1				5		6
2d 155mm How Bn		1				1		2
7th 155mm Gun Bn		1				6		7
9th Def Bn						5		5
14th Def Bn		2		5	3	38	3	45
3d Mar Div								
Hq Bn	5	28	1	15	19	140	25	183
Med Bn						4		4
MT Bn				3		9		12
Ser Bn		3		2	2	17	2	22
Tk Bn		5		2	6	56	6	63
3d Mar								
H&S Co		5		1	4	9	4	15
Wpns Co		2		2	2	32	2	36
1st Bn	9	43	1	30	6	217	16	290
2d Bn	3	70	2	17	10	221	15	308
3d Bn		77		20	17	282	17	379
9th Mar								
H&S Co		4		2	2	12	2	18
Wpns Co		13		1	1	40	1	54
1st Bn	2	38	2	13	9	175	13	226

See footnotes at end of table.

178

Marine Organizations [1]	KIA		DOW		WIA		Total	
	OFF	ENL	OFF	ENL	OFF	ENL	OFF	ENL
3d Mar Div—Continued								
9th Mar—Continued								
2d Bn	4	60	1	23	14	316	19	399
3d Bn	5	28	1	16	11	170	17	214
12th Mar								
H&S Btry	1	1		3	1	22	2	26
1st Bn	2	6		8	2	41	4	55
2d Bn	1	11		4	7	52	8	67
3d Bn		6		2	6	27	6	35
4th Bn		7			9	29	9	36
19th Mar								
H&S Co		1		1	4	11	4	13
1st Bn	1	17	1	5	4	85	6	107
2d Bn	1	4		1	2	54	3	59
21st Mar								
H&S Co		5		1	2	17	2	23
Wpns Co	1	7	2	1	1	36	4	44
1st Bn	7	68	1	30	12	360	20	458
2d Bn	5	78		18	14	392	19	488
3d Bn	3	56	1	21	9	242	13	319
1st Prov Mar Brig								
Brig Trps	1	9		1	4	28	5	38
1st Prov Repl Co						6		6
4th Mar								
H&S Co	1	7		1	1	14	2	22
Eng Co	1	6		2	3	38	4	46
Med Co						1		1
MT Co		2				2		4
Pion Co					2	24	2	24
Tk Co		1			1	21	1	22
Wpns Co		4		1	2	29	2	34
1st Bn	5	53		6	6	166	11	225
2d Bn	2	27		5	11	175	13	207
3d Bn	1	50		13	8	205	9	268
Pk How Bn		2			5	14	5	16
22d Mar								
H&S Co					1	8	1	8
Eng Co		3		4		25		32
Med Co								
MT Co		1				5		6
Pion Co		5		2		20		27
Tk Co	1	4			3	12	4	16
Wpns Co		3			2	24	2	27
1st Bn	5	82	1	24	12	242	18	348
2d Bn	2	48		20	13	247	15	315
3d Bn	2	43	1	13	14	213	17	269
Pk How Bn		5		2	1	34	1	41
Is Com								
Hq Bn	2					3	2	3
5th Fld Dep		4		2		27		33
Mar Air Gru–21		1			1	5	1	6
Misc Units		3		1		12		16
Naval Medical Personnel Attached to Marine Units [2]	1	42	1	3	10	170	12	215

See footnotes at end of table.

	KIA		DOW		WIA		Total	
	OFF	ENL	OFF	ENL	OFF	ENL	OFF	ENL
Navy Organizations [3]								
Lion 6								
5th Const Brig Hq								
2d Spec Const Bn		2			1	7	1	9
13th Spec Const Bn								
25th Const Bn		1				2		3
53d Const Bn						3		3
59th Const Bn						2		2
Const Det 1010								
Comm Unit 41								
Argus 17								
Army Organizations [4]								
77th Inf Div								
Div Trps	1	5			4	43	5	48
305th Inf	2	71			15	274	17	345
306th Inf	2	37			11	93	13	130
307th Inf	3	49			10	188	13	237
Atchd Trps		7			2	22	2	29
254th Sig Const Co								
726th Air Wrn Co								
746th Air Wrn Co								
Grand Total	87	1,283	16	361	334	5,719 [5]	437	7,363 [6]

[1] Marine casualty figures furnished by the Personnel Accounting Section, Records Branch, Personnel Department, Headquarters, U. S. Marine Corps on 12Dec52 and cover the period 21Jul–10Aug44.

[2] Naval medical casualty figures furnished by the Medical Statistics Division, Bureau of Medicine and Surgery, Navy Department on 15Oct52 and cover the period 21Jul–10Aug44. For this same period 49 casualties (5 KIA, 3 DOW, 41 WIA) were listed as having occurred in the Marianas without specifying the island; of this group some men were attached to ships and some were assigned to Marine units.

[3] Navy casualty figures were taken from the IIIAC SAR, PersRpt and cover the period 21Jul–11Aug44.

[4] Army casualty figures for the 77th InfDiv and attached troops were taken from the 77th InfDiv G–1 Jnl and cover the period 21Jul–10Aug44. Available Army records do not provide a breakdown comparable to that used for Marine units. Casualty information for those Army troops attached to STLF was taken from the IIIAC SAR, PersRpt and cover the period 21Jul–11Aug44.

[5] Owing to the method of reporting and recording Marine casualties, most of the DOW totals are repeated in the WIA figures.

[6] Twenty-two enlisted men (18 Marine and 4 Army) are still listed as missing in action, presumed dead.

Command and Staff List of Major Units

APPENDIX IV

21 JULY 1944–10 AUGUST 1944[1]

EXPEDITIONARY TROOPS

Commanding General_	LtGen Holland M. Smith
Chief of Staff_____	BrigGen Graves B. Erskine
G–1_____	LtCol Albert F. Metze
G–2_____	Col St. Julien R. Marshall
G–3_____	Col John C. McQueen
G–4_____	Col Raymond E. Knapp
G–5_____	Col Joseph T. Smith

SOUTHERN TROOPS AND LANDING FORCE

Commanding General_	MajGen Roy S. Geiger
Chief of Staff_____	Col Merwin H. Silverthorn
C–1_____	Col William J. Scheyer
C–2_____	LtCol William F. Coleman
C–3_____	Col Walter A. Wachtler
C–4_____	LtCol Frederick L. Wieseman

III AMPHIBIOUS CORPS TROOPS

III Corps Headquarters and Service Battalion

Commanding Officer__	LtCol Floyd A. Stephenson
Executive Officer_____	Capt Harry O. Buzhardt
Bn–3_____	(none assigned)

III Corps Medical Battalion

Commanding Officer__	LCdr William H. Rambo (MC)
Executive Officer_____	Lt William E. Dierking (MC)
Bn–3_____	(not shown)

[1] Command and staff lists for Marine organizations were taken from the muster rolls of these units filed at Headquarters, U. S. Marine Corps. Letters from officers of the 77th InfDiv supplemented information supplied by The Adjutant General's Office to provide the listing for Army units. War diaries for the period of the operation furnished the data needed to complete the Island Command section.

III Corps Motor Transport Battalion

Commanding Officer___	Maj Franklin H. Hayner
Executive Officer_____	Maj Kenneth E. Murphy
Bn–3_____	Maj Kenneth E. Murphy

III Corps Signal Battalion

Commanding Officer__	LtCol Robert L. Peterson
Executive Officer_____	LtCol Allan Sutter
Bn–3_____	Maj Hubert C. Lattimer, Jr.

1st Armored Amphibian Battalion

Commanding Officer___	Maj Louis Metzger
Executive Officer_____	Capt Richard G. Warga
Bn–3_____	1stLt Thomas M. Crosby

2d Separate Engineer Battalion

Commanding Officer___	LtCol Charles O. Clark
Executive Officer_____	Maj Hooper A. Williams, Jr.
Bn–3_____	2dLt Francis P. McCormick

3d Amphibian Tractor Battalion

Commanding Officer___	LtCol Sylvester L. Stephan
Executive Officer_____	Maj Erwin F. Wann, Jr.
Bn–3_____	Capt George M. Foote

4th Amphibian Tractor Battalion

Commanding Officer___	LtCol Clovis C. Coffman
Executive Officer_____	Maj Arnold S. Dane
Bn–3_____	Capt Ralph J. Parker, Jr.

III AMPHIBIOUS CORPS ARTILLERY

Commanding General_	BrigGen Pedro A. del Valle
Chief of Staff_____	Col John A. Bemis
A–1_____	Maj James A. Tatsch
A–2_____	WO David G. Garnett
A–3(FA)_____	LtCol Frederick P. Henderson

A–3 (AA) _____ LtCol Edgar O. Price
A–4 _____ Maj Frederick W. Miller

1st 155mm Howitzer Battalion

Commanding Officer ___ Col James J. Keating
Executive Officer _____ Maj George H. Ford
Bn–3 _____ Maj Marshall J. Hooper

2d 155mm Howitzer Battalion

Commanding Officer ___ LtCol Marvin H. Floom
Executive Officer _____ Maj Gene N. Schraeder
Bn–3 _____ Maj Earl J. Fowse

7th 155mm Gun Battalion

Commanding Officer ___ LtCol John S. Twitchell
Executive Officer _____ Maj Dale H. Heely
Bn–3 _____ Maj Alfred L. Owens

9th Defense Battalion

Commanding Officer ___ LtCol Archie E. O'Neil
Executive Officer _____ LtCol Frank M. Reinecke
Bn–3 _____ Maj Allan R. Miller

14th Defense Battalion

Commanding Officer ___ LtCol William F. Parks
Executive Officer _____ LtCol William F. Kramer
Bn–3 _____ LtCol Jack H. Brown

3D MARINE DIVISION

Commanding General __ MajGen Allen H. Turnage
ADC _____ BrigGen Alfred H. Noble
Chief of Staff _____ Col Ray A. Robinson
D–1 _____ LtCol Chevey S. White (KIA 22J)
               Maj Irving R. Kriendler (From 22J)
D–2 _____ LtCol Howard J. Turton (To 28J)
               LtCol Ellsworth N. Murray (From 29J)
D–3 _____ Col James A. Stuart (To 28J)
               LtCol Howard J. Turton (From 29J)
D–4 _____ LtCol Ellsworth N. Murray (To 28J)
               Col W. Carvel Hall (From 29J)

Headquarters Battalion

Commanding Officer ____ LtCol Newton B. Barkley
Executive Officer _____ Maj William L. Clauset, Jr.
Bn–3 _____ (Not shown)
Hq Co _____ 1stLt George F. De Falco
Recon Co _____ 1stLt Arthur Salgo
MP Co _____ Maj Richard Tonis
Sig Co _____ Maj William N. Loftin
JASCO _____ Maj John H. Ellis (WIA 21J)*

---

*WIA. Records show returned to duty.

3d Medical Battalion

Commanding Officer ____ Cdr Raymond R. Callaway (MC)
Executive Officer _____ LCdr Delbert H. McNamara (MC) (WIA 26J)*
               Cdr Abraham Kaplan (MC) (From 3A)
S–3 _____ LCdr Delbert H. McNamara (MC) (WIA 26J)*
               Cdr Abraham Kaplan (MC) (From 3A)
H&S Co _____ LCdr Delbert H. McNamara (MC) (WIA 26J)*
               Cdr Abraham Kaplan (MC) (From 3A)
A Co _____ LCdr George L. Butler (MC) (KIA 21J)
               Lt William B. Harkins (MC) (From 22J)
B Co _____ LCdr Julius Simon (MC) (WIA 21J)*
               Lt Edmond A. Utkewicz (MC) (From 1A)
C Co _____ LCdr Daniel B. Landau (MC)
D Co _____ LCdr Clarence C. Piepergerdes (MC)
E Co _____ LCdr Stanley B. Haraburda (MC)

3d Motor Transport Battalion

Commanding Officer ____ LtCol Thomas R. Stokes
Executive Officer _____ Maj Ira E. Harrod, Jr.
Bn–3 _____ 1stLt Marshall W. Henry
H&S Co _____ Capt Herbert C. Bumgardner
A Co _____ Capt Garl A. Wilson
B Co _____ 1stLt Donald A. Lloyd
C Co _____ Capt Walter R. O'Quinn

3d Service Battalion

Commanding Officer ___ LtCol Durant S. Buchanan
Executive Officer _____ Maj Paul G. Chandler
Bn–3 _____ Capt Warren E. Smith
Hq Co _____ Capt Warren E. Smith
Ord Co _____ 1stLt Joseph M. Broderick
S&S Co _____ Maj William M. Roosevelt

3d Tank Battalion

Commanding Officer ___ LtCol Hartnoll J. Withers
Executive Officer _____ Maj Holly H. Evans
Bn–3 _____ Capt Victor E. Wade (To 22J)
               Capt David M. Graham (From 23J)
H&S Co _____ Capt David M. Graham
A Co _____ Capt William D. Stone (WIA 21J)*
B Co _____ Capt Bertram A. Yaffe (WIA 26J)*
C Co _____ Capt Julius O. Lemke

3d Marines

Commanding Officer___ Col W. Carvel Hall (To 28J)
                         Col James A. Stuart (From 29J)
Executive Officer_____ Col James Snedeker
R–1_____ Maj John E. MacDonald
R–2_____ Capt John W. Foley, Jr.
R–3_____ Maj John A. Scott (WIA 6A)*
R–4_____ Maj Grant Crane
H&S Co_____ Capt Victor J. Bachman (WIA 22J)
                         Capt Francis M. Blodget, Jr. (From 23J)
Wpns Co_____ Maj Laurence D. Gammon

1st Battalion, 3d Marines

Commanding Officer___ Maj Henry Aplington, II
Executive Officer_____ Maj John A. Ptak (KIA 1A)
Bn–3_____ Capt John B. Erickson
Hq Co_____ 1stLt George R. Nash (To 9A)
                         2dLt Charles R. Weissberger (From 10A)
A Co_____ Capt Geary B. Bundschu (KIA 21J)
                         Capt Robert L. Patterson (From 23J)
B Co_____ Capt Joseph V. Millerick
C Co_____ Capt David I. Zeitlin (WIA 25J)*

2d Battalion, 3d Marines

Commanding Officer___ LtCol Hector de Zayas (KIA 26J)
                         Maj William A. Culpepper (From 26J)
Executive Officer_____ Maj William A. Culpepper (To 26J)
                         Maj Howard J. Smith (From 26J)
Bn–3_____ Maj Howard J. Smith
Hq Co_____ 1stLt Matthew J. Cole, Jr.
E Co_____ Capt William E. Moore, Jr. (WIA 25J)
                         1stLt French R. Fogle (From 25J)
F Co_____ Capt Paul H. Groth
G Co_____ Capt Stetson S. Holmes (WIA 21J)
                         1stLt Alex H. Sawyer (From 21J)

3d Battalion, 3d Marines

Commanding Officer___ LtCol Ralph L. Houser (WIA 22J)
                         Maj Royal R. Bastian (From 24J)

Executive Officer_____ Maj Royal R. Bastian (To 23J)
                         Capt William R. Bradley (From 24J)
Bn–3_____ Capt Paul T. Torian
Hq Co_____ Capt William R. Bradley
I Co_____ Capt Lowell H. Smith (WIA 7A)*
K Co_____ Capt Anthony A. Akstin (WIA 23J)
                         Capt Paul C. Trammell (WIA 26J)*
L Co_____ Capt William G. H. Stephens, Jr.

9th Marines

Commanding Officer___ Col Edward A. Craig
Executive Officer_____ LtCol Jaime Sabater (WIA 21J)
                         LtCol Ralph M. King (From 30J)
R–1_____ Capt Charles C. Henderson (WIA 21J)
                         1stLt Charles H. Schofield (From 21J)
R–2_____ Capt Douglas Whipple
R–3_____ Capt Evan E. Lips
R–4_____ LtCol Frank Shine
H&S Co_____ Capt James M. Farrington
Wpns Co_____ Maj Jess P. Ferrill, Jr. (To 1A)
                         Capt Robert A. Campbell (From 1A)

1st Battalion, 9th Marines

Commanding Officer___ LtCol Carey A. Randall
Executive Officer_____ Maj Harold C. Boehm
Bn–3_____ Capt Francis H. Bergholdt
Hq Co_____ WO Douglas W. Diggers
A Co_____ Capt Conrad M. Fowler
B Co_____ Capt Burtis W. Anderson (To 8A)
                         Capt John B. Clapp (From 9A)
C Co_____ Capt Frank C. Finneran

2d Battalion, 9th Marines

Commanding Officer___ LtCol Robert E. Cushman, Jr.
Executive Officer_____ Maj William T. Glass
Bn–3_____ Capt Laurance W. Chacroft
Hq Co_____ Capt Francis L. Fagan (To 27J)
                         Capt Luther S. Kjos (From 28J)
E Co_____ Capt Lyle Q. Peterson (DOW 25J)
                         Capt Maynard W. Smith (From 25J)

F Co _____ Capt Louis H. Wilson, Jr. (WIA 25J)*

G Co _____ Maj Fraser E. West (WIA 26J)

Capt Francis L. Fagan (From 28J)

3d Battalion, 9th Marines

Commanding Officer ___ LtCol Walter Asmuth, Jr. (WIA 21J)

Maj Donald B. Hubbard (WIA 1A)

Maj Jess P. Ferrill, Jr. (From 1A)

Executive Officer _____ Maj Donald B. Hubbard (To 22J)

Capt Calvin W. Kunz, Jr. (From 22J)

Bn–3 _____ Capt Calvin W. Kunz, Jr.

Hq Co _____ 1stLt George G. Robinson

I Co _____ Capt Harry B. Parker (KIA 21J)

1stLt Raymond A. Overpeck (From 21J)

K Co _____ Capt William G. Smith (KIA 21J)

1stLt David H. Lewis (From 21J)

L Co _____ Capt Walter K. Crawford

21st Marines

Commanding Officer ___ Col Arthur H. Butler

Executive Officer _____ LtCol Ernest W. Fry, Jr.

R–1 _____ Capt Walter R. White

R–2 _____ Capt Blair A. Hyde

R–3 _____ Maj James H. Tinsley

R–4 _____ Capt Norman S. Chase

H&S Co _____ Capt Albert L. Jensen

Wpns Co _____ Maj Robert H. Houser

1st Battalion, 21st Marines

Commanding Officer ___ LtCol Marlowe C. Williams

Executive Officer _____ LtCol Ronald R. Van Stockum

Bn–3 _____ Capt Leslie A. Gilson, Jr. (WIA 22J)

Capt Edward H. Voorhees (From 23J)

Hq Co _____ Capt Edward H. Voorhees

A Co _____ Capt William G. Shoemaker (KIA 3A)

Capt Fred F. Harbin (From 4A)

B Co _____ Capt Donald M. Beck (WIA 21J)*

C Co _____ Capt Henry M. Helgren, Jr.

2d Battalion, 21st Marines

Commanding Officer ___ LtCol Eustace R. Smoak

Executive Officer _____ Maj Lowell E. English

Bn–3 _____ Capt Andrew Hedesh

Hq Co _____ Capt James A. Michener

E Co _____ Capt Sidney J. Altman (WIA 22J)*

1stLt William R. Williams (From 1A)

F Co _____ Capt Gerald G. Kirby

G Co _____ Capt William H. McDonough (DOW 21J)

1stLt Maurice G. Austin (WIA 5A)

1stLt Howard L. Cousins, Jr. (From 5A)

3d Battalion, 21st Marines

Commanding Officer ___ LtCol Wendell H. Duplantis

Executive Officer _____ Maj Edward A. Clark

Bn–3 _____ 1stLt James C. Corman (To 21J)

Maj Paul M. Jones (From 21J)

Hq Co _____ Capt Clayton S. Rockmore (WIA 26J)*

2dLt Coleman C. Jones (From 4A)

I Co _____ Capt Rodney L. Heinze (WIA 3A)*

K Co _____ Capt Clarence W. McCord

L Co _____ Capt Frederick I. Ptucha

12th Marines

Commanding Officer ___ Col John B. Wilson

Executive Officer _____ LtCol John S. Letcher

R–1 _____ Capt Edwin M. Gorman

R–2 _____ Maj Oliver E. Robinett

R–3 _____ LtCol William T. Fairbourn

R–4 _____ Maj Lytle G. Williams (Rear Ech)

H&S Btry _____ 1stLt Robert Stutz

1st Battalion, 12th Marines

Commanding Officer ___ LtCol Raymond F. Crist, Jr. (WIA 22J)*

Executive Officer _____ Maj George B. Thomas

Bn–3 _____ Capt Luther A. Bookout, Jr.

H&S Btry _____ Capt Carl H. Senge

A Btry _____ Capt Joshua C. West, III

B Btry _____ Capt James L. Cullen

C Btry _____ Capt Clarence E. Brissenden

2d Battalion, 12th Marines

Commanding Officer ___ LtCol Donald M. Weller

Executive Officer _____ Maj Henry E. W. Barnes

Bn–3 _____ Maj William P. Pala

H&S Btry _____ Capt Norman V. McElroy

D Btry _____ Capt Robert H. O'Meara

E Btry _____ Capt James Leffers

F Btry _____ Capt David S. Randall

3d Battalion, 12th Marines

Commanding Officer___ LtCol Alpha L. Bowser, Jr.
Executive Officer_____ Maj Claude S. Sanders, Jr.
Bn–3_____ Capt Wilbur R. Helmer
H&S Btry_____ 1stLt William G. Reid
G Btry_____ Capt Joe B. Wallen
H Btry_____ Capt James H. P. Garnett
I Btry_____ Capt Robert E. Rain, Jr.
    (WIA 23J)
    1stLt Reuben W. Estopinal
    (From 23J)

4th Battalion, 12th Marines

Commanding Officer___ LtCol Bernard H. Kirk (WIA
    21J)*
Executive Officer_____ Maj Thomas R. Belzer
Bn–3_____ Capt Lewis E. Poggemeyer
H&S Btry_____ 2dLt John T. Nute
K Btry_____ Maj Benjamin O. Cantey, Jr.
    (WIA 21J)
    Capt Charles O. Schrodt
    (From 21J)
L Btry_____ Capt Robert S. Wilson (WIA
    21J)*
M Btry_____ Capt Lonnie D. McCurry
    (WIA 21J)*

19th Marines

Commanding Officer___ LtCol Robert E. Fojt
Executive Officer_____ LtCol Edmund M. Williams
R–1_____ WO John J. Beaumont (WIA
    22J)*
R–2_____ Capt Clarence B. Allen, Jr.
    (WIA 31J)*
R–3_____ Maj George D. Flood, Jr.
R–4_____ Capt Julius S. Conrad
H&S Co_____ Maj Ward K. Schaub

1st Battalion, 19th Marines

Commanding Officer___ LtCol Walter S. Campbell
Executive Officer_____ Maj Virgil M. Davis
Bn–3_____ Capt Arthur J. Waldrep, Jr.
Hq Co_____ Capt Jack B. Wehner (To
    26J)
    1stLt Felix D. Kuzwicki
    (From 27J)
A Co_____ Capt Charles H. Horn
B Co_____ Capt Robert K. Higgins
C Co_____ Capt Charles M. Hunter, Jr.
    (To 8A)
    1stLt John T. McFadden, Jr.
    (From 8A)

2d Battalion, 19th Marines

Commanding Officer___ Maj Victor J. Simpson
Executive Officer_____ Maj Howard A. Hurst

Bn–3_____ Capt Jack R. Edwards
Hq Co_____ 1stLt Waldemar Meckes
D Co_____ Capt Claude D. Hamill, Jr.
E Co_____ Capt Charles F. Ingram
F Co_____ Capt Charles Z. Yonce

25th Naval Construction Battalion

Commanding Officer___ LCdr George J. Whelan
    (CEC)
Executive Officer_____ LCdr Brett W. Walker (CEC)
Hq Co_____ Lt John L. Walker, Jr. (CEC)
G Co_____ Lt Philip P. Nelson (CEC)
H Co_____ Lt John V. Frankenthal
    (CEC)
I Co_____ Lt Joseph H. Gehring (CEC)

1ST PROVISIONAL MARINE BRIGADE

Commanding General__ BrigGen Lemuel C. Shepherd,
    Jr.
Chief of Staff_____ Col John T. Walker
B–1_____ Maj Addison B. Overstreet
B–2_____ Maj Robert W. Shaw
B–3_____ LtCol Thomas A. Culhane, Jr.
B–4_____ LtCol August Larson
Hq Co_____ 2dLt Daniel B. Brewster, Jr.
MP Co_____ 1stLt Fred Henetz
Sig Co_____ Capt Edward P. Nugent

4th Marines

Commanding Officer___ LtCol Alan Shapley
Executive Officer_____ LtCol Samuel D. Puller (KIA
    27J)
    Capt Charles T. Lamb (From
    27J)
R–1_____ Capt Charles T. Lamb
R–2_____ Maj Clyde P. Ford
R–3_____ Maj Orville V. Bergren
R–4_____ 1stLt Noble W. Ferren
H&S Co_____ Capt Ralph L. Summeril
Eng Co_____ Capt Albert S. Guerard, Jr.
Med Co_____ Lt John T. Sacco (MC)
Pion Co_____ Capt John G. Dibble
Tk Co_____ Capt Philip C. Morell
Trans Co_____ WO Louis L. Barnhardt
Wpns Co_____ Maj John T. Rooney (WIA
    21J)*

1st Battalion, 4th Marines

Commanding Officer___ Maj Bernard W. Green
Executive Officer_____ Maj Robert S. Wade (temp.
    atchd.)
Bn–3_____ 1stLt Clinton B. Eastment
Hq Co_____ 2dLt Charles O. Diliberto
A Co_____ 1stLt Frank A. Kemp
B Co_____ 1stLt Thad N. Dodds (WIA
    29J)*
C Co_____ 1stLt Lawrence S. Bangser
    (WIA 21J)*

2d Battalion, 4th Marines

Commanding Officer___ Maj John S. Messer
Executive Officer_____ Maj Roy S. Batterton, Jr. (WIA 21J)
Capt Lincoln N. Holdzcom (From 21J)
Bn-3_____ Capt Lincoln N. Holdzcom (To 21J)
Capt Raymond L. Luckel (From 21J)
Hq Co_____ 1stLt Arthur C. Fix
E Co_____ 1stLt Leonard W. Alford
F Co_____ 1stLt Eric S. Holmgrain
G Co_____ Capt Archie B. Norford

3d Battalion, 4th Marines

Commanding Officer___ Maj Hamilton M. Hoyler
Executive Officer_____ Maj Hugh J. Chapman
Bn-3_____ Maj Anthony Walker
Hq Co_____ 1stLt Frank G. Lyte (To 1A)
1stLt Edward A. Harwood (From 2A)
I Co_____ Capt Robert G. McMaster
K Co_____ 1stLt Martin J. Sexton
L Co_____ Capt William J. Stewart (WIA 7A)*

22d Marines

Commanding Officer___ Col Merlin F. Schneider
Executive Officer_____ LtCol William J. Wise
R-1_____ Capt Alfred H. Benjamin
R-2_____ 1stLt Chauncey B. Chapman, Jr.
R-3_____ LtCol Horatio C. Woodhouse, Jr.
R-4_____ Maj Frederick A. Seimears
H&S Co_____ Capt David E. Cruikshank (To 6A)
Capt Elliot R. Lima (From 7A)
Eng Co_____ Capt Frederick C. Bloomfield
Med Co_____ Lt James V. Barrett (MC)
Pion Co_____ Maj Allen W. Hazard (To 4A)
1stLt Harold L. Manley (From 5A)
Tk Co_____ Capt Harry Calcutt (WIA 21J)*
Trans Co_____ Capt William F. A. Trax
Wpns Co_____ Maj John F. Schoettel (To 27J)
Capt John H. Mallory (From 28J)

1st Battalion, 22d Marines

Commanding Officer___ LtCol Walfried H. Fromhold (To 31J)
Maj Crawford B. Lawton (From 1A)

Executive Officer_____ Maj Crawford B. Lawton (To 1A)
Maj William E. Sperling, III (From 5A)
Bn-3_____ Capt Charles P. Delong
Hq Co_____ Maj Hudson E. Bridge (KIA 21J)
Capt Lacey Buckner (Rear Ech)
A Co_____ Capt Glenn E. Martin
B Co_____ Maj Robert Y. Stratton
C Co_____ Capt Charles F. Widdecke (WIA 25J)
1stLt Warren F. Lloyd (From 25J)

2d Battalion, 22d Marines

Commanding Officer___ LtCol Donn C. Hart (To 27J)
Maj John F. Schoettel (WIA 27J)*
Executive Officer_____ Maj Robert P. Felker
Bn-3_____ Maj John A. Copeland
Hq Co_____ Capt John E. Waddill (WIA 27J)
1stLt Thomas J. Jones (From 27J)
E Co_____ Capt Donald B. Goverts (WIA 27J)
Capt John P. Lanigan (From 28J)
F Co_____ Capt Ben L. Hoover
G Co_____ Capt Maurice R. Amundson (KIA 27J)
1stLt Carl W. Tuell (From 28J)

3rd Battalion, 22d Marines

Commanding Officer___ LtCol Clair W. Shisler (WIA 27J)*
Executive Officer_____ Maj Earl J. Cook
Bn-3_____ Capt Samuel A. Todd (To 1A)
Capt Robert P. Neuffer (From 1A)
Hq Co_____ 2dLt Buenos A. W. Young (To 1A)
Capt George F. Bloom (From 1A)
I Co_____ Capt Robert A. McCabe (WIA 25J)
Capt Jack J. Monroe (WIA 25J)*
Capt Samuel A. Todd (From 1A)
K Co_____ Capt Harry D. Hedrick (KIA 25J)
1stLt Walter G. Barrett (From 25J)

L Co_____ Capt Robert L. Frank (DOW
                    27J)
                    Capt George F. Bloom (To 1A)
                    2dLt Powless W. Lanier, Jr.
                    (From 1A)

Brigade Artillery Group

Commanding Officer___ LtCol Edwin C. Ferguson

Pack Howitzer Battalion, 4th Marines

Commanding Officer___ Maj Robert F. Armstrong
Executive Officer_____ Maj Thomas C. Jolly, III
Bn–3_____ Capt Henry Matsinger (To
                    1A)
                    Capt John E. Shepherd, Jr.
                    (From 1A)
H&S Btry_____ 2dLt Paul K. Lynde (To 1A)
                    2dLt Spencer V. Silverthorne,
                    Jr. (From 1A)
A Btry_____ Capt William E. Curtis (To
                    1A)
                    1stLt Benjamin S. Read
                    (From 2A)
B Btry_____ Capt John E. Shepherd, Jr.
                    (To 1A)
                    1stLt James H. Boyd (From
                    1A)
C Btry_____ Capt Herman Poggemeyer, Jr.
                    (WIA 26J)*
                    1stLt Herbert T. Fitch (From
                    1A)

Pack Howitzer Battalion, 22d Marines

Commanding Officer___ Maj Alfred M. Mahoney
Executive Officer_____ Maj Nathan C. Kingsbury
Bn–3_____ Capt Robert T. Gillespie
H&S Btry_____ Capt Morris McM. Garrett
A Btry_____ Capt Robert P. Yeomans
B Btry_____ Capt James R. Haynes
C Btry_____ Capt Gordon R. Worthington,
                    Jr.

53d Naval Construction Battalion

Commanding Officer___ Cdr Edward M. Denbo (CEC)
Executive Officer_____ LCdr Charles A. Thompson
                    (CEC)
Hq Co_____ Lt Thomas L. Milligan (CEC)
A Co_____ Lt Edward Keen (CEC)
B Co_____ Lt Felix W. Reeves (CEC)
C Co_____ Lt Phillip A. Peller (CEC)
D Co_____ Lt Gustav T. Oien (CEC)

77TH INFANTRY DIVISION (USA)

Commanding General__ MajGen Andrew D. Bruce
ADC_____ BrigGen Edwin H. Randle

Chief of Staff_____ Col Douglas C. McNair (KIA
                    6A)
                    LtCol Guy V. Miller (From
                    6A)
G–1_____ Maj James F. Doyle
G–2_____ LtCol F. Clay Bridgewater
G–3_____ LtCol Frank D. Miller
G–4_____ LtCol Guy V. Miller (To 5A)
                    LtCol Henry J. O'Brien (From
                    6A)

302d Engineer Combat Battalion

Commanding Officer___ LtCol Leigh C. Fairbank, Jr.
Executive Officer_____ Maj Thomas J. Scott, Jr.
S–3_____ Maj Edward W. Peake, Jr.

302d Medical Battalion

Commanding Officer___ Maj Abraham S. Jacobsen
Executive Officer_____ Capt Herman J. Halperin
S–3_____ 1stLt William W. Kirk

305th Infantry Regiment

Commanding Officer___ Col Vincent J. Tanzola
Executive Officer_____ LtCol Ward W. Caddington
S–3_____ Maj Robert J. M. Frye, Jr.

1st Battalion, 305th Infantry Regiment

Commanding Officer___ LtCol James E. Landrum, Jr.
Executive Officer_____ Maj Spencer E. Nurkin
S–3_____ 1stLt Milton Fineman

2d Battalion, 305th Infantry Regiment

Commanding Officer___ LtCol Robert D. Adair
Executive Officer_____ Capt Charles T. Hillman
                    (DOW 8A)
S–3_____ Capt Edward L. Davis

3d Battalion, 305th Infantry Regiment

Commanding Officer___ LtCol Edward Chalgren, Jr.
Executive Officer_____ Maj Robert J. Brink
S–3_____ Capt Edward W. Hopkins

306th Infantry Regiment

Commanding Officer___ Col Aubrey D. Smith
Executive Officer_____ LtCol John L. Keefe
S–3_____ Maj Marion G. Williams

1st Battalion, 306th Infantry Regiment

Commanding Officer___ LtCol Joseph H. Remus
Executive Officer_____ Capt James F. Love
S–3_____ Capt Stephen K. Smith

2d Battalion, 306th Infantry Regiment

Commanding Officer___ LtCol Charles F. Greene
Executive Officer_____ Maj William D. Cavness
S–3_____ Capt Charles T. Caprino

3d Battalion, 306th Infantry Regiment

Commanding Officer___ LtCol Gordon T. Kimbrell
Executive Officer_____ Capt Eugene Cook
S-3_____ Capt Charles P. Mailloux

307th Infantry Regiment

Commanding Officer___ Col Stephen S. Hamilton (To 1A)
LtCol Thomas B. Manuel (From 1A)
Col Stephen S. Hamilton (From 10A)
Executive Officer_____ LtCol Thomas B. Manuel (To 1A)
LtCol Thomas B. Manuel (From 10A)
S-3_____ Maj Ernest C. Dameron

1st Battalion, 307th Infantry Regiment

Commanding Officer___ LtCol Joseph B. Coolidge (WIA 2A)
Maj Gerald G. Cooney (From 2A)
Executive Officer_____ Maj Gerald G. Cooney (To 2A)
S-3_____ Capt William W. Kreis

2d Battalion, 307th Infantry Regiment

Commanding Officer___ LtCol Charles F. Learner (WIA 3A)
Maj Thomas R. Mackin (From 3A)
Executive Officer_____ Maj Thomas R. Mackin (To 3A)
S-3_____ Capt Richard O. Ballschmider

3d Battalion, 307th Infantry Regiment

Commanding Officer___ Maj John W. Lovell (To 3A)
Maj Joseph W. Hanna (From 3A)
Maj John W. Lovell (From 6A)
Executive Officer_____ Maj Joseph W. Hanna (To 3A)
Maj Joseph W. Hanna (From 6A)
S-3_____ Capt Boyce B. Burley, Jr.

77th Infantry Division Artillery

Commanding General__ BrigGen Isaac Spalding
Executive Officer_____ Col Royal L. Gervais
S-3_____ LtCol Charles L. Davis

304th Field Artillery Battalion

Commanding Officer___ LtCol Elbert P. Tuttle
Executive Officer_____ Maj Daniel A. Shaefer
S-3_____ Maj Lloyd D. Upshaw

305th Field Artillery Battalion

Commanding Officer___ LtCol Edward B. Leever
Executive Officer_____ Maj Joe M. Dietzel
S-3_____ Maj Stanford I. Hoff

306th Field Artillery Battalion

Commanding Officer___ LtCol Jackson P. Serfas
Executive Officer_____ Maj Charlie F. Talbot
S-3_____ Maj William P. Shelley, Jr.

902d Field Artillery Battalion

Commanding Officer___ LtCol Leo B. Burkett
Executive Officer_____ Maj Eugene R. Smyth
S-3_____ Maj Robert E. Hand

706th Tank Battalion

Commanding Officer___ LtCol Charles W. Stokes
Executive Officer_____ Maj John H. Kellett
S-3_____ Maj Byron M. Olson

132d Engineer Combat Battalion

Commanding Officer___ LtCol Richard G. Morossy
Executive Officer_____ Maj William H. Hardin
S-3_____ Capt Henry J. Moses

233d Engineer Combat Battalion

Commanding Officer___ Maj Orlan A. Johnson
Executive Officer_____ Capt William D. Long, Jr.
S-3_____ Capt Richard S. Stevick

242d Engineer Combat Battalion

Commanding Officer___ Maj Perry E. Borchers, Jr.
Executive Officer_____ Capt Charles R. Googe
S-3_____ Capt Sherwood A. Sutton

7th Antiaircraft (Automatic Weapons) Battalion

Commanding Officer___ LtCol Robert F. Murphy
Executive Officer_____ Maj William B. Bogue
S-3_____ Maj Thomas E. Steere, Jr.

ISLAND COMMAND

Commanding General__ MajGen Henry L. Larsen
Chief of Staff_____ Col Robert Blake
A-1_____ Col Lee N. Utz
A-2_____ Col Francis H. Brink
A-3_____ Col Benjamin W. Atkinson (To 8A)
LtCol Shelton C. Zern (From 9A)
A-4_____ Col James A. Mixson
A-5_____ Col Charles L. Murray

1st Provisional Base Headquarters Battalion

Commanding Officer___ LtCol Victor A. Barraco
Hq Co_____ 1stLt Emerson S. Clark, Jr.
MP Co_____ Capt Paul J. Swartz

5th Field Depot

Commanding Officer___ LtCol Walter A. Churchill
Executive Officer_____ LtCol Patrick J. Haltigan, Jr.
Operations Officer_____ Maj John W. Allen

Marine Air Group 21

Commanding Officer___ Col Peter F. Schrider
Executive Officer_____ LtCol James A. Booth, Jr.
Operations Officer_____ LtCol Robert W. Clark
Hq Sq_____ Maj Robert F. Higley
Ser Sq_____ Maj Charleton B. Ivey
AWS-2_____ Capt George T. C. Fry
VMF-216_____ Maj John Fitting, Jr.
VMF-217_____ Maj Max R. Read, Jr.

VMF-225_____ LtCol James A. Embry, Jr.
VMF(N)-534_____ Maj Ross S. Mickey
VMO-1_____ Maj Gordon W. Heritage

Lion 6 Advance Naval Base

Commanding Officer___ Capt Adolph E. Becker, Jr.
Executive Officer_____ Cdr David H. Hammer
(D-V(G))

5th Naval Construction Brigade

Commanding Officer___ Capt William O. Hiltabiddle,
Jr. (CEC)
Executive Officer_____ Cdr Henry G. Clark (CEC)
B-3_____ Cdr Henry G. Clark (CEC)
26th NC Regt_____ Cdr Em B. Cavallo (CEC)
27th NC Regt_____ Cdr Robert W. Denbo (CEC)
28th NC Regt_____ Cdr William H. Fitzgerld
(D-V(S))

United States Ships Participating in the Guam Operation[1]

APPENDIX V

KEY TO SHIP DESIGNATIONS

AGC—Amphibious Force Flagship
AGS —Surveying Ship
AH —Hospital Ship
AK —Cargo Ship, Auxiliary
AKA—Cargo Ship, Attack
AM —Mine Sweeper
AN —Net Laying Ship
AO —Fuel Oil Tanker
AP —Transport
APA —Transport, Attack
APc —Coastal Transport (small)
APD—Transport (high speed)
ARD—Auxiliary Repair Dock (Floating Drydock)
ARL—Repair Ship, Landing Craft
ARS —Salvage Vessel
ATF —Ocean Tug, Fleet
BB —Battleship
CA —Heavy Cruiser

CL —Light Cruiser
CM —Mine Layer
CV —Aircraft Carrier
CVE —Aircraft Carrier, Escort
CVL —Aircraft Carrier, Small
DD —Destroyer
DE —Destroyer Escort
DMS —Mine Sweeper (converted DD)
IX —Miscellaneous Unclassified
LCI(G)—Landing Craft, Infantry Gunboat
LCT(6)—Landing Craft, Tank (Mark VI)
LSD —Landing Ship, Dock
LST —Landing Ship, Tank
PC —Patrol Vessel, Submarine Chaser (173′)
PCS —Patrol Vessel, Submarine Chaser (136′)
SC —Submarine Chaser (110′)
SS —Submarine
YMS —Motor Mine Sweeper

* Vessels awarded the Presidential Unit Citation for service including the Guam campaign.

** Vessels awarded the Navy Unit Commendation for service including the Guam campaign.

BATTLESHIPS

Alabama (BB–60)
California (BB–44)
Colorado (BB–45)
Idaho (BB–42)
Indiana (BB–58)
Iowa (BB–61)
New Jersey (BB–62)
New Mexico (BB–40)
Pennsylvania (BB–38)**
Tennessee (BB–43)**
Washington (BB–56)

CARRIERS

Anzio (CVE–57)**
Belleau Wood (CVL–24)
Bunker Hill (CV–17)*

Cabot (CVL–28)*
Chenango (CVE–28)**
Corregidor (CVE–58)
Essex (CV–9)*
Franklin (CV–13)
Gambier Bay (CVE–73)
Hornet (CV–12)*
Kalinin Bay (CVE–68)
Kitkun Bay (CVE–71)
Kwajalein (CVE–98)
Langley (CVL–27)**
Lexington (CV–16)*
Midway (CVE–63)
Monterey (CVL–26)
Nehenta Bay (CVE–74)
Princeton (CVL–23)
Sangamon (CVE–26)*

San Jacinto (CVL–30)*
Santee (CVE–29)
Wasp (CV–18)**
Yorktown (CV–10)*

CRUISERS

Biloxi (CL–80)
Birmingham (CL–62)
Boston (CA–69)
Canberra (CA–70)
Cleveland (CL–55)
Denver (CL–58)
Honolulu (CL–48)
Houston (CL–81)
Indianapolis (CA–35)
Louisville (CA–28)
Miami (CL–89)

Minneapolis (CA–36)
Mobile (CL–63)
Montpelier (CL–57)
New Orleans (CA–32)
Oakland (CL–95)
Reno (CL–96)
St. Louis (CL–49)
San Diego (CL–53)
San Francisco (CA–38)
San Juan (CL–54)
Santa Fe (CL–60)
Vincennes (CL–64)
Wichita (CA–45)

DESTROYERS

Abbott (DD–629)
Acree (DE–167)

[1] Compiled from NavPers 15,790 (Revised), *Decorations, Medals, Ribbons, and Badges of the United States Navy, Marine Corps, and Coast Guard 1861–1948.* The period of entitlement to the battle participation star on the Asiatic-Pacific Theater Ribbon is 12Jul44–15Aug44.

Anthony (DD–515)
Auliek (DD–569)
Charles F. Ausburne
  (DD–570)
Aylwin (DD–355)
Bagley (DD–386)
Bangust (DD–739)
Baron (DE–166)
Bell (DD–587)
Benham (DD–796)
Bennett (DD–473)
Black (DD–666)
Boyd (DD–544)
Bradford (DD–545)
Clarence K. Bronson
  (DD–668)
Brown (DD–546)
Bullard (DD–660)
Burns (DD–588)
Cabana (DE–260)
Callaghan (DD–792)
Caperton (DD–650)
Capps (DD–550)
Case (DD–370)
Cassin (DD–372)
Charrette (DD–581)
Chauncy (DD–667)
Cloues (DE–265)
Coggswell (DD–651)
Colahan (DD–658)
Conner (DD–582)
Converse (DD–509)
Conway (DD–507)
Conyngham (DD–371)
Cotten (DD–669)
Cowell (DD–547)
Craven (DD–382)
Dale (DD–353)
Dashiell (DD–659)
Deede (DE–263)
Dewey (DD–349)
Dionne (DE–261)
Dortch (DD–670)
Dyson (DD–572)
Eisele (DE–34)
Elden (DE–264)
Ellet (DD–398)
Erben (DD–631)
Evans (DD–552)
Fair (DE–35)
Farenholt (DD–491)
Farragut (DD–348)
Fleming (DE–32)
Franks (DD–554)
Fullam (DD–474)
Gatling (DD–671)
Gridley (DD–380)
Guest (DD–472)
Haggard (DD–555)
Hailey (DD–556)
Hale (DD–642)
Halford (DD–480)
Paul Hamilton (DD–590)
Lewis Hancock (DD–675)
Harrison (DD–573)
Healy (DD–672)
Helm (DD–388)
John D. Henley (DD–553)
Hickox (DD–673)
Hilbert (DE–742)
Hudson (DD–475)
Hull (DD–350)
Hunt (DD–674)
Ingersoll (DE–652)
Irwin (DD–794)
Izard (DD–589)

Johnston (DD–557)
Kidd (DD–661)
Knapp (DD–653)
Lamons (DE–743)
Lang (DD–399)
Lansdowne (DD–486)
Lardner (DD–487)
Levy (DE–162)
Longshaw (DD–559)
MacDonough (DD–351)
Manlove (DE–36)
Marshall (DD–676)
Maury (DD–401)
McCall (DD–400)
McCalla (DD–488)
McConnell (DE–163)
McDermut (DD–677)
McGowan (DD–678)
McKee (DD–575)
McNair (DD–679)
Meade (DD–602)
Melvin (DD–680)
Mertz (DD–691)
Samuel S. Miles (DE–183)
Miller (DD–535)
Mitchell (DE–43)
Monaghan (DD–354)
Monssen (DD–798)
Mugford (DD–389)
Murray (DD–576)
O'Flaherty (DE–340)
Osterhaus (DE–164)
Owen (DD–536)
Parks (DE–165)
Patterson (DD–392)
Porterfield (DD–682)
Stephen Potter (DD–538)
Halsey Powell (DD–686)
Preston (DD–795)
Prichett (DD–561)
Pringle (DD–477)
Renshaw (DD–499)
Ringgold (DD–500)
Robinson (DD–562)
John Rodgers (DD–574)
Saufley (DD–465)
Schroeder (DD–501)
Sederstrom (DE–31)
Selfridge (DD–357)
Shaw (DD–373)
Sigsbee (DD–502)
Spence (DD–512)
Stanly (DD–478)
Stembel (DD–644)
Sterett (DD–407)
Stevens (DD–479)
Stockham (DD–683)
The Sullivans (DD–537)
Swearer (DE–186)
David W. Taylor (DD–551)
Terry (DD–513)
Thatcher (DD–514)
Tingey (DD–539)
Tisdale (DE–33)
Wadsworth (DD–516)
Walker (DD–517)
Waller (DD–466)
Waterman (DE–740)
Weaver (DE–741)
Wedderburn (DE–684)
Wesson (DE–184)
Whitman (DE–24)
Wileman (DE–22)
Williamson (DD–244)
Wilson (DD–408)
Yarnall (DD–541)

MINE VESSELS

Caravan (AM–157)
Hamilton (DMS–18)
Hogan (DMS–6)
Hopkins (DMS–13)
Long (DMS–12)
Motive (AM–102)
Palmer (DMS–5)
Perry (DMS–17)
Sheldrake (AM–62)
Skylark (AM–63)
Spear (AM–322)
Stansbury (DMS–8)
Starling (AM–64)
Terror (CM–5)
YMS–136
YMS–151
YMS–184
YMS–195
YMS–216
YMS–237
YMS–241
YMS–242
YMS–260
YMS–266
YMS–270
YMS–272
YMS–281
YMS–291
YMS–292
YMS–295
YMS–296
YMS–302
YMS–317
YMS–321
YMS–322
YMS–323
YMS–396
Zane (DMS–14)

PATROL VESSELS

PC–549
PC–555
PC–581
PC–1079
PC–1080
PC–1125
PC–1126
PC–1127
PC–1136
PCS–1396
PCS–1457
SC–504
SC–521
SC–667
SC–724
SC–727
SC–1052
SC–1273
SC–1319
SC–1325
SC–1326
SC–1328

SUBMARINE

Tarpon (SS–175)

FLEET AUXILIARIES

Agenor (ARL–3)
Aloe (AN–6)
Apache (ATF–67)
ARD–16
ARD–17
Astabula (AO–51)
Bountiful (AH–9)

Cache (AO–67)
Cahaba (AO–82)
Caliente (AO–53)
Chowanoe (ATF–100)
Cimarron (AO–22)
City of Dalhart (IX–156)
Concrete Barge 1321
Concrete Barge 1324
Enoree (AO–69)
Grapple (ARS–7)
Guadalupe (AO–32)
Holly (AN–19)
Hydrographer (AGS–2)
Kaskaskia (AO–27)
Kennebago (AO–81)
Lackawanna (AO–40)
Lipan (ATF–85)
Manatee (AO–58)
Marias (AO–57)
Mascoma (AO–83)
Monongahela (AO–42)
Neosho (AO–48)
Neshanic (AO–71)
Owklawaha (AO–84)
Pakana (ATF–108)
Pautuxent (AO–44)
Pecos (AO–65)
Pennant (Motor Ship)
Platte (AO–24)
Sabine (AO–25)
Samaritan (AH–10)
Saugatuck (AO–75)
Schuylkill (AO–76)
Sebec (AO–87)
Solace (AH–5)
Tallulah (AO–50)
Tappahannock (AO–43)
Takesta (ATF–93)
Tomahawk (AO–88)
Tupelo (AN–56)
Typhoon (IX–145)
Zuni (ATF–95)

TRANSPORTS AND
CARGO VESSELS

Alcyone (AKA–7)**
Alkes (AK–110)
Almaack (APA–10)
Alpine (APA–92)**
Alshain (AKA–55)
APc–46
Appalachian (AGC–1)
Acquarius (AKA–16)
Ara (AK–136)
William P. Biddle (APA–8)
Bolivar (APA–34)
William Ward Burrows
  (AP–6)
Centaurus (AKA–17)
Clemson (APA–31)
George Clymer (APA–27)
Comet (AP–166)
Cor Caroli (AK–91)
Crescent City (APA–21)**
Custer (APA–40)
Degrasse (AP–164)
Dickerson (APD–21)
Doyen (APA–1)
Draco (AK–79)
Du Page (APA–41)
Elmore (APA–42)
Fayette (APA–43)
Feland (APA–11)
Frederick Funston (APA–89)
Golden City (AP–169)

Kane (APD–18)
Lamar (APA–47)
Harry Lee (APA–10)
Leedstown (APA–56)
Libra (AKA–12)**
Monrovia (APA–31)**
Noa (APD–24)
Ormsby (APA–49)
President Adams
    (APA–19)**
President Hayes
    (APA–20)**
President Jackson
    (APA–18)**
President Monroe
    (APA–104)
President Polk (APA–103)
Rixey (APH–3)
Sheridan (APA–51)
Starlight (AP–175)
Sterope (AK–96)
Titania (AKA–13)**
Vega (AK–17)
Virgo (AKA–20)
Warhawk (AP–168)
Warren (APA–53)
Waters (APD–8)
Wayne (APA–54)
Wharton (AP–7)
Windsor (APA–55)

Zeilin (APA–3)**

LANDING SHIPS
AND CRAFT

Carter Hall (LSD–3)
Epping Forrest (LSD–4)
Gunston Hall (LSD–5)
LCI(G)–345**
LCI(G)–346**
LCI(G)–348**
LCI(G)–365**
LCI(G)–366**
LCI(G)–437**
LCI(G)–438**
LCI(G)–439**
LCI(G)–440**
LCI(G)–441**
LCI(G)–442**
LCI(G)–449**
LCI(G)–450**
LCI(G)–451**
LCI(G)–455**
LCI(G)–457**
LCI(G)–464
LCI(G)–465
LCI(G)–466
LCI(G)–467
LCI(G)–468
LCI(G)–469

LCI(G)–471
LCI(G)–472
LCI(G)–473
LCI(G)–474
LCI(G)–475
LCT(6)–962
LCT(6)–964
LCT(6)–965
LCT(6)–966
LCT(6)–968
LCT(6)–982
LCT(6)–989
LCT(6)–995
LCT(6)–1059
LCT(6)–1061
LCT(6)–1062
LST–24
LST–29
LST–38
LST–41
LST–70
LST–71
LST–78
LST–117
LST–118
LST–122
LST–123
LST–125
LST–207

LST–219
LST–220
LST–221
LST–227
LST–241
LST–243
LST–244
LST–247
LST–269
LST–270
LST–276
LST–334
LST–341
LST–343
LST–398
LST–399
LST–446
LST–447
LST–449
LST–476
LST–477
LST–478
LST–479
LST–481
LST–482
LST–488
LST–684
LST–731
LST–986

Southern Troops and Landing Force, Order of Battle for Guam[1]

APPENDIX VI

FORCE TROOPS—Major General Roy S. Geiger

Headquarters and Service Battalion, III Amphibious Corps (less detachments)

Signal Battalion, III Amphibious Corps (less detachments)

4th Marine Ammunition Company

Detachment, Argus 17 (Shore-based Fighter Director Unit)

Detachment, Marine Air Warning Squadron–2

Detachment, 756th Air Warning Company (Army)

Communication Unit 41 (Navy)

III AMPHIBIOUS CORPS ARTILLERY—Brigadier General Pedro A. del Valle

Headquarters and Headquarters and Service Battery, III Amphibious Corps Artillery

1st 155mm Howitzer Battalion (less Battery C attached to Brigade Artillery Group on landing)

2d 155mm Howitzer Battalion

7th 155mm Gun Battalion

3D MARINE DIVISION (Reinforced)—Major General Alan H. Turnage

a. 9th Combat Team

9th Marines

1st Battalion (less Companies B and C), 19th Marines (Engineers)

Company D, 19th Marines (Pioneers)

Company G, 25th Naval Construction Battalion (plus detachment, Headquarters Company)

3d Tank Battalion (less Companies B and C)

Reconnaissance Company (less 2 platoons), 3d Headquarters Battalion

1st Messenger Dog Section (less 1 squad), 2d War Dog Platoon

1st Scout Dog Section (less 1 squad), 3d War Dog Platoon

Company A, 3d Motor Transport Battalion

Company A, 3d Medical Battalion

1st Band Section

Detachment, 3d Joint Assault Signal Company

b. 21st Combat Team

21st Marines

Company B, 19th Marines (Engineers)

2d Battalion (less Companies D and F), 19th Marines (Pioneers)

Company H, 25th Naval Construction Battalion (plus detachment, Headquarters Company)

1st and 2d Platoons, Company B, 3d Tank Battalion

2d Platoon, Reconnaissance Company, 3d Headquarters Battalion

2d Messenger Dog Section (less 1 squad), 2d War Dog Platoon

2d Scout Dog Section (less 1 squad), 3d War Dog Platoon

Company B, 3d Motor Transport Battalion

Company B, 3d Medical Battalion

2d Band Section

Detachment, 3d Joint Assault Signal Company

c. 3d Combat Team

3d Marines

Company C, 19th Marines (Engineers)

Company F, 19th Marines (Pioneers)

25th Naval Construction Battalion (less Companies G and H and 2 detachments, Headquarters Company)

Company C, 3d Tank Battalion

3d Messenger Dog Section (less 1 squad), 2d War Dog Platoon

3d Scout Dog Section (less 1 squad), 3d War Dog Platoon

Company C, 3d Motor Transport Battalion

Company C, 3d Medical Battalion

3d Band Section

Detachment, 3d Joint Assault Signal Company

---

[1] Order of Battle information was taken from task organization appendices of the operation plans of units assigned to STLF and shows only those units assigned at the time of the landing.

d. 12th Marines (Reinforced)
  12th Marines
  14th Defense Battalion (less 155mm Seacoast Artillery group, 2 90mm batteries, 1 searchlight platoon, and detachments, Headquarters and Service Battery)
  Artillery Liaison Group, III Amphibious Corps
e. 1st Armored Amphibian Battalion (less Companies A and B)
f. 3d Amphibian Tractor Battalion (Reinforced)
g. Motor Transport Battalion (less Company C), III Amphibious Corps (DUKW's)
h. Reserve Group
  3d Headquarters Battalion [less 3 Band Sections and 3d Reconnaissance Company (less 4th Platoon)]
  Company B (less 2 platoons), 3d Tank Battalion
  2d War Dog Platoon (less 6 squads)
  3d War Dog Platoon (less 6 squads)
  3d Joint Assault Signal Company (less detachments)
  Detachment, Signal Battalion, III Amphibious Corps
i. Engineer Group
  19th Marines (less 1st and 2d Battalions)
  2d Separate Engineer Battalion
  Company B, 2d Special Naval Construction Battalion
  Garrison Beach Party
j. Service Group
  3d Service Battalion (less detachments)
  3d Medical Battalion (less Companies A, B, and C)
  3d Motor Transport Battalion (less Companies A, B, and C)
  Detachment, Service Group, 5th Field Depot
  2d Marine Ammunition Company (less 4th Platoon)

1ST PROVISIONAL MARINE BRIGADE (Reinforced)—Brigadier General Lemuel C. Shepherd, Jr.
a. Brigade Troops
  Headquarters and Headquarters Company, 1st Provisional Marine Brigade
  Military Police Company (less 1st and 2d Platoons), 1st Provisional Marine Brigade
  Signal Company (less detachments), 1st Provisional Marine Brigade
b. 4th Combat Team
  4th Marines
  Tank Company, 4th Marines
  Engineer Company, 4th Marines
  Pioneer Company, 4th Marines
  Medical Company, 4th Marines
  Motor Transport Company, 4th Marines
  Reconnaissance Platoon, 4th Marines
  Ordnance Platoon, 4th Marines
  Service and Supply Platoon, 4th Marines
  1st Platoon, Military Police Company, 1st Provisional Marine Brigade

4th Platoon, 2d Marine Ammunition Company
Detachment, 5th Field Depot
1st War Dog Platoon
1st Joint Assault Signal Party, Signal Company, 1st Provisional Marine Brigade
c. 22d Combat Team
  22d Marines
  Tank Company, 22d Marines
  Pioneer Company, 22d Marines
  Engineer Company, 22d Marines
  Medical Company, 22d Marines
  Motor Transport Company, 22d Marines
  Reconnaissance Platoon, 22d Marines
  Ordnance Platoon, 22d Marines
  Service and Supply Platoon, 22d Marines
  Band Section, 22d Marines
  2d Platoon, Military Police Company, 1st Provisional Marine Brigade
  1st Provisional Replacement Company
  Detachment, 5th Field Depot
  Construction Battalion Maintenance Unit 515 (Navy)
  2d Joint Assault Signal Party, Signal Company, 1st Provisional Marine Brigade
d. Companies A and B, 1st Armored Amphibian Battalion
e. Amphibian Tractor Group
  4th Amphibian Tractor Battalion (Reinforced)
  Company C, Motor Transport Battalion, III Amphibious Corps (DUKW's)
f. Artillery Group
  Artillery Headquarters Detachment, 1st Provisional Marine Brigade
  75mm Pack Howitzer Battalion, 4th Marines
  75mm Pack Howitzer Battalion, 22d Marines
  305th Field Artillery Battalion (attached on landing)
  Battery C, 1st 155mm Howitzer Battalion (attached on landing)
g. 305th Combat Team (USA)
  305th Infantry
  305th Field Artillery Battalion (detached on landing)
  Battery A, 7th Antiaircraft Artillery (Automatic Weapons) Battalion (detached on landing)
  Company C, 706th Tank Battalion (less 1 platoon)
  242d Engineer Combat Battalion
  Company A, 302d Engineer Combat Battalion
  Company A and 1 platoon, Company D, 302d Medical Battalion
  1 platoon, Company A, 88th Chemical Battalion
  Detachment, 77th Signal Company
  Detachment, 777th Ordnance Company
  Detachment, 292d Joint Assault Signal Company
  Detachment, Prisoner of War Interrogation Team
h. Antiaircraft Group
  9th Defense Battalion (less 155mm Seacoast Artillery Group, 90mm Antiaircraft Group, and detachments, Headquarters and Service Battery)
  Battery A, 7th Antiaircraft Artillery (Automatic Weapons) Battalion (attached on landing)

i. 53d Naval Construction Battalion
j. Medical Battalion, III Amphibious Corps (Reinforced)

77TH INFANTRY DIVISION (Reinforced) (USA) —
Major General Andrew D. Bruce
a. Division Troops
Headquarters, 77th Infantry Division
Special Troops
    Headquarters Company, 77th Infantry Division
    Military Police Platoon, 77th Infantry Division
    777th Ordnance Company (Light Maintenance)
      (less detachments)
    77th Quartermaster Company
    77th Signal Company (less detachments)
    77th Infantry Division Band
    77th Reconnaissance Troop
Headquarters and Headquarters Battery, 77th Infantry Division Artillery
306th Field Artillery Battalion
302d Engineer Combat Battalion (less Companies A, B, and C)
302d Medical Battalion (less Companies A, B, C, and 1 platoon, Company D)
36th Field Hospital (less 2 platoons)
95th Portable Surgical Hospital
Company A (less 1 platoon), 88th Chemical Battalion
92d Bomb Disposal Squad
292d Joint Assault Signal Company (less detachments)
7th Antiaircraft Artillery (Automatic Weapons) Battalion [less Companies A, B, and C (less 1 platoon)]
404th Ordnance Company (Medium Maintenance)
Prisoner of War Interrogation Team (less detachments)
Detachment, Counter Intelligence Corps
Joint Intelligence Center, Pacific Ocean Areas Team
Signal Photo Sections 1 and 2
b. 306th Combat Team
306th Infantry
304th Field Artillery Battalion
Company B, 302d Engineer Combat Battalion

132d Engineer Combat Battalion
Detachment, 292d Joint Assault Signal Company
Company B, 302d Medical Battalion
Battery B, 7th Antiaircraft Artillery (Automatic Weapons) Battalion
Detachment, 77th Signal Company
Detachment, 777th Ordnance Company
Company B, 706th Tank Battalion
1st Platoon, 36th Field Hospital
c. 307th Combat Team
307th Infantry
902d Field Artillery Battalion
Company C, 302d Engineer Combat Battalion
233d Engineer Combat Battalion
Detachment, 292d Joint Assault Signal Company
Company C, 302d Medical Battalion
Battery C, 7th Antiaircraft Artillery (Automatic Weapons) Battalion
Company A, 706th Tank Battalion
Detachment, 77th Signal Company
Detachment, 777th Ordnance Company
2d Platoon, 36th Field Hospital

GARRISON FORCE (when released by Southern Troops and Landing Force) — Major General Henry C. Larsen
1st Provisional Base Headquarters Battalion
3d Marine Division (Reinforced)
14th Defense Battalion (less detachments)
9th Defense Battalion (less detachments)
2d Special Engineer Battalion
25th Naval Construction Battalion
53d Naval Construction Battalion
Company B, 2d Special Naval Construction Battalion
Communication Unit 41
5th Field Depot
Detachment, 5th Naval Construction Brigade
Detachment, Marine Air Group 21
Detachment, Lion 6 Advance Naval Base
Detachment, Argus 17
Detachment, Marine Air Warning Squadron 2
Detachment, 746th Air Warning Company
Army defense troops
Other units as assigned.

Japanese Order of Battle on Guam

APPENDIX VII

ESTIMATED STRENGTH AS OF 21 JULY 1944[1]

ARMY UNITS

Forward Echelon, 13th Infantry Division—Capt Iki. Advance detachment from most units of the division. Since the 13th Div never reached Guam, the troops were probably attached to 29th Div headquarters units and may possibly be included in totals below_____ 200

Southern Marianas Group and 29th Infantry Division Headquarters — LtGen Takashina. Takashina's command included Guam and Rota plus Tinian after the fall of Saipan. LtGen Obata, 31st Army Commander, was present on the island but did not take over actual control of the defense until after Takashina's death___ 220

29th Division Signal Unit—Capt Suda. Understrength, like most division headquarters units as some men were lost in the sinking of the 18th Regt transport and others were with the 50th Regt on Tinian which was originally part of the division _____ 186

29 Division Ordnance Unit—Lt Kamei_____ 45

29th Division Intendance Unit—LtCol Mitzutani. This unit handled finance and quartermaster activity and may have acted as the control agency for conscripted civilian labor_____ 133

29th Division Transport Unit—Lt Mori_____ 97

29th Division Field Hospital—LtCol Morimoto__ 290

24th Tank Company—Capt Sato. Assigned as division tank unit with nine light tanks, eight tanks having been lost in sinking of 18th Regt transport _____ 117

265th Independent Motor Transport Company—Lt Takeuchi. Probably assigned to division headquarters _____ 180

---

[1] Figures shown are mainly from IIIAC Final Order of Battle, dtd 8Aug44. Any revisions and deletions have been made in light of intelligence data available following the campaign.

18th Infantry Regiment (minus 1st Battalion)—Col Ohashi. Unit lost almost 50% of personnel and all heavy equipment in submarine attack enroute to Saipan. After reorganization, headquarters and two battalions moved to Guam, leaving 1st Bn on Saipan and tank unit on Tinian. Each battalion had three rifle companies, a trench mortar company, and a pioneer unit ----------------------------------- 1,300

38th Infantry Regiment—Col Suenaga. Regimental headquarters, signal, medical, intendance, transport, and engineer units. Three infantry battalions, each with three rifle companies, an infantry gun company, and a machine-gun company. One mountain artillery battalion with four companies_____ 2,894

48th Independent Mixed Brigade Headquarters—MajGen Shigematsu. Originally the 11th Div Infantry Group Headquarters which came to Guam in the 6th Expeditionary Force_____ 149

48th IMB Engineer Company—Capt Miyake____ 187

48th IMB Medical Company—Capt Kitazawa__ 164

48th IMB Signal Company—Lt Kamakura____ 109

48th IMB Artillery Unit—Capt Kato. Headquarters and three companies, formerly 3d Bn, 11th MtArty Regt of the 11th Div_____ 368

319th Independent Infantry Battalion—Capt Miyanashi. Formed from the fourth rifle company taken from the three infantry battalions of the 11th Div which came to Guam with the 6th Expeditionary Force_____ 360

320th Independent Infantry Battalion—Capt Nakamura. Three rifle companies, an infantry gun company, and a machine-gun company, formerly 3d Bn, 12th InfRegt of the 11th Div_____ 486

321st Independent Infantry Battalion—Capt Furukawa. Three rifle companies, an infantry gun company, and a machine-gun company, formerly 3d Bn, 43d InfRegt of the 11th Div_____ 488

322d Independent Infantry Battalion—Maj Hamada. Three rifle companies, an infantry gun company, and a machine-gun company, formerly 1st Bn, 44th InfRegt of the 11th Div_____ 500

10th Independent Mixed Regiment (minus 1st Battalion)—LtCol Kataoka. Formed from the units of the 1st Div in the 6th Expeditionary Force. Regimental headquarters, engineer, and signal companies. Two infantry battalions, each with three rifle companies, an infantry gun company, and a machine-gun company. An artillery unit with two companies. The 1st Bn with one artillery company and an engineer platoon was on Rota_____ 1,912

52d Field Antiaircraft Battalion (minus 1st and 3d Companies)—LtCol Ishii. Headquarters and the 2d Company plus the AA unit of the 18th InfRegt_____ 250

45th Independent Antiaircraft Company—Assigned to the 52d FAA Bn_____ 140

1st Company, 9th Tank Regiment—Lt Ko. Twelve to fifteen light tanks, assigned to 38th RCT_____ 122

2d Company, 9th Tank Regiment—Lt Kumagai. Ten to eleven mediums and two to three light tanks, assigned to 48th IMB_____ 122

*2d Company, 7th Independent Engineer Regiment*_____ 225

2d Company, 16th Shipping Engineer Regiment—Lt Ogawa_____ 200

*Detachment, 60th Anchorage Headquarters*____ 20

          Total Army_____ [2] 11,464

[2] The original C-2 figure for Army troops was 12,744, but it included several units that definitely were not present. For example, elements of the 11th AA Regt and the 55th IndEngBn were identified and given a tentative troop strength of 650; however, the first unit was reorganized into the 52d FAA Bn in Manchuria and the second into the 16th ShpgEngRegt in the Philippines. In addition, there is insufficient evidence now to include four miscellaneous units with a total estimated strength of 726 that were carried on the original list.

NAVY GROUND UNITS

54th Naval Guard Force—Capt Sugimoto. Headquarters and 21 coast defense and antiaircraft units_____ 2,300

60th Antiaircraft Defense Unit—Lt(jg) Mochimitsu _____ 259

217th Construction Battalion—Capt Sugimoto__ 900

*218th Construction Battalion*_____ 900

Land Reclamation Unit—Mostly Japanese civilian males impressed for labor and lightly armed in the later stages of the campaign_____ 300

          Total Navy Ground_____ 4,659

NAVY AIR UNITS

*Guam Branch, Southeast Area Air Depot*_____ 100

263d (Hyo) Air Group—Cdr Tamai. All air groups consisted of ground elements hastily organized for airfield defense_____ 800

521st (Otori) Air Group—Cdr Kamai_____ 400

755th (Genzan) Air Group—Cdr Kusumoto____ 700

          Total Navy Air_____ [3] 2,000

Total Army (rounded out) _____ 11,500

Total Navy Ground (rounded out)_____ 5,000

Total Navy Air (rounded out)_____ 2,000

          Grand Total (rounded out)_____ [4] 18,500

[3] Original C-2 estimate of enemy air unit strength was 600; however, the strength of the three air groups in May 1944 is listed in CinCPac-CinCPOA Translation No. 12,541 as 3,100. Since the only casualties were to flying personnel and those killed in preinvasion bombardments and there is no evidence to indicate that any substantial number of ground crewmen were evacuated, a more reasonable estimate of group strength is included above. Of the original assigned plane strength of 80 fighters and 80 bombers, all were lost, either shot down in dogfights over Guam, demolished on the ground, or missing in battles over Biak Island.

[4] The figures have been rounded out to avoid the appearance of exactness, since the strengths of many units are only estimates. In view of the final enemy casualty figures on Guam this figure is, if anything, a minimum estimate.

APPENDIX VIII Navy Unit Commendations

THE SECRETARY OF THE NAVY
WASHINGTON

The Secretary of the Navy takes pleasure in commending the

FIRST PROVISIONAL MARINE BRIGADE

for service as follows:

"For outstanding heroism in action against enemy Japanese forces during the invasion of Guam, Marianas Islands, from July 21 to August 10, 1944. Functioning as a combat unit for the first time, the First Provisional Marine Brigade forced a landing against strong hostile defenses and well camouflaged positions, steadily advancing inland under the relentless fury of the enemy's heavy artillery, mortar and small arms fire to secure a firm beachhead by nightfall. Executing a difficult turning movement to the north, this daring and courageous unit fought its way ahead yard by yard through mangrove swamps, dense jungles and over cliffs and, although terrifically reduced in strength under the enemy's fanatical counterattacks, hunted the Japanese in caves, pillboxes and foxholes and exterminated them. By their individual acts of gallantry and their indomitable fighting teamwork throughout this bitter and costly struggle, the men of the First Provisional Marine Brigade aided immeasurably in the restoration of Guam to our sovereignty."

James Forrestal

JAMES FORRESTAL,
Secretary of the Navy.

All personnel serving in the First Provisional Marine Brigade, comprised of: Headquarters Company; Brigade Signal Company; Brigade Military Police Company, 4th Marines, Reinforced; 22nd Marines, Reinforced, Naval Construction Battalion Maintenance Unit 515; and 4th Platoon, 2nd Marine Ammunition Company, during the above mentioned period are hereby authorized to wear the NAVY UNIT COMMENDATION Ribbon.

The Secretary of the Navy takes pleasure in commending the

TWENTY-FIRST MARINES, REINFORCED, serving as the TWENTY-FIRST REGIMEN-TAL COMBAT TEAM, THIRD MARINE DIVISION

consisting of: the Twenty-First Marines; Company "B", Nineteenth Marines (Combat Engineers); Company "B", Third Tank Battalion; Second Band Section,

for service as follows:

"For outstanding heroism in action against enemy Japanese forces during the assault, seizure and occupation of Guam, Marianas Islands, from July 21 to August 10, 1944. Landing as the center Regimental Combat Team of the Division at Asan, the Twenty-First Marine Regiment, Reinforced, serving as the Twenty-First Regimental Combat Team, swept rapidly over enemy beach defenses toward a strategic high ridge which afforded the enemy observation of the Division landing area and enabled him to deliver accurate mortar and artillery fire on the beaches. Under heavy mortar and small-arms fire as they stormed the two narrow defiles which constituted the only approach to the vertical cliffs, these gallant Marines established two bridgeheads covering the defiles and, by midafternoon, had consolidated the Combat Team's position atop the cliffs, thus materially reducing the volume and accuracy of hostile fire and facilitating establishment of the Division artillery ashore and the landing of supplies and equipment. Halted by direct, short-range enfilade artillery fire from commanding terrain in an adjacent zone, they held tenaciously to their vital position in the face of continuous mortar fire by day, sharp nightly counterattacks and mounting casualties. When the enemy launched a full-scale counterattack with his remaining organized forces in the pre-dawn hours of July 26, wiping out one company of the Combat Team and penetrating the front lines, these officers and men waged a furious battle in the darkness; they annihilated approximately 2,000 Japanese troops in front of and within their position; and, by their individual heroism and gallant fighting spirit, dealt a crushing blow to organized enemy resistance on Guam, thereby upholding the finest traditions of the United States Naval Service."

All personnel attached to and serving with the Twenty-First Regimental Combat Team on Guam from July 21 to August 10, 1944, are authorized to wear the NAVY UNIT COMMENDATION Ribbon.

JOHN L. SULLIVAN,
Secretary of the Navy.

The Secretary of the Navy takes pleasure in commending the

TWELFTH MARINES, THIRD MARINE DIVISION

for service as follows:

"For outstanding heroism in action against enemy Japanese forces in the Empress Augusta
Bay Beachhead, Bougainville, Solomon Islands, from November 1, 1943, to January 12, 1944;
and in the invasion and seizure of Guam, Marianas, July 21 to August 10, 1944. Divided
for landing into small elements dispersed over 5,000 yards of beach at Empress Augusta Bay,
the TWELFTH Marines overcame perilous surf and beach conditions and an almost impenetrable wall of jungle and swampy terrain to land their pack howitzers, initial ammunition
and equipment by hand, to occupy firing positions, emplace guns, set up all control facilities
and deliver effective fire in support of the THIRD Marine Division beachhead by afternoon of
D-Day. In action for 73 days while under continual Japanese air attacks, the TWELFTH
Marines aided in smashing an enemy counterattack on November 7–8, silenced all hostile fire
in the Battle of Cocoanut Grove on November 13, and delivered continuous effective fire in
defense of the vital beachhead position. At Guam, they landed in the face of enemy mortar
and artillery fire through treacherous surf and, despite extreme difficulties of communication,
supply and transportation, and the necessity of shifting from one type of fire to another, rendered valuable fire support in night and day harassing fires, counterbattery fires and defensive
barrages, including the disruption of an organized counterattack by seven Japanese battalions
on the night of July 26–27. By their individual heroic actions and their skilled teamwork,
the officers and men of the TWELFTH Marines served with courage and distinction during
the THIRD Marine Division's missions to secure the Empress Augusta Bay Beachhead and
to aid in the recapture of Guam, thereby enhancing the finest traditions of the United States
Naval Service."

All personnel attached to and serving with the TWELFTH Marines during these periods are
hereby authorized to wear the NAVY UNIT COMMENDATION Ribbon.

JAMES FORRESTAL,
Secretary of the Navy.

The Secretary of the Navy takes pleasure in commending the

NINTH MARINE DEFENSE BATTALION

for service as follows:

"For outstanding heroism in action against enemy Japanese forces at Guadalcanal, November 30, 1942, to May 20, 1943; Rendova-New Georgia Area, June 30 to November 7, 1943; and at Guam, Marianas, July 21 to August 20, 1944. One of the first units of its kind to operate in the South Pacific Area, the NINTH Defense Battalion established strong seacoast and beach positions which destroyed 12 hostile planes attempting to bomb Guadalcanal, and further engaged in extensive patrolling activities. In a 21-day-and-night training period prior to the Rendova-New Georgia assault, this group calibrated and learned to handle new weapons and readily effected the conversion from a seacoast unit to a unit capable of executing field artillery missions. Joining Army Artillery units, special groups of this battalion aided in launching an attack which drove the enemy from the beaches, downed 13 of a 16-bomber plane formation during the first night ashore and denied the use of the Munda airfield to the Japanese. The NINTH Defense Battalion aided in spearheading the attack of the Army Corps operating on New Georgia and, despite heavy losses, remained in action until the enemy was routed from the island. Elements of the Battalion landed at Guam under intense fire, established beach defenses, installed antiaircraft guns and later, contributed to the rescue of civilians and to the capture or destruction of thousands of Japanese. By their skill, courage and aggressive fighting spirit, the officers and men of the NINTH Defense Battalion upheld the highest traditions of the United States Naval Service."

All personnel attached to and serving with the NINTH Defense Battalion during the above mentioned periods are authorized to wear the NAVY UNIT COMMENDATION Ribbon.

JOHN L. SULLIVAN,
Secretary of the Navy.

The Secretary of the Navy takes pleasure in commending the

III AMPHIBIOUS CORPS SIGNAL BATTALION

for service as set forth in the following

CITATION:

"For extremely meritorious service in support of military operations, while attached to the I Marines Amphibious Corps during the amphibious assault on Bougainville, and attached to the III Amphibious Corps during operations at Guam, Palau and Okinawa, during the period from November 1, 1943, to June 21, 1945. The first American Signal Battalion to engage in amphibious landings in the Pacific Ocean Areas, the III Amphibious Corps Signal Battalion pioneered and developed techniques and procedures without benefit of established precedent, operating with limited and inadequate equipment, particularly in the earlier phase of these offensive actions, and providing its own security while participating in jungle fighting, atoll invasions and occupation of large island masses. Becoming rapidly experienced in guerrilla warfare and the handling of swiftly changing situations, this valiant group of men successfully surmounted the most difficult conditions of terrain and weather as well as unfamiliar technical problems and, working tirelessly without consideration for safety, comfort or convenience, provided the Corps with uninterrupted ship-shore and bivouac communication service con tinuously throughout this period. This splendid record of achievement, made possible only by the combined efforts, loyalty and courageous devotion to duty of each individual, was a decisive factor in the success of the hazardous Bougainville, Guam, Palau and Okinawa Campaigns and reflects the highest credit upon the III Amphibious Corps Signal Battalion and the United States Naval Service."

All personnel attached to the III Amphibious Corps Signal Battalion who actually participated in one or more of the Bougainville, Guam, Palau and Okinawa operations are hereby authorized to wear the NAVY UNIT COMMENDATION Ribbon.

JAMES FORRESTAL,
Secretary of the Navy.

THE RECAPTURE OF GUAM

Index

203

U. S. GOVERNMENT PRINTING OFFICE: 1953